D0758946

A clinical and counselling psychologist and Fellow of the Australian Psychological Society, Chris Mackey has 35 years' psychotherapy experience in public and private mental health settings. He is the principal psychologist at Chris Mackey and Associates, his private psychology practice in Geelong. He was previously the senior clinical psychologist at the Geelong Hospital and at the Heidelberg Repatriation Hospital, where he helped establish a group programme for veterans of the Vietnam War.

Chris has presented at numerous national and international scientific conferences over the past 20 years on such topics as the assessment and treatment of psychological trauma and the evaluation of effectiveness of psychological therapy for anxiety and depression. He has a particular interest in positive psychology and has offered free public talks in this area over the past ten years. He also consults on applying positive psychology strategies to enhance business and organizational success. Chris is particularly interested in promoting more optimistic approaches to mental health. Throughout his career, and in his everyday life, he has been fascinated by synchronicity and the opportunities for personal development offered by this phenomenon.

For more about Chris, as well as extensive information about a wide range of mental health issues, visit:
www.chrismackey.com.au

SYNCHRONICITY

Empower Your Life with the
Gift of Coincidence

Chris Mackey

WATKINS

Sharing Wisdom Since
1893

This edition published in the UK and USA 2015 by
Watkins, an imprint of Watkins Media Limited
19 Cecil Court
London WC2N 4EZ

enquiries@watkinspublishing.co.uk

Design and typography copyright © Watkins Media Limited 2015

Text copyright © Chris Mackey 2015

9 8 7 6 5 4 3 2 1

Designed and typeset by JCS Publishing Services Ltd,
www.jcs-publishing.co.uk

Printed and bound in Europe

A CIP record for this book is available from the British Library

UK ISBN: 978-1-78028-795-9
US ISBN: 978-1-78028-808-6

www.watkinspublishing.com

To Ross, my dear spiritual friend and mentor.
In appreciation of your exceptional guidance and support
over all these years. You truly are one of a kind.

Acknowledgments

Firstly, I would like to thank Sandra Rigby, my commissioning editor at Watkins Media, for contacting me out of the blue to ask whether I'd like to write a book, convincing me to write about synchronicity, and helping guide me through the first draft and into the second. Thanks also to Melissa Faulkner, my sister, who helped make writing this book seem less daunting from the outset.

I am indebted to my friends and colleagues whose feedback on the manuscript, from parts to full drafts, was invaluable, including Megan Henderson, Emily Hill, Amber Denehey, Rod Carne, Charlotte Kerr, Sue Mackey, Margie Beasley, Andrew Bigelow, Ken Jarvis, Kerry Gemmell and Denise Cromer, among others. I also especially thank my spiritual friends, Trent Barry and Danny Taylor, whose wise comments helped me negotiate the most challenging sections to write.

Many people helped me tell my personal story more than they might realize, including Laura Capitanio, Mary Dimovski, Clare Heaney, Les Duck, Rod Jones, Craig Mackey, Alison Jones, Liz Barson, Andrew Fuller and Vicki Jones.

Thank you to Andrew Griffiths for his ever-generous writing guidance, my writing buddies, Gerard Spriet and Maree Herath, and Mick Ragg for his Nirvana advice.

I am especially grateful to the Watkins editors Fiona Robertson and Bob Saxton for their key role in guiding the manuscript to its final shape. Bob's editing was always thoughtful and often inspired in paring and clarifying the text and in helping integrate my personal story with other material. I also thank John Tintera and all other

Watkins staff for their valuable contribution at various stages in producing this book and bringing it to others' attention.

I thank my clinical and administrative colleagues at Chris Mackey and Associates for their active support throughout this project and for helping make work a joy.

I am indebted to my family – Rowan, Joanna, Ellie and especially Sue, my wife, friend, colleague and soul-partner – for their love, forbearance and encouragement. I am blessed to have my life path intertwined with theirs.

Finally, I should like to express my heartfelt gratitude to my clients, who have provided me with a most satisfying career and taught me the vast majority of what I truly understand.

Contents

Introduction   1

Part One: Life, Chance and Destiny   7
  1 What Is Synchronicity?   9
  2 Spooky Action at a Distance – Synchronicity, Science and Spirituality   25
  3 Ghostly Encounters – Seeing the Future, Healing the Past   38
  4 Synchronicity and Your Life Path   48

Part Two: Early Signals   59
  5 Shifting Worldviews   61
  6 Something Is Happening – A Career Shaped by Coincidence   72
  7 The Synchronistic Matchmaker – Flirting with Numerology   83
  8 Revealing Dreams – Watch Out for the Shark!   92
  9 A Wider World – Blessings and Mishaps   103
  10 Hell on Earth – Into the Abyss   112

Part Three: Tuning into the Universe   123
  11 Return to the Light – The Self Regained   125
  12 Wisdom on Tap – Learning from a Mentor   134
  13 A Confession – Hypomanic Wellness   144
  14 Doing a Daedalus   153
  15 Seeing the Sun   167

16 Signposts to Enlightenment – From Anaheim
      to Findhorn   175
17 Synchronicity and Brain Science – Making Sense
      of It All   188
18 A Free Kick from the Universe – From Global
      to Local   196

Part Four: Loud and Clear   203
19 It's Time for Positive Psychiatry   205
20 Going to California   217
21 Told in Confidence – Client Stories   230
22 Unwrapping a Gift from the Universe   241

Notes   245
Bibliography   260

Introduction

Have you ever been astonished by a striking coincidence? Indeed, so awestruck that you can't help wondering whether there's some kind of hidden order or organizing force at large in the universe? You might be a very rational-minded person, but this thought strikes you nonetheless. I'd call that kind of coincidence 'synchronicity'.

Synchronicity is an uncanny timing of events that seems to go beyond pure chance, in a compelling way that seems mysteriously meaningful, or numinous. I believe there's more to it than coincidence. In my view, synchronicity is a gift from the universe: a most valuable one. Synchronicity is often a helpful pointer, affirming that you're going in the right direction in your life. It's a bit like coming across a marker on a lengthy bush track indicating that you're on the right path.

But I'd go further than that. I believe that there's meaning within the mysterious gift of synchronicity, and that if the meaning is missed, the present is left unwrapped. Patterns can emerge in uncanny coincidences, especially over time. And patterns have messages for us. A pattern, at the very least, can make you stop and think. It invites you into a mental space in which to consider one or more aspects of your life. More than that, you might be prompted to consider the possible implications of the coincidence: if it *were* a message of wisdom from a source of external wisdom, what would that message be saying to you? Would it be affirming some decision you'd taken or were thinking about taking? In my experience, synchronicity often does that.

This book is designed to help you uncover the symbolic meanings behind uncanny coincidences, and especially the ones you experience personally. It takes a bit of work, though. It's like cracking your own personal Da Vinci Code. You have to be prepared to struggle with uncertainty. You need a little knowledge, and skill, and practice, and persistence. But the effort can be well worthwhile. This book is written to help you navigate the path of synchronicity in your life.

Since synchronistic messages tend to be affirmative, they can help us to correct imbalances in our lives. They can restore our belief in ourselves when that belief has been damaged by painful experiences. They can make us feel more vital, more energetic, more determined, more hopeful. They can reawaken us to what it really means to be ourselves, alive in the present with prospects for the future, following a path we believe is right for us.

Actually, I'm not the kind of person you'd expect to find writing about synchronicity. I'm mainly known as a clinical psychologist who uses mainstream cognitive-behavioural therapy (CBT). This discipline follows a scientist-practitioner approach: we always aim to objectively test our beliefs. I love the rigour of CBT. I love the commitment the field shows to demonstrating the effectiveness of its interventions. So it's probably not surprising that when I first came to explore synchronicity, a paranormal phenomenon, it was from the position of a committed sceptic.

I first encountered the term 'synchronicity' after attending a 'Wellness' seminar with Dr John Travis of Johns Hopkins University. To my rational mind at the time, Dr Travis's claim that a transpersonal, or spiritual, dimension underpinned our health and wellbeing seemed wildly extravagant. However, he made a convincing case for his ideas. It was shortly after that experience that I read about synchronicity, and then, soon afterwards, as you'll discover, experienced an explosion of remarkable coincidences that stopped me in my tracks!

Today I'd consider synchronicity to be as valid an influence as any upon the course of my own life, and the lives of many others, including my clients. This book is full of examples of synchronistic experiences, many of my own among them. I hope to show how such incidents establish meaningful patterns across a lifetime. This will also, I hope, encourage others to be open in relating their own synchronistic or other unusual experiences, since it's only talking about such things that will bring about greater acceptance of them.

The early chapters in this book describe some of the background theory relevant to a fuller understanding of synchronicity, including its overlap with findings from quantum physics. Some readers may prefer to skip the theory-based chapters at first, but reading them should provide a useful context for more deeply appreciating the phenomenon of synchronicity, which in later chapters I illustrate mainly in terms of my own life story. This book is, in part, a detailed case study on synchronicity and its capacity to shape a person's life.

When it comes to meaning in life generally, I can scarcely improve on what I learned from my grandmother. Her view, quite simply, is that life is like a jigsaw puzzle – and the longer you live, the more the jigsaw pieces fall into place. This fits: at least it fits for me. And when I pause to contemplate this thought, it strikes me that what has most helped to illuminate my life path, at times like a set of bright signposts, is the experience of synchronicity. I see synchronicity as an affirming sign that you're on an optimal life path. This is invaluable for providing extra energy and a clearer sense of purpose and direction, even when you're facing challenging situations.

Since I started to write this book, so many people have come forward with their own experiences. 'I haven't told anyone else this, but …', they'd begin … and then go on to divulge a remarkably coincidental experience appearing to defy rational explanation. Often they'd describe a remarkable coincidence as 'weird'. But it would seem to niggle away at them, leaving the feeling that there might be something else going on. Others I've met are so convinced about the reality of synchronicity that they simply say that there's no such thing as coincidence. Others again are openly sceptical.

Sceptics might be surprised to learn that Carl Jung, the great psychiatrist who coined the term 'synchronicity', came up with his theory about it after a series of conversations with Albert Einstein, and that he wrote his first monograph on synchronicity only after receiving active encouragement from Wolfgang Pauli, one of the fathers of quantum theory.

If you're sceptical but curious, I hope this book will enlarge your horizons and encourage you to explore the potential relevance and meaning of any inexplicable coincidences in your personal experience. If you're doubtful about the reality of synchronicity, or spiritual experiences in general, I hope at least that you'll see why others have some justification for taking a different view.

If, like myself, you're working in the health professions, I hope this book will prompt you to consider whether synchronicity might be a helpful and meaningful way of exploring a spiritual dimension in people's lives, which many consider as integral to their experience as their physical wellbeing.

Experiences that can't easily be explained in rational terms, regardless of how powerfully they impact on our minds, are often dismissed or ignored. This applies not only to synchronistic experience, but also to dreams, intuitions and psychic phenomena such as premonitions. However, I believe that there's potentially great benefit in considering the meaning of any such experiences that strongly draw our attention. If they make us reflect on our lives in ways we find helpful, then surely there's no case to answer. This book aims to help you develop your intuitive awareness and understanding, so that you can derive more benefit from synchronicity and other related phenomena when you experience them.

To help in this regard, I shall describe how a number of people, including myself, have drawn on what I call 'supra-rational' thinking – that is, advanced intuitive thought processes which seem to offer more advantageous outcomes in various situations than are likely to be achievable using logic or reason alone.

I believe that drawing on the benefit and meaning of synchronistic experience can be integrated with other methods of helping to find life direction and purpose, such as those used in the field of positive psychology.

There's a subplot to this book, or perhaps a not-so-hidden agenda. As I reflect on 35 years' experience as a clinical psychologist, gained in both public and private mental health settings, it's clear to me that our most common mental health approaches, particularly those that come from psychiatry, are failing. Explanations of mental health conditions appear to be overly mechanical and pessimistic. This, in my opinion, has taken the soul out of psychiatry – which is especially unfortunate given that 'psychiatry' literally means 'soul-doctoring'.

The usual psychiatric approaches explain people's problems in terms of genes and biochemical imbalances and address them through long-term medication. Such strategies, especially when rigidly applied, discourage hope of transformative change and personal growth. These themes are highlighted in Chapter 19, 'It's Time for Positive Psychiatry'.

An unfolding synchronistic theme in my personal and professional life is a desire to help discredit rigid, simplistic and pessimistic explanations of mental health problems. My everyday work involves helping people transform psychological problems into personal growth. My higher purpose, so to speak, is to promote transformation in the area of mental health, both individually and system-wide. Working towards this goal, I draw on my experiences not only as a therapist, but also as a patient: I was once hospitalized for severe depression.

The autobiographical material in this book gives an example of how synchronicity can be incorporated as a guide along one's life path. My coverage of personal experience includes a chapter on interpreting dreams, which illustrates the interplay between inner and outer worlds in the search for personal meaning – an interplay that's also explored when interpreting synchronistic experience.

The benefits of synchronistic experience become most clear when it's paired with *kairos*, the opportune or right moment to take a particular action. In archery, *kairos* literally refers to a long tunnel-like opening through which the archer's arrow has to pass.[1] The arrow needs to be shot not only accurately, but also with enough power to penetrate. *Kairos* also historically relates to weaving: there's a critical time when the yarn must be drawn through a momentary gap.[2] Taking the two meanings together, *kairos* is a passing instant when an opening appears that must be driven through strongly for the most successful outcome.

Synchronicity illuminates *kairos* in a way that's highly beneficial. If you face a challenge or an opportunity that seems to call for immediate action, and if around the same time you experience a markedly uncanny coincidence, that amounts to an affirmation, a 'tick from the universe' – a cue to forge ahead with your chosen action.

This echoes Carlos Casteneda's description in *Journey to Ixtlan* of the lesson taught by the shaman warrior, Don Juan, to his student: the difference between a warrior and a mere mortal is that a warrior remains ready to strike when encountering a 'cubic centimetre of chance'. This book relates many such examples of acting immediately on intuition, informed by synchronistic experience. As one writer, Joe Jaworski, puts it, this can lead to 'predictable miracles'.[3] I call it, to use a metaphor from football, getting 'a free kick from the universe'.

In my experience, drawing on synchronicity in opportune or challenging life moments provides an effective way of acting with authority and empowering your life path. The key motivation in writing this book is to assist others to do the same.

PART ONE

Life, Chance and Destiny

1

What Is Synchronicity?

Carl Jung, the eminent Swiss psychiatrist, coined the term *synchronicity* in the mid-1920s.[1] He didn't lecture or write about it until the 1950s, partly because it was so complex and difficult to explain. Nevertheless, he believed that synchronicity was of great importance not only for his patients' wellbeing and fuller self-understanding but also for his own, and he experienced it more and more frequently throughout his life.

Jung defined synchronicity as the 'simultaneous occurrence of two meaningfully but not causally connected events'.[2] More broadly, the word can refer to any uncanny and meaningful coincidence that connects our inner and outer worlds, in a manner that suggests that our inner life and outer reality are somehow more synchronized than we might previously have imagined.

For example, Jung noted many well-authenticated reports of clocks mysteriously stopping at the exact time of their owner's death. This apparently occurred with a pendulum clock in the palace of Frederick the Great.[3] An even more striking example reportedly occurred in Winnipeg, Canada. A grandfather clock stopped when its 72-year-old owner died. There was no male heir to pass it on to, following traditional practice. Several years later the man's widow noticed that the clock had inexplicably started again. Moments afterwards, she received a phone call announcing that her first grandson had been born 15 minutes earlier.[4]

A synchronistic experience involves such uncanny timing that we feel unable to dismiss it as mere coincidence. We have a deep-seated belief in a connection between our inner self and the things that happen all around us, and the event justifies our holding this belief; or, if we're borderline sceptical, it sways us towards acceptance. Even though great minds such as Carl Jung's have been working on synchronicity for almost century, it remains a mystery, even to those who accept it as a genuine phenomenon.

Particularly striking examples of synchronicity commonly involve a person thinking about something, and then experiencing a situation that seems inexplicably related to what they'd been thinking. For example, Jung described the case of a young female patient who, at a particularly poignant stage of therapy, told him about a dream in which she was given a golden scarab – a piece of jewellery.[5] Just at that moment he heard a gentle tapping on the closed window behind him. He opened the window and in flew a winged insect, which he caught. It was a scarab-like beetle with a greeny golden sheen: a common rose chafer.

Seemingly against habit, it had flown into a dark room. Jung noted that this beetle was the closest thing to a golden scarab in his part of the world. Jung remarked that nothing like this had ever happened to him, before or since. The timing had seemed strangely meaningful, as the patient had seemed at that point stuck in therapy, owing to her rigidly rationalistic worldview. Jung had previously been unable to shift her way of thinking by his usual methods. However, this fortuitous experience 'punctured the desired hole in her rationalism and broke the ice of her intellectual resistance'.[6]

This is not to suggest that anything in their conversations had caused the beetle to fly through the window. However, the timing seemed too remarkable to be random. It suggested there might be some kind of pattern, or order, in the unfolding of events that is not immediately obvious. It suggested that our consciousness could somehow intersect with our outer reality, without directly causing it.

The scarab example demonstrates another key feature of synchronicity: it relates to coincidence that's *meaningful*. In this case, Jung saw the meaningfulness of the incident deriving from ancient symbolism that he fully understood. The scarab beetle is a classic symbol of rebirth, or transformation, in Egyptian mythology. How appropriate, then, that it should manifest itself at this moment of transformation in Jung's patient's outlook. A symbolic meaning, however, will not always be so readily evident (just as the significance of a dream might never be discerned), regardless of how powerfully affecting the experience might have been. Sometimes a coincidence will seem meaningful purely because it's so improbable, pointing to a different conception of reality from the more limited view arrived at by reason or logic.

It's often suggested by sceptics that synchronicity is not a genuine phenomenon, but results purely from people looking out for coincidences and therefore inevitably perceiving more of them. The implication is that those who believe in synchronicity are unduly suggestible. This argument is tested by such remarkable but true stories as Monsieur de Fortgibu and the plum pudding, as described by Jung.[7]

The French poet Émile Deschamps recalled first tasting plum pudding as a boy in 1805, after his neighbour, M. de Fortgibu, brought back the novel treat from England. Deschamps next encountered plum pudding ten years later when asking for a piece of it in a Paris restaurant. However, he couldn't have it, as the one remaining piece had already been ordered by a M. de Fortgibu. Many years later, in 1832, the poet and other guests were invited to share some plum pudding while at a friend's house. When it was produced, he declared that the only thing missing was M. de Fortgibu. At that moment, an old and disoriented man walked into the house as a result of a mistaken address. It proved to be M. de Fortgibu! It turned out that M. de Fortgibu was present on each of the only three occasions that Deschamps had ever encountered plum pudding. It's difficult to see how sceptics could credibly dismiss such an example, as well as the extensive documentation, by Jung and others, of countless other compelling examples.

In addition to Jung, a number of authors have documented a run of synchronistic incidents experienced by one individual. Roderick Main has described approximately 90 of them out of hundreds recorded over a three-year period by James Plaskett, a former

British chess champion.[8] Plaskett wished to be completely objective about whether his synchronistic experiences could reasonably be attributed to chance, so he invited a committed sceptic to review them for him. He chose a fellow chess champion who was also a Cambridge-educated mathematician and industrial psychologist: William Hartston.

The content of the experiences was striking enough. For example, Plaskett and a friend independently recorded having a similar dream, about synchronized swimming, on the same evening. There were no references in the news or other media to synchronized swimming around that time that could explain the coincidence.

Perhaps even more remarkably, there proved to be synchronistic connections between Plaskett and his reviewer. Several of Plaskett's examples were uncannily related to an uncommon castling manoeuvre late in a chess game, leading a player to very narrowly

---

How to Recognize Synchronicity

When a coincidence is uncommonly strong, or occurs more than once, or seems to relate to an especially relevant theme in your life, it could be synchronicity. Other identifying features that are commonly found are that the event:

- has a numinous, or strongly mysterious, feeling
- interrupts your regular trains of thought and makes you think differently for a moment
- gives you a sense of wonder, or at least seems pleasingly or curiously unusual
- makes you feel momentarily that a message has been sent to you from some mysterious source
- causes you to imagine that something beyond the usual operation of cause and effect has occurred.

miss out on a rare achievement in chess called a 'grandmaster norm'. As it turned out, Hartston had missed out on achieving a grandmaster norm himself by the smallest margin possible. While reading the chess anecdotes, Hartston was surprised to notice that the TV programme he was simultaneously watching introduced a dream sequence about a chess game in which one of the characters said, 'I don't even know how to castle.' Hartston was no longer a sceptic by the end of his review.[9]

In his explorations in this field, Jung came to the conclusion that synchronistic events commonly have universal symbolic meanings attached to them. He'd previously noticed that certain powerful images or personifications worked within our unconscious minds, shaping our experience. At first he thought these were genetically inherited, but later he came to believe they equated to ancient cultural concepts, shared in different forms by various peoples around the world. Powerful symbols, such as the cross and the star, and figures, such as the Great Mother and the Child, appeared in both religious symbolism and in myth – two aspects of culture that blended into each other. Symbols of this kind could crop up in people's dreams or synchronistic experiences – as in the scarab example described above.

One of Jung's psychotic patients once invited him to look out through a window where he too might squint and see an upright tail, like a phallus, attached to the sun.[10] It was this that supposedly made the wind blow. Years later, Jung read an obscure Mithraic liturgical text – one of the so-called 'Greek Magical Papyri' – in which the wind was described as originating form a pipe hanging from the solar disc. Jung's poorly educated schizophrenic patient could not have read about this, as it was published after their conversation. Jung thought the coincidence too great for the idea to have simply come from his patient's own thoughts. He believed it must have arisen from a broader consciousness that subliminally influenced his patient.

Jung believed that such symbols could only have been repeated so often across many cultures throughout history because of their potential value at a fundamental level of human experience. Presumably the most useful or relevant symbols, or symbolic themes, developed and strengthened through evolution. He referred to the most enduring symbolic forms, or motifs, as 'archetypes'.[11] Jung believed that the influence of the archetypes emanated from a universal consciousness – a kind of universal pool of resonant images we can all somehow tap into at a subliminal level. He called this the 'collective unconscious'.

Jung suggested that a symbol or image in a dream, or in a synchronistic experience, could be interpreted by a technique he called 'amplification', to help identify symbolic meaning beyond the most immediately obvious associations. Rather than free-associating around the image following Freud's usual method, Jung worked by comparing the person's dream's image with images in myth or culture, to bring out any parallels with the archetypes. Although the archetypes don't have fixed or strict interpretations, they could point to a potentially fuller meaning of any dream or synchronistic experience, especially when an intimate knowledge of the individual's circumstances is brought into play.

Examples of archetypes include: trees, which might represent growth; winged figures, which might relate to transcendence; and mandalas, or circles or squares divided into quadrants, which might represent wholeness and the integration of complementary personality characteristics. Common archetypal forms also include sun symbols and various animals, including snakes and birds. Archetypes can also appear as larger-than-life characters, or life roles, such as a wise old man, a beautiful goddess, a saviour, a creative artist or a mystical healer. They can also relate to situations, such as falling, being chased by wild animals or finding treasure.

Jung suggested that archetypes, although lacking a rigidly defined meaning, represent an 'instinctive trend' to perceive things according to a particular motif.[12] In this respect, they were akin to the impulse of birds to build nests, or ants to form colonies.

Jung was very much open to seeking out experience that was anomalous, or unexpected or unusual, and looking for meaning in it. He was fascinated by the wisdom of the ancient Chinese sages, reflected in the I Ching.[13] This Chinese system of divination, which included writings attributed to Confucius, highlighted the role of 'acausal co-occurrence' – two events connected in a way that isn't merely causal – in attempting to explain the link between one event and another. Jung experimented with the I Ching, prompting his patients to cast yarrow sticks to compose hexagrams in a seemingly random fashion, yet finding that the standard interpretation of the resulting hexagrams uncannily fitted his patients' circumstances. For example, a patient whose primary concern was about being dominated by a woman he might have married was offered the interpretation, 'The maiden is powerful. One should not marry such a maiden.'

Jung was eager to embrace a holistic scientific worldview, emphasizing the profound interconnectedness of all things. He believed that many scientific approaches, including those within the field of psychology, missed this core understanding of the nature of life. His meetings with leading scientists of his day, including Einstein and Pauli, led him to believe that there were new themes emerging from cutting-edge physics that fitted more closely with a holistic view of reality.[14]

Synchronicity can be differentiated from another concept, ser-endipity, in that it goes beyond mere coincidence or happenstance. Serendipity tends to be a matter of making a fortunate discovery – for example, in a second-hand bookstore you happen to come across a biography of someone your friend had mentioned to you the previous day. That would be a coincidence, but not an astonishing one, and not a significant one if you had not been particularly interested in the figure your friend had talked about. Synchronicity implies an additional layer of meaning – the coincidence is not just lucky, but charged with meaning. If you were determined, after learning about this character, to find out more about him or her, on the grounds that their life story might have connections with your own, then the bookstore find could be more than a coinci-dence: it could be synchronicity.

Chance and Destiny: The I Ching

A number of structured systems exist that relate to synchronicity and have a strong underpinning of philosophy around spiritual themes and personal transformation. The I Ching and the Tarot are commonly seen as systems of divination, or prophecy. However, each can also be regarded as a store of accumulated wisdom on the nature of life change processes. They are future oriented – that is, designed to support your purpose or optimal direction.

Each follows a method that, on the surface at least, relies on a chance mechanism. The I Ching is based on the way in which yarrow sticks or coins fall when thrown.

Such seemingly chance outcomes, however, are not random. They are meaningful, and therefore synchronistic. The meaning may or may not be readily apparent to us, but latent meaning is assumed. Making sense of the result, however, requires active, creative interpretation.

The I Ching, also known as The Book of Changes, has been widely used for 2,500 years, becoming increasingly popular in the West over the past 100 years under Carl Jung's influence. Roderick Main describes in *Revelations of Chance* how Jung viewed the I Ching as relating to synchronicity, providing a number of compelling examples to help account for Jung's belief in its potency.

Confucius was clearly taken with the I Ching as well. He reportedly used his copy so often that he wore out the binding several times. The supplementary annexe to the I Ching, known as the Ten Wings, is understood to have been written by Confucius, perhaps assisted by his disciples based on Confucius's direct teachings. This addition more explicitly shifted the I Ching from a divination system to a work related to philosophy and personal meaning.

The difference between serendipity and synchronicity is not, however, clear-cut. For example, many scientific discoveries are commonly attributed to serendipity, or fortunate coincidence, when there seems to have been something more uncanny involved. For example, in the 19th century August Kekulé, a German organic chemist, reportedly discovered the ring-like structure of the benzene molecule after dreaming of a snake swallowing its tail, a common archetypal image across many cultures. As another example, the discovery of penicillin by Alexander Fleming followed an astonishingly fortunate series of interconnected events, including extreme weather, the location of an open window and the nature of bacteria he was experimenting with, combined with remarkably uncanny timing.

The Jungian psychoanalyst Roderick Main, in his book *Revelations of Chance: Synchronicity as Spiritual Experience*, points out that synchronistic experiences often have a spiritual quality. Almost by definition they are numinous – imbued with a sense of mystery, fascination or awe. Often they have a miraculous or revelatory quality, and may be thematically linked to some kind of transformation – as with Jung's scarab beetle. A synchronistic experience may suggest a profound interconnectedness between people, and perhaps a sense of an overarching, indivisible consciousness; or it may relate to the theme of personal destiny.

Synchronistic experiences are often joyful, leading to the compelling impression of a benevolent order in the universe. They commonly lead to the belief that 'the universe provides' – for example, by uncannily facilitating scientific discoveries.

As a more personal example of the universe providing, my friends Margie and Chris described how once, while sailing, they expressed their concern that they'd been unable to fill their propane gas bottles. Within the next half-hour they tacked around an object floating in the expanse of ocean: it proved to be a large, almost full, gas bottle. They found such experiences affirming – perhaps in some way validating their unconventional life choice to spend many years sailing around the world.

A particularly meaningful kind of synchronicity is that of providentially meeting someone who's uncommonly well equipped to teach us a timely lesson. Throughout this book there are numerous examples of my own and others' experiences that fit the saying, 'When the pupil is ready, the teacher will come.' Other provident examples of uncanny timeliness include finding new insights in other ways – such as from a book, or a movie, or something you might overhear in conversation.

A common form of synchronicity is propinquity – a coincidence reflecting the psychological connection between people. A rationally minded and usually sceptical friend, Ian, has described to me how, on a more or less weekly basis, when his finger is reaching to call someone on his mobile phone, the other person rings him first. He interprets this in terms of a sense of connection with the other person.

A fellow school parent named Cameron, learning from a dinner conversation that I was writing about synchronicity, suggested I should include something on propinquity. When we met at school next morning, he told me he'd just driven to a service station to re-check the air in his car tyres, recognizing that this might have seemed excessive, given that he'd checked them the previous day. He explained that over recent weeks he'd been feeling stressed about a business issue: there was a particular individual he needed to negotiate with. Fortuitously, he'd just met that very same man at the service station and had resolved the issue. It was all the more striking as they were in a town called Mansfield several hours' drive from home.

Strikingly, some months after writing about these two examples to illustrate the concept of propinquity, I learned that Ian and Cameron shared a house when they were students at university. I met them 25 years apart under very different circumstances and was surprised to find out much later that they knew each other. Propinquity, surely, strikes again!

When I emailed Cameron months later to ask his permission to use this anecdote, he replied that he'd just returned that very day from New Zealand, specifically to meet the man he'd negotiated with in Mansfield. In my email I'd referred to a strange dream I'd had about him months earlier, which revolved around the word 'bow'. I associated this word with *kairos*, with the implication of acting on intuition in a timely manner, as Cameron did when he re-checked his car tyres. When Cameron read my email about this association, he added that he was meeting with the Mansfield contact in the Long Bow restaurant. Perhaps the concept of psychic propinquity is not such a long shot after all.

Sometimes propinquity is evident in the therapist–client relationship. My friend Margie also provided an amusing story, about a former supervisor, a psychotherapist named Peter O'Connor. Dr O'Connor had apparently been seeing a client who requested that he also help him with a flying phobia. He explained that the client would be best advised to see another therapist, since treating that problem was outside his areas of expertise. Some time later Dr O'Connor was sitting on a plane, and who should be seated next to him? It was evident the client had made progress.

This story illustrates how synchronistic experiences sometimes seem to have a playful quality, perhaps reflecting the idea that we can't control everything in our lives. I like to think of this tendency as the 'cosmic prankster' at work.

A personal example of therapist–client propinquity is that of the thousands of clients I have seen in Geelong over 35 years, there were three in particular I initially had in mind to refer to in this book. Each of the three fortuitously and independently made contact with me after I chose to write about them, despite our most recent contact having been approximately 30, 20 and 5 years earlier. Few other clients I'd worked with long ago contacted my practice to book further appointments with me during that period.

Sometimes a synchronistic connection is a sad one. Synchronicity can reflect a connection with someone deceased – perhaps someone particularly close, such as a parent. A tennis friend, Mark, volunteered the following example. A number of years earlier, Mark's father had died from a fall while climbing ruins in Turkey. Mark is an airline pilot. The very next time he was flying in that part of the world, his plane was deviated from its usual flight path to London. This is in itself not an uncommon occurrence, owing to circumstances such as military operations. However, the direction in which his plane was re-routed deviated far from the usual adjusted course. He'd not undertaken a similar re-routing in the last 50 or so equivalent flights. As a consequence his plane flew directly above the ruins where his father had fallen.

The category of synchronicity also covers instances of psychic ability, or other paranormal phenomena, that involve uncanny timing. This includes precognition, or premonitions – a particular interest of Jung's, due in part to his own direct experience.

Jung described a most striking example involving visions associated with his near-death experience following a heart attack.[15] He envisaged entering a rock temple, suspended in space, whereupon an image of the doctor responsible for his treatment floated up to him and gave him the message that he was meant to return. At first Jung felt aggrieved that his doctor had brought him back to life, ending such a transcendent experience. Then he became distressed about his doctor having presented to him in his 'primal form', as a king from the temple of Asclepius, the god of healing: Jung feared this delirious vision meant that the doctor must die. Such thinking might normally be dismissed as being extremely superstitious or delusional. However, on the first day that Jung was able to sit up in his bed, his doctor became bedridden with a fever from which he never recovered. Jung was his last patient.

My uncle described a similarly grim premonition – one that involved a fatal accident. While part of a search-and-rescue operation after an aircraft crash near Sydney in 1990, he had the feeling that another such accident would happen. He mentioned this to colleagues, who dismissed the idea. When the crew of two young men walked to their aircraft to set out for the search area, he had a compelling sense that one of them would not return. He said to some pilots with him that one of them would not be alive in ten minutes, but given that they agreed there was no logical reason for such an outcome, there seemed no need to act on this concern.

Not long after the aircraft took off, the group waiting together received a mayday call on their radio. The aircraft had suffered catastrophic engine failure and hit the ground, resulting in a number of fatalities, including one of two young men. When a mother was soon given the news that her son had perished, my uncle, despite hearing of no further details, confidently told her not to worry: her son would be fine, since it was someone else who'd died in the accident. He based this on the seemingly inexplicable intuition he had that the other man wouldn't return.

My uncle's reassurance to the parent proved accurate. When the names of the deceased were announced, her son had indeed survived: it was the other man who'd perished. Such stories illustrate that even though synchronicity is often a joyful experience associated with fortuitous outcomes, it can have its tragic side as well.

Over the course of a lifetime, repeated synchronistic experiences can revolve around specific themes related to the individual's sense of purpose. Jung's autobiography, *Memories, Dreams, Reflections*, offers the best-known account of one person's extended experience of synchronicity. For Jung, many of his synchronistic experiences seemed to relate to his interest in promoting a deeper understanding of the human psyche. In James Plaskett's case (see p.12), his collective synchronistic experience appeared to revolve around the theme of pushing the limits of human intelligence. Joe Jaworski, in *Synchronicity: The Inner Path of Leadership*, describes synchronistic experiences that often related to his interest in developing enlightened models of leadership. Jean Shinoda Bolen, a psychiatry professor who wrote *The Tao of Psychology: Synchronicity and the Self,* tells us how synchronistic experiences helped her pursue her interest in paranormal phenomena. Her interest in synchronicity and psychic phenomena, like mine, was stimulated by encounters with patients.

In my own case, some of my most striking synchronistic experiences have related to themes associated with mental health. I believe it's time for mainstream psychology to pay more attention to synchronicity. Although this would take scientists into the realm of what's sometimes described as 'intellectual intuition', as opposed to logical or rational thinking, in my view that would be a far from bad thing.

Synchronicity relates to our inner experience as much as to any objective outer experience. Its significance to us can be quite private and personal, and difficult to convey to others. Much can be lost in translation. This means that the most useful learning you can do about synchronicity will result from your own personal experiences. If synchronicity is defined in terms of uncanny and meaningful coincidences, this means experiences that seem like a coincidence *to you*, seem uncanny *to you* and seem meaningful *to you*. As Jung emphasized, synchronicity is meant to be interpreted from the subjective viewpoint of the person experiencing it.

As an example of such subjectivity, I recall an experience that I felt was both synchronistic and highly motivating when starting to write this book. Along with a few friends, I'd just returned from China, where our host had given us some pre-arranged tasks. My task was to weave in the theme of Australian bush poetry while introducing some Australian wines at an expatriate wine club in Nanjing. To introduce the theme, I recited the first two lines of Banjo Patterson's 1890 poem, 'The Man from Snowy River'. Within days of returning home, my ears pricked up when I heard a radio interview in which the same two lines were recited, a most unexpected occurrence. I can't recall ever before hearing a reference to that poem on radio, let alone a recital of just the same two lines.

The person being interviewed was a first-time author. The theme of the interview was whether the subject of his book, the story depicted in the poem, was truth or fiction. I saw parallels to my own experience of offering an Australian voice, as a first-time author, to a subject of which the reality was in question. The interviewer told the author, whose passion was readily evident, that he seemed to have many more books left in him. The initial message I took from this was that writing could be well achievable for new authors and the task could be greatly satisfying.

Regardless of how appropriate or meaningful this interpretation might seem to others, it was certainly meaningful to me. I saw it as

How to Interpret Synchronicity

A synchronistic experience, like a dream, will have potential meanings that are not always easy to discover. Ambiguity may be at work. To interpret an example satisfactorily it helps to:

- notice what stands out most to you in the situation – that is, 'notice what you notice'
- open up your intuition and apply your imagination
- look for symbolism – that is, the shades of possible meanings that surround a name, an event, an object or any other phenomenon
- interpret any symbolism in a subjective way, looking for personal associations
- allow intuitive associations to develop over time, without too much deliberate effort – associations are likely to be more meaningful if they pop into your mind unbidden (this is more likely to happen when you're in a reflective mood, as I tend to be while jogging or in the shower)
- consider any alternative interpretations that come to mind and sift between them to see which one intuitively seems to fit, or to feel more right, taking into account what's happening in your life at the time
- be alert to possible archetypal meanings – which you can find in a dictionary of symbols, or online
- write up the circumstances in a notebook or journal if you can't find any significance in them, while allowing the experience to sit in the back of your mind. In other words, file it away – just because you don't identify any particular meaning at the time doesn't mean that you won't later on.

a tick from the universe that I was on the right track. Along with a clearly noticeable increase in synchronistic experiences around that time, I felt encouraged by some kind of power beyond myself.

Anything we pay attention to and appreciate will tend to be enhanced by synchronicity. We naturally pay attention to the things that contribute positive energy to our experience – that's what gives purpose and value to our lives. In many people's experience, synchronicity adds an additional layer of energy. It illuminates priorities. It emphasizes connections that otherwise we might have missed. It confirms us in taking one direction rather than another. It can help us realize our potential. In short, it can help us be more fully ourselves.

Appreciating synchronicity is a complex process that's difficult to sum up in words, but I've given some guidance in the boxes on pp.12 and 23. Gathering meaning from a synchronistic experience can feel like receiving individual guidance from an unimaginably wise and benevolent mentor – one who is exquisitely attuned to your particular needs and interests. When I have this experience, and act swiftly and confidently on the guidance given, then the combination of synchronicity with *kairos* gives me a strongly numinous feeling, and a sense of being in harmony with myself. And then I often go on to experience further synchronicity, which provides additional benefits – further free ticks from the universe.

As with many other things, I believe one gets better at drawing on synchronicity with practice. Many people find that reflecting on synchronicity is a practical life skill that can be developed, like emotional intelligence or the ability to brainstorm.

2

Spooky Action at a Distance

Synchronicity, Science and Spirituality

Synchronicity is often seen as a mystical phenomenon, which leads many people to reject it as a superstitious, unscientific notion. Perhaps surprisingly, however, it was a pioneer of quantum physics, Wolfgang Pauli, who convinced Carl Jung to write about the subject, partly by offering to co-author a book with Jung, *The Interpretation of Nature and the Psyche*, to which Pauli contributed his own essay about archetypes.[1] Pauli and Jung corresponded often over 25 years until Pauli's death in 1958, and their interchanges helped to shape Jung's theories about synchronicity.

It is not as though Pauli was superstitious, or anything but rigorous in his thinking. As a schoolboy bored in class, he read Einstein's papers on relativity, under the cover of his desk. Aged 18, with a reputation as an intellectual prodigy, he was invited to join a Munich physics research team.[2] In fact, a number of quantum physics pioneers had an explicit interest in mystical beliefs,[3] and a number of prominent physicists, past and present, have turned to traditional Eastern mystical teachings to help make sense of what they've learned about the nature of physical reality.[4]

In this chapter, attempting to describe some of the concepts related to my understanding of synchronicity, I explore aspects of the relationship between science and spirituality – and between logical reasoning and intuitive insight. I hope this will provide a suitable grounding for ideas expressed in this book that extend beyond mainstream psychology and conventional mental health approaches. The subjective experience of synchronicity becomes more meaningful, I believe, if you engage with this kind of material. I will try to show that synchronicity is not as alien to a scientifically informed approach as it may at first sight seem. And if I'm successful, I hope this will prompt a number of my colleagues in the health professions to consider more seriously the potential relevance of synchronicity in their clients' lives.

In 1975 Fritjof Capra, in his book *The Tao of Physics*, highlighted the overlap between quantum physics and traditional mystical beliefs. He suggested that science and mysticism represent two complementary aspects of the human mind, namely the rational and intuitive faculties.[5] Both quantum physicists and mystics have made observations that were not accessible to the ordinary senses. Between their different viewpoints there's not so much a chasm as a connection. There's a striking overlap – a kinship, a congruence.

What did the quantum physicists discover that was so challenging to their worldviews that they started to look more favourably on mystical beliefs? Firstly, despite appearances, they learned that the physical world was not made of any type of solid stuff. Physical matter is formed of molecules, atoms and elementary particles. Such matter only manifests as an object at some point in time and space when it's observed or measured. Until it's observed, the basic building block of matter, an elementary particle, exists only as a kind of potential. Because the act of observation stems from consciousness, this means that it's ultimately consciousness that leads to matter becoming manifest.

No less surprising perhaps is this scientific discovery: before it's observed, a particle has the potential to be located in any number of positions at one and the same time, a principle called 'superposition'.[6] It first exists as a kind of potential with varying probability of being in one location rather than another. It's only after it's been observed that it becomes fixed in one position, and could no longer exist anywhere else at that point in time. Furthermore, a particle may function either as a wave of energy, or as a form of localized matter. When it's observed by an experimenter, what happens is described as a 'collapse of the wave function'[7] – a transition from a probability to an actuality, a measurable physical existence in space.

The fact that the building blocks of matter can be either wave or particle, or can be located in any number of positions at one and the same time until observed, reflects an ambiguity, or uncertainty, inherent in physical reality. The German scientist Werner Heisenberg highlighted the limitations of any objective knowledge or measurement of reality in his reference to the 'uncertainty principle'.[8] He demonstrated that the more accurately the position of an electron could be determined, the less accurately its momentum could be known, and vice versa. The quantum physicists also recognized that the uncertainty of what they observed was influenced not only by the apparatus they used for their measurements,[9] but also by the theories they adopted when designing their experiments in the first place.[10]

The observers' choices, and therefore their consciousness, had a fundamental impact on what was observed. There was no such thing as an objective external reality separate from the observer's consciousness: human involvement was needed to 'collapse' a potential into something observable in the first place. Other challenging conclusions were that mass and energy were interchangeable, and that particles could move backwards, as well as forwards, in time.

Many of these notions had long been recognized by certain Eastern spiritual traditions.[11] For example, Indian and Chinese mystics from Vedanta and Taoist traditions had articulated beliefs about the physical world being an illusion, the primacy of consciousness in creating reality, the fundamental impact of subjective perception in the manifest world, the idea of physical matter being interchangeable with energy, and the potential for time to go backwards as well as forwards. Somehow the mystics intuited such conclusions through practices including deep meditation, as they sought to refine and expand their awareness in their search for enlightenment.

To place their developing understanding of science in a broader, holistic context, a number of quantum physics pioneers appeared to develop a particular interest in the Upanishads, the central scriptures of Vedanta philosophy, the most intellectual school of the Hindu religion. For example, Erwin Schrödinger, who won the Nobel Prize in 1933 for his wave equation, in his book *My View of the World* relates his mystical and metaphysical views to Vedanta philosophy. He referred to the 'ancient wisdom of the Upanishad'[12] as giving support to his scientific conclusion that individual consciousness was a manifestation of an undivided universal consciousness pervading the universe.[13]

Werner Heisenberg reportedly confided to Fritjof Capra that he was greatly encouraged to learn that some of the challenging ideas emerging from quantum physics were consistent with mystical teachings, so that 'some of the ideas that seemed so crazy suddenly made much more sense'.[14] Niels Bohr, the great Danish physicist, was so struck by the way that quantum physics chimed with Chinese mystical views that he adopted the Yin Yang symbol for his family coat-of-arms when he received a knighthood for his scientific work.[15]

Albert Einstein became concerned that some of his peers were seeming to veer too much towards mysticism. He publicly challenged Niels Bohr for doing so, prompting Bohr to defend himself.[16] Einstein himself had expressed similar ideas, claiming to believe, for example, 'that the cosmic religious feeling is the strongest and noblest motive for scientific research'.[17] However, it seems that in Einstein's view Bohr had ventured too far in this direction.

Einstein's challenge to Bohr reflects a general cultural tendency, continuing in scientific fields to this day, to challenge or dismiss beliefs that seem irrational, however much they might fit with people's subjective experiences. Peer pressure can lead people to express themselves differently in public and in private. Heisenberg was renowned as one of the more positivist, or rigorously scientific, quantum physicists.[18] However, when Fritjof Capra went through every chapter of his book *The Tao of Physics* with an elderly Heisenberg, asserting the relevance of Eastern mystical beliefs, Heisenberg apparently nodded his assent: 'basically,' he said, 'I am in complete agreement with you.'[19]

Heisenberg confided to Capra that he too had been accused of 'getting too much into philosophy'.[20] 'You know, you and I', he told him, 'are physicists of a different kind, but every now and then we just have to howl with the wolves' – in other words, one has to conform to the expectations of one's social group. Capra was so heartened by such comments that he felt ready to 'take on the rest of the world'. Highlighting in his book the overlapping conclusions from quantum physics and mystical wisdom would, he hoped, encourage a shift towards an expanded worldview, with greater acknowledgment of the relevance of intuition. This could help people transcend the all-too-common mechanically rationalistic perspectives that prevailed in all the various sciences and in the wider culture.

In a similar vein, a contemporary theoretical physicist, Amit Goswami, has studied the connections between quantum physics and Indian mysticism, and the implications of these for physical and mental health. In his books *The Quantum Doctor* (2004) and *Quantum Creativity* (2013), he suggested that principles of quantum physics such as superposition also apply to the manifestation of thoughts, feelings and intuitions. He suggested that such subjective experiences are similarly derived from infinite alternatives emanating from a realm of consciousness: they become manifest, as a particular thought, or feeling, or intuition, when 'collapsed' at the point of being observed. In accord with the uncertainty principle, the extent to which we literally create our own reality seems consistent with the elegant Mexican proverb, 'Nothing is false and nothing is true: it depends on the crystal that we look through.'[21]

Given this affinity between modern physics and mysticism, we might wonder about the current tendency in the fields of psychology and mental health to downplay mystical or spiritual phenomena. Much of this can be attributed to the continuing influence of the Cartesian–Newtonian paradigm, based on the combined analytical and scientific methods of René Descartes and Isaac Newton established in the 17th century.[22]

Descartes (1596–1650) developed strategies for analytical thinking, which involved breaking a problem into its parts and analysing it using logic and reason. He considered that the mind and body were fundamentally divided, and viewed the universe as a machine that was completely separate from consciousness. Isaac Newton (1642–1727) also viewed the world as a huge mechanical system. His conception of the universe based upon natural and rationally understandable laws became one of the seeds of Enlightenment thinking.

According to the Cartesian–Newtonian paradigm, the world is subject to predictable mechanical laws independent of an observer. The consequent separation between the scientific and spiritual domains became a major cultural limitation: science advanced by leaps and bounds but ignored whatever failed to succumb to its experimental method. This lack of integrated understanding is probably one of the reasons Sigmund Freud dismissed religious beliefs as a form of neurosis.

This separation of science and spirit seems to go well beyond what Descartes or Newton intended. Far from rejecting spiritual beliefs, Descartes put forward as one of his claimed 'proofs' the idea that God exists.[23] He attributed his discovery of his scientific method to divine inspiration, as it was strongly based on a revelatory vision confirmed by a symbolic dream.[24] Similarly, Newton believed it was God who created the universe in the first place. And Newton's interests, outside the natural sciences, included numerology, biblical prophecy and alchemy.[25] Indeed, he wrote more about alchemy, a quasi-mystical activity that involved attempting to transform base metals into gold, than physics.[26]

Many scientific fields have done well by the Cartesian–Newtonian approach, using disciplined objective observations and logical, analytical thought to achieve amazing advances that have changed our lives for the better. However, there are so many aspects of life that don't lend themselves to that kind of analysis. We live our lives by faith and by intuition, more than we might imagine. And there's so much we don't understand even about commonplace experiences such as healing, dreaming and falling in love.

Albert Einstein, along with many of his fellow scientists, believed that the scientific method did not discredit religious or spiritual beliefs. Such beliefs, it was thought, could be important for motivation, personal values and appreciating the importance of those aspects of life that are simply not reducible to science, such as art and music. Nevertheless, Einstein and many others believed that science and spirituality were two very different ways of relating to the world, and should be kept separate.[27]

Following this, there has been an excessive tendency in some fields of science to devalue not only the spiritual but also the subjective. In psychology, behaviourism showed a total disregard for not only spiritual and mystical phenomena but even thoughts and feelings. In its aim of using objective measurement to test falsifiable theory, it focused so exclusively on outwardly observable behaviour that it seemed to promote the idea that an individual is nothing more than a complex assembly of predetermined biological responses, at the mercy of environmental triggers. Free will, personality, personal growth and spirit are devalued in such a mindset. And events that aren't causally connected can have no connection at all: a coincidence is just a coincidence. Fortunately, humanistic and transpersonal psychology approaches have allowed a fuller appreciation of human experience.

It's now 100 years since the core findings of quantum physics started to emerge, and we're still struggling to understand their implications. As some scientists have argued, the universe is not just stranger than we imagine – it's stranger than we *can* imagine.[28] This should remind us of the importance of not dismissing extremely surprising or seemingly irrational notions too readily. We should by now know enough to welcome the weird into our world, rather than unreflectingly reject it. As Niels Bohr humorously suggested, if a new theory doesn't at first appear crazy or absurd, then most likely it's doomed to failure.[29]

I hope that the foregoing overview will be useful when it comes to considering the implications of another mind-boggling finding from quantum physics that most closely relates to synchronicity: the phenomenon of entanglement. As a concept, this was seemingly the one that most strained credibility. Despite mounting evidence, even Einstein rejected the idea, setting him apart from his fellow pioneers in science.

The term 'entanglement' describes a relationship between two or more particles, or other objects, that have interacted with each other and then been separated. Bell's Theorem hypothesized that two or more such objects would somehow remain connected with each other, functioning as a single system. This meant that any induced change in one twinned particle, such as an electron, would lead to an instantaneous and complementary change in the other, regardless of how vast the distance that separated them.

Einstein simply couldn't accept the idea of 'spooky action at a distance', as he called it. He didn't believe that any influence between physical objects could occur faster than the speed of light, let alone instantaneously. However, numerous experiments from the 1970s have progressively established the reality of entanglement – or instantaneous, non-local influence.[30]

Einstein's scepticism shows that those who find it difficult to accept this notion as a reality are in good company. Entanglement doesn't mean that a change in one object directly causes a change in the other; however, it does mean that there's a pre-existing invisible connection between the two objects. Given that all physical matter supposedly emanated from one point, at the time of the Big Bang, this suggests that all physical matter might be entangled, or instantaneously connected, in some way. Just like synchronicity, entanglement implies a transcendence of our everyday notions of time, space and direct causal influence.

In my view, the scientific evidence for entanglement lends some support to the existence of telepathy, precognition and other paranormal phenomena. There seem to be obvious parallels. If physical objects can be instantaneously connected at any distance, then why can't the same be true of people's minds? There seems to be a clear overlap between entanglement and psychic propinquity.

Entanglement is often seen as the most profound discovery ever made in the physical sciences. I believe its potential implications are yet to be integrated in the social sciences, and in the psychological and mental health fields in particular. This would include giving more serious consideration to the potential reality of paranormal, or 'psi', phenomena.

It isn't as though psychology has always turned its back on mystical experience.[31] William James (1842–1910), one of the most influential psychologists of his time, believed that any theory of personality that didn't take alternative states of consciousness into account, including mystical experience, was incomplete – it would ignore a core aspect of human experience.[32] (This is also a basic premise of this book.)

In *The Varieties of Religious Experience*, published in 1902, James detailed his interest in practical and subjective aspects of mystical experience in everyday life. He defined mystical experience as being extraordinary experience that's marked by a number of key features. It's ineffable: that is, it's impossible to describe the experience adequately in words. It's noetic, in that it conveys seemingly significant insight beyond that available to the intellect. It's transient, being unsustainable for a long period. And it shows passivity: a sense of being influenced by something beyond our own will. These features clearly apply to synchronicity.

James initially explored such personal mystical experiences by inhaling nitrous oxide.[33] However, he later emphasized practices such as yoga, meditation and hypnosis as offering more reliable and lasting ways to access different states of consciousness.

From the late 1960s onwards, the emerging field of transpersonal psychology has developed to explore spiritual experiences and transcendental states of consciousness, including mystical experience and paranormal phenomena. Carl Jung's core influence on this field is reflected in its adoption of his term 'transpersonal', which he coined to refer to the collective unconscious.[34] Other influential precursors, apart from William James, include Abraham Maslow, well known for his ideas about self-actualization and peak experiences.

A contemporary leader in this field, Ken Wilber, has described a ten-stage psycho-spiritual model to help integrate mystical experience into psychological and personality development.[35] This model includes several 'pre-egoic' stages, from pre-birth to early infancy, several 'egoic' stages commonly associated with normal personality development, and several more advanced 'trans-egoic' stages, related to the process of enlightenment.

Most psychological theories of personality development describe the most mature levels as occurring when a person has gone through stages of conformity, conscientiousness and autonomy to become a highly functioning and differentiated individual who is nonetheless well integrated into society. However, a transpersonal model suggests that further personal and spiritual development may occur, accompanied by mystical experience, and involving progressive stages of enlightenment.

According to this model, there are several recognized traps that people can fall into around the more advanced, trans-egoic stages. One is to be fearful of recognizing, or taking seriously, mystical experiences in the first place. For example, a person having an accurate premonition, seeing a vision or having an out-of-body experience might suddenly feel overwhelmed. They could then retreat, blocking out or denying such experience, in a manner that disrupts their further personal and spiritual development. Maslow suggested that this could interfere with people recognizing or pursuing their destiny.

On the other hand, people could also fall into the trap of becoming overly fixated on their seemingly mystical illuminations or insights. For example, if you were to be overly focused on the seemingly miraculous nature of psychic phenomena, including synchronistic experiences, this could distract you from the important goal of pursuing your personal and spiritual development, beyond concerns of the ego. At worst, feeling you'd been uniquely singled out by the miraculous, you might get caught up in a sense of specialness or grandiosity and suffer from so-called 'psychic inflation'. The story of winged Icarus falling from the heavens after donning a pair of wings and flying too close to the sun (causing the adhesive wax to melt) is a mythological warning for people to remain grounded in the face of extraordinary experience.

Castaneda and Psychic Inflation

The colourful life story of Carlos Castaneda warns against the dangers of psychic inflation. Castaneda sold over 10 million books about his reported mystical encounters with a Yaqui Indian shaman. Castaneda's works, including *The Teachings of Don Juan* and *Journey to Ixtlan*, became so influential that he was described by *Time* magazine in 1973 as the 'Godfather of the New Age'. However, even though he was awarded a doctoral degree in anthropology for his work, it turned out that his books were fictionalized.[36]

Arguably, Castaneda's elegant teachings about following 'a path with a heart', and being ready for a 'cubic centimetre of chance', still conveyed meaningful truths in a metaphorical guise. However, there seems little doubt that Castaneda lapsed into psychic inflation when he established himself as a cult leader, encouraged the separation of his followers from their families and allegedly urged some of his closest followers to attempt suicide after his death. He apparently concealed his eventually fatal liver cancer from all but his closest followers, because sorcerers weren't meant to get sick. Castaneda's story points to the potential importance of having a mentor as a grounding influence when exploring mystical phenomena or seeking enlightenment. Castaneda, I imagine, would have been less likely to succumb to psychic inflation if he'd been guided by a real mentor, as opposed to a fictional one.

The final stage of enlightenment would presumably be the preserve of such figures as Jesus Christ and the Buddha. It might also apply to those mystics who have seemingly experienced the true mystery of the physical universe – the ineffable reality to which quantum physics gives us a mere sketch map. At this level, people are said to have direct experience of themselves in an unmanifest form, while still being able to differentiate a world of manifest form. I wouldn't pretend to understand this – it goes well beyond any stage I might be at. However, this description reminds me of Jung's striking account of his near-death experience associated with a mystical encounter with his doctor (see p.20).

Mystical experience can be misinterpreted in mainstream psychiatry and psychology as psychosis, with which it shares many features, at least superficially. However, according to Eastern spiritual perspectives, mystical experience accompanied by a sense of the boundaries dissolving between yourself and the world around you might be seen instead as enlightenment – or *satori*.[37] The latter alternative is rarely considered, but I think it's often the most fitting.

Whereas mainstream psychology continues to be wary of mystical experience, typically considering it to be pre-scientific, there's increasing recognition of the potential relevance of broader notions of spirituality. In the fields of physical and mental health, many doctors and therapists today are drawn to Eastern disciplines of mind, body and spirit, and particularly yoga, meditation and mindfulness techniques.

Interest in spirituality has also increased in response to evidence that religious faith confers physical and mental health benefits – including a reduced incidence of and quicker recovery from depression, lower alcohol and drug abuse, lesser suicide risk, reduced risk from physical illnesses such as heart disease and cancer, and greater longevity.[38] Having faith, an involvement in some kind of spiritual practice or belief, promotes individual happiness and family wellbeing in adults, as well as better academic performance and emotional self-regulation in children.[39]

Such findings are increasingly acknowledged in medical schools, and in such fields as positive psychology. There are also increasing signs of interest in spirituality and faith in cognitive-behavioural therapy (CBT), beyond the widespread adoption of mindfulness techniques. For example, Donald Meichenbaum, a prominent leader in the field, recently urged a greater focus on spirituality, which he suggested had been just as much ignored in the present day as cognition had been in the behaviour-focused psychology training of the 1960s.[40] Faith has been found to help people after trauma, facilitating hope and helping them to find meaning, even in the most challenging of circumstances.

In psychology, a distinction is sometimes made between extrinsic religiosity, which involves participating in institutionalized religious practice, and intrinsic religiosity, which is more of an internal commitment.[41] These aspects commonly, but not always, occur together. Health benefits appear to be most associated with intrinsic religiosity, which overlaps with broader definitions of spirituality, related to personal meaning and connectedness.

It's valid to think of synchronicity as a spiritual experience, particularly in the ways it can promote a sense of connection, meaning and purpose in your life. It can help to point to a worthwhile life direction – the theme of the next chapter.

I'll finish this overview of synchronicity, science and spirituality with a personal story. On the morning I started writing this chapter, I felt daunted. To write about synchronicity I believed I had to venture into quantum physics. Did I know enough about the subject? Was I going to be somewhat out of my depth? I procrastinated. I looked up emails. I clicked into one that had an interesting link I'd never seen before: 'Divergent Minds: a weekly podcast about creativity, design and shaping life in the 21st century'. I clicked on the most recent podcast. It had a section on quantum mechanics! I clicked into that. It had a quote attributed to the physicist Richard Feynman: 'If you think you understand quantum mechanics, then you don't!' Phew! I was in good company. From then on the task didn't seem quite so daunting.

3

Ghostly Encounters

Seeing the Future, Healing the Past

Jung's interest in the connection between our inner, mental, and external, physical, reality was not just confined to synchronicity: he also studied such other experiences as precognition, psychokinesis and poltergeist phenomena. He was especially interested in J.B. Rhine's research in the 1930s on extra-sensory perception, which he believed provided scientific evidence for additional phenomena that couldn't be explained by usual notions of space, time and causality. Jung considered that any such evidence, just like recent findings from quantum physics, could provide at least indirect support for the notion of synchronicity.

Further evidence for such psychic (also known as 'psi') phenomena is extensively documented by accredited scientists, including Mario Beauregard,[1] a neuroscientist, and Dean Radin, a scientist who was appointed by the US government to investigate psychic phenomena.[2] (See box on psi phenomena, p.46.)

Often my clients who report synchronistic experiences also convincingly report other psychic phenomena. Their experiences of such phenomena often seem to be beneficial, providing further evidence for the 'power of supra-rational thinking'. They include reported visions or encounters with ghosts, a different – perhaps more literal – form of 'spooky action'.

In his autobiography, *Memories, Dreams, Reflections*, Jung described having numerous dreams or visions that uncannily anticipated events such as the death of his mother, doctor, former patients and others.[3]

For example, after a dream involving a gravesite and an audible death sigh, Jung had the feeling that someone associated with his wife (he didn't know who) had died at 3am. He learned a few hours later that his wife's cousin had died at that precise time.[4]

Jung didn't claim that such events, as numerous as they were, amounted to objective proof of psychic phenomena, but they gave him 'a certain respect for the potentialities and arts of the unconscious'.[5] Jung's openness to the idea of some form of consciousness beyond the purely personal, and potentially beyond death, was prompted by a dream six weeks after his father died. His father suddenly appeared before him and announced that he'd recovered and was coming home. Jung wrote that his father's appearance in the dream, repeated two days later, was so real and unforgettable that 'it forced me for the first time to think about life after death.'[6]

Jung's interest in such matters was further piqued after he came across literature on spiritualistic phenomena that seemed to contain authentic and objective accounts of events he'd heard about in his rural childhood. The material included encounters with ghosts or dreams that foresaw death. Jung was surprised by the extent to which his peers, including his closest friends, seemed so confident in dismissing such accounts, despite potential support for them from modern physics.

After much extensive study and many personal experiences, Jung came to believe that such 'images of the unconscious are not produced by consciousness, but have a reality and spontaneity of their own.' He lamented that they were regarded as 'mere marginal phenomena',[7] since he believed that openness to this kind of experience could contribute vitality and meaning in one's life.

I shall now describe two accounts of such phenomena from among my own clients. In both cases, apparent encounters with the deceased occurred with uncanny timing, enhancing the motivation and life purpose experienced by these individuals. I might add that it is only clients who learned that I was writing a book on synchronicity who have divulged such examples.

Gary, a skilled tradesmen and father of three adult children, had lost a daughter as a result of a rare blood condition a day after she was born 20 years earlier. I saw him on account of his limited recovery from his 'severe clinical depression', despite having received combined psychiatric and psychological treatment over the previous eight years. He continued to be plagued by guilt from having allowed undignified funeral arrangements for his daughter, including a seemingly unnecessary and macabre viewing of her corpse, and the transportation of her coffin on the back seat of an ordinary car rather than in a hearse. He still admonished himself for not attending better to the upkeep of her headstone and gravesite. However, he feared that if he attempted to rectify this neglect, he might give in to fantasies of taking his life at the gravesite.

We pursued a therapy approach with an initial aim of alleviating his chronic post-traumatic stress reactions. We used a therapy technique, Eye Movement Desensitization and Reprocessing (EMDR), which involved a deliberate re-living of painful memories to help defuse their negative emotional impact. Whereas his response to EMDR in our fourth and fifth sessions appeared favourable from the outset, a new and fortuitous development at the time of those sessions strongly bolstered his progress.

At the end of our fourth session, Gary became my first client ever to directly ask me, 'Do you believe in synchronicity?' I responded that I did, and was in fact writing a book about it. We laughingly shared that we both found that in itself to be synchronistic. There seemed little doubt that he was ready from that point on to report unusual experiences to me that he might typically have kept to himself.

Over the next two weeks, Gary confided to me that on the night after our first EMDR session he was very distressed and couldn't get out of his mind a worry about whether his daughter was 'OK'. At that point he had the vivid experience of feeling a pat on his head that could not have come from his wife, who was asleep beside him. After the following session he'd again gone to bed, again wondering whether his daughter was OK. He awoke at 3am to notice his bedside clock flashing as though the household power had failed.

He got up to check, and by the time he climbed back into bed, after finding nothing amiss, he noticed that the flashing had incomprehensibly stopped. He then described the profound experience of 'putting two and two together', recognizing that the pat he'd unmistakably felt the week before was his infant daughter 'saying everything is all right'. He believed that the flashing clock, occurring at precisely the time he tended to wake up at night, along with the pat on the head the week before, was his daughter sending a sign or signal that 'seemed too coincidental'. He concluded, 'she knows I care about her, she knows that I know she's OK.'

At his sixth therapy session he described an even more vivid spiritualistic encounter. He began, 'I saw Anna last night … I had a chat before I went to sleep. Around 3am there was some noise. I could see a faint young person's head hovering just above [my wife's] head.' He added that it was definitely his daughter's face – he looked at her two or three times to confirm this. At first he'd thought it was his wife's face, and was about to respond to her, but then he'd seen that his wife's head was turned away.

Gary described feeling much lighter in spirits after these experiences that he felt were unambiguously connected with his deceased daughter. He felt absolved of guilt, stating that if she'd felt any grievance against him, then she wouldn't have reassuringly appeared. He added, 'It is a happy thing to know she's around … She can pop in any time she wants!'

An objective check of Gary's symptomatic distress showed that his post-traumatic stress and depressive symptoms had by then reduced to a minimal level. He became more motivated and efficient at work, his energy levels lifted, and his family relationships improved. 'I probably would have written it off as stupid 10 years ago,' he said. 'Now it's all happening for a reason … The timing is perfect … Coming to see you … That night it happens … It all happens for a reason. It's put me in a fantastic mindset.' He added, 'Not so many things worry me any more … I have a lot of living ahead of me.'

Gary later volunteered that his wife had often felt that her deceased grandmother was 'following her around'. Apparently one of her relatives encountered ghostly presences almost daily, including a man who visited her home and a cat that sometimes sat at the end of her bed. Gary described having more frequent and intense synchronistic experiences that 'happen too often to dismiss', including going to make a phone call to a work colleague or family member who rang him themselves at that precise time. He attributed this to having a 'clearer mind' and being 'more open to stuff like this'. The increased number of synchronistic experiences contributed to his feeling that 'I'm on the right track … Things are definitely pointing in the right direction.'

We'd probably never have had such intriguing conversations without a fortunate happenstance. Gary later explained that his question as to whether I believed in synchronicity was initially prompted by my requesting him to change our next appointment to a particular day when I don't normally see clients. Unbeknownst to me, just beforehand he'd asked our reception staff for the exact same change in date, but had been denied as they didn't know that I planned to request this exceptional change myself. This coincidence could be described as merely lucky. But given that we both felt the timing was meaningful, as though facilitating events that were meant to be, I'd call it synchronicity.

Another client, Diana, a woman in her early 40s, came to me after the end of a marriage marked by years of physical and emotional abuse. She'd also suffered a harsh childhood with similar, frequent abuse. She aimed to rise above her relatively impoverished emotional and socio-economic background by actively setting herself goals and 'planning everything I want in future'.

Over the two years (to date) of our typically monthly therapy contact, her single-minded determination and clear focus have shone through (not least in undertaking full-time study in social work, while raising two children, and being offered a mentoring role to new students at the end of her first year).

She was helped on this new path by remarkable synchronistic experiences, which I learned about long after our initial contact, after telling her I was writing a book on the subject.

Ghostly Contact

A 2012 poll has shown that 45 per cent of Americans believe in ghosts, or that the spirits of the dead can return to the realm of the living in certain circumstances.[8] Mourners who have a vision of the deceased are often concerned that they are becoming mentally unhinged, and for this reason they often they keep their experiences to themselves. Such secrecy explains why it's generally thought that such communications are rare, perhaps reflecting psychological problems. Jung warned against interpreting such reported experiences as providing objective evidence of super-natural phenomena, such as life beyond death. However, many anecdotal reports indicate that information gained from encounters with ghosts has proved uncannily accurate, often in circumstances where there was no rational explanation for how that person could otherwise have gained the information. This seems to indicate that, at least sometimes, ghostly encounters can't be readily dismissed as merely an individual's projected fantasies.

As the cases in this chapter suggest, what counts most in a therapy setting is what's of most benefit to the client. These examples indicate that it can be profoundly helpful, in at least some situations, for a person to actively reflect on their transpersonal experience with someone else who's attuned to them, including when dealing with grief.

She described a poignant incident that played a key role in setting her on her new life direction: a synchronistic ghostly encounter. At one point, Diana sensed that she might gain assistance for her future path from her ancestors. She had a strong interest in her family tree but her researches into the subject turned up nothing of value.

Frustrated, she prayed for some information about her ancestors. As Diana was in her bathroom preparing for bed, she was startled to see a vision of a little old man, hunched over, standing before her. His clothes were old-fashioned, including black pants, a pinstripe shirt, waistcoat, cap and hobnailed boots. He looked at her and said, 'The information you require you will have in the morning.' Then he vanished, and she went to bed. When she awoke, she wondered whether she'd been hallucinating. However, the man's message prompted her to renew her search for information that morning.

Within half an hour she stumbled across an internet website which detailed information about a 'well-to-do' branch of her family with a number of accomplished relatives. They included a celebrated associate of the Duke of Wellington and a prominent Justice of the Peace, her great-grandfather. It was clear that many family members had been well connected and enjoyed an uncommonly privileged education, in contrast to her modest schooling. The benefits of such privilege had been disrupted by an ancestor's fall from grace in committing forgery. Having found evidence of an academic streak in her heritage, Diana determined to build on that, while remaining faithful to her working-class roots.

Despite her early success in a new career direction, Diana was nonetheless susceptible at times to tolerating at least mildly abusive or exploitative relationships with men. However, on one occasion a premonition associated with a synchronistic dream assisted her to break free. In the dream a female face appeared to her and told her to look at the top of a particular bathroom cupboard at her boyfriend's house. She didn't act on this when she woke up, but received 'loud messages' in her mind to go to the cupboard and find some papers. After removing clothes and other things from the top of the cupboard, she found a hotel receipt that revealed her partner's infidelity, which eventually he couldn't deny. She ended the relationship.

Diana reported other uncanny premonitions. She was once with her mother in a cemetery when they took a photo including a headstone. They were later struck by what they both agreed was an image of a male relative of theirs on the photographed headstone, which hadn't been visible on the headstone itself. They guessed that the relative might face imminent death, even though they had no reason to suspect this on the grounds of his health. He died six months later.

Diana's synchronistic experiences, in premonitory visions and dreams, seem consistent with Jung's idea that such material can't easily be dismissed as emanating from a personal consciousness based on intuitive insights alone. She felt she was receiving external assistance or information from another source, and at least in part she attributed this to guidance from deceased ancestors.

Currently, Diana is going from strength to strength, continuing her studies, extending her social network and moving confidently in business, professional and political circles. She matter-of-factly told me, 'I feel I'm on some journey to help with healing people ... And helping people to transition in life and heal ... I feel that I'm going to develop a voice in society ... I don't know how.' Her fortuitous social contacts have been 'meant to be'. 'Synchronicity', she said, 'is the universe telling you that you're getting warmer.'

Being open to messages from outside herself, and acting on her synchronistic premonitions, have clearly strengthened Diana in her determination to make a vocation for herself in social work, as well as in building a more confident individual self. Combining synchronicity with *kairos*, she has created her own path.

Jung believed that 'the unconscious helps us by communicating things to us ... It has other ways of informing us of things which by all logic we could not possibly know.'[9] Diana might agree with his claim that 'the unconscious ... possesses better sources of information than the conscious mind.'[10]

Jung felt that his own synchronistic experiences, including premonitory visions and dreams, helped to clarify his direction in life, which seemed strongly based on promoting further understanding of the psyche. His inner images helped him to 'see the line which leads through my life into the world, and out of the world again.'[11] Synchronicity is linked to personal destiny: it can show you your life's path, like a carpet being rolled out in front of you.

Psi Phenomena – Can Time Travel Backwards?

As Jung described in *Synchronicity: An Acausal Connecting Principle*, J.B. Rhine and colleagues provided evidence for psychic phenomena from numerous scientific experiments that challenged usual notions of cause and effect. One such task involved people guessing which of five geometrical designs would be revealed on each of 25 shuffled cards. The results across numerous experiments resulted in a greater number of correct hits than expected by chance (approximately double). Rhine used the term 'extra-sensory perception' (ESP) to describe such phenomena.

Nowadays, psychic phenomena are referred to as 'psi' phenomena. They include telepathy (transfer of thought between people), clairvoyance (gaining information, but not through the known senses), psychokinesis (mentally influencing a physical action) and precognition. Mario Beauregard, a neuroscientist, has documented extensive evidence for psi phenomena in his book *Brain Wars*, as has another scientist, Dean Radin, in *Supernormal*. They each conclude that the combined results of all known research on psi effects strongly support the reality of psi phenomena, at odds of billions to one against the findings resulting from lucky guesses.

Psi research has now entered mainstream psychology owing to the research of eminent psychologist Professor Daryl Bem of Cornell University.[12] He conducted nine experiments on 1,000 student participants that provided evidence for such phenomena as precognition. He found that students could correctly guess (that is, better than chance) which of two curtains an erotic picture would appear behind, *even before* a computer randomly determined where the picture would appear. Another experiment showed that the benefits of practice could go backwards in time: when students were asked to recall 48 words that had appeared on a screen for three seconds each, and straight afterwards did practice drills involving 24 of those words selected at random, it turned out after the practice that *during the test* they'd showed better recall of those 24 words they later practised than of the words they hadn't practised.

These findings are the first findings in the mainstream psychology literature to suggest that future events can influence past events (known as 'retrocausal' effects), or that time can seemingly travel backwards. This anomalous idea is nonetheless reminiscent of the findings from quantum physics described in Chapter 2.

4

Synchronicity and Your Life Path

Do you believe in destiny? Do you have a sense of your fate unfolding? Do you believe that many things that have happened in your life were not random but have led you to a particular path or calling that's somehow meant for you? Modern psychology generally considers such notions to be pre-scientific or superstitious. However, as described by James Hillman in *The Soul's Code: In Search of Character and Calling*, many cultures have used specific terms to refer to a hidden tendency that guides us to our personal destiny. He associated this with the 'acorn theory', whereby everyone has a seed within himself or herself; if nurtured and supported, this could grow metaphorically into a great oak tree, reflecting one's unique nature.[1]

The Greeks referred to being guided by your daimon; the Romans called it genius; Christians refer to having a guardian angel; shamans believe that they're guided by their animal-soul.[2] The Chinese value the Tao, or Way, meaning an inner spiritual path, aligned with the harmony of nature, to be consciously followed.[3] Buddhists might describe your life purpose in terms of fulfilling your dharma.[4] William James, the American pioneer of psychology, referred to a 'higher self'[5] and Jung, similarly, to an archetypal 'Self' as an inner guide.[6]

Your daimon may guide you towards your calling or destiny in numerous ways, not always welcome at the time. For example, if you're heading in a direction in conflict with your calling, you might experience prolonged dissatisfaction, restlessness, illness or misfortune. On the other hand, when committing to a direction consistent with your destiny, then satisfaction, motivation and uncommon opportunity, or good fortune, will accompany you.

Joseph Campbell, the American mythologist, summed up his encouragement to people to find their calling in the elegantly simple expression, 'Follow your bliss.' In a famous series of interviews with Bill Moyers, entitled *The Power of Myth*, Campbell elaborated that when you follow your bliss, 'you put yourself on a kind of track that has been there all the while, waiting for you, and the life you ought to be living is the one you are living ... When you can see that, you begin to meet people who are in your field of bliss, and they open doors for you ... Follow your bliss and don't be afraid ... Doors will open where you didn't know they were going to be.'[7] This fits my own experience of uncommon opportunities arising in my life, marked by a feeling of strong synchronicity; and I've met many others with similar stories to tell. In my view, such experiences are a reliable indication of being on the right track for one's calling or destiny, representing a 'tick from the universe'; when such experiences lead to an obvious boon, I also refer to it as getting a 'free kick from the universe'.

Even painful experiences involving misfortune can ultimately prove to have been extremely helpful in redirecting oneself, and perhaps clarifying a life direction that's ultimately more meaningful and fulfilling.

From that perspective, synchronicity is not especially meaningful in itself, regardless of how intriguing it may be. It's especially beneficial in helping us see a larger picture, guiding us towards our optimal life path, or encouraging us that we're on the right track. In my view, synchronicity is a message from your daimon to 'keep on going'.

Deepak Chopra's suggestively titled book *Synchrodestiny* describes synchronicity as a path to meaning and purpose in one's life, connecting to the 'nonlocal intelligence of the universe'.[8] There's no such thing, Chopra claims, as meaningless coincidence. Moreover, 'the more attention you put on coincidences and the more you enquire into their significance, the more often coincidences occur,

Follow Your Bliss

Joseph Campbell summed up so much in a single phrase: 'Follow your bliss.' This is another way of saying to follow your daimon. Do what you're passionate about. Focus on what moves you. If you devote yourself to tasks and roles that draw on your passions, you'll be motivated, energized and engaged. You'll be more likely to be in a state of 'flow' for more of the time. You'll most probably be more effective in what you do. You'll tend to derive a strong sense of gratification from your chosen purpose. This applies to recreation and hobbies, but also, more importantly, it applies to the work and life roles in which we spend a large proportion of our waking hours. As Confucius said, if you choose a job you love, you will never have to work a day in your life.

Alternatively, if we're struggling with what we're doing and finding it difficult to become focused and motivated, this might be a pointer that we could be better off following a different path. Sometimes we might need to perform tasks or undertake roles that aren't the most satisfying to us. It might be important to do so, at least temporarily, to gain an income, meet certain obligations and responsibilities, or as a stepping stone to something better. Under such circumstances it might be important in the meantime to follow our bliss in other ways, while committing to doing our best even with activities that aren't voluntary. We should be truthful with ourselves if what we're doing isn't moving us. It's part of a full life to experience many ups and downs: they all combine to make us who we are. Synchronicity typically seems less common during the downs, or flat spots. The absence of synchronicity might be a clue that we could do more to follow our bliss.

and the more clearly their meaning comes into view.'[9] When a coincidence occurs, he suggests you ask, 'What is the message here?' An answer might emerge in the form of a sudden insight. But it could also emerge later, through some encounter, or some other experience, that throws retrospective illumination on the coincidence, making sense of it for the first time.[10]

Joseph Jaworski's personal account in *Synchronicity: The Inner Path of Leadership* provides a particularly colourful example of these themes. Jaworski describes leaving his job as a well-established partner in a law firm to become an expert in organizational leadership. Aged 41, Jaworski faced a crisis after his wife told him she wanted a divorce. He took time off work, travelled, and reflected extensively on his life's meaning and purpose. At one point he had a mysteriously profound encounter with a weasel in the snowy wilds of Alaska. It made lengthy eye contact with him, before appearing to perform various tricks especially for him. He then felt what he could only describe as 'a kind of transcendence of time and a feeling of oneness with all the universe'.[11]

As positive as this experience was, Jaworski was unsettled by its strangeness. A psychiatrist friend reassured him that he wasn't in fact going mad: he'd had an enlightenment experience of the kind described by all major religions. Jaworski then felt he had a developing awareness of 'relatedness' as the organizing principle of the universe, an awareness he felt was missing in contemporary views of leadership.[12] He felt a compelling desire to create a training programme for creative and visionary leadership that emphasized serving others.

At first Jaworski felt coy about sharing his grand personal dream with others. However, he later felt inspired by a vision of his deceased nephew sitting atop his funeral casket saying, 'Go for it!' That prompted Jaworski to commit himself to leaving his law firm and pursuing his dream of establishing a leadership training centre, despite having no prior training or recognized expertise in this area.

Jaworski's progress was bolstered by a fortuitous encounter with David Bohm, perhaps the pre-eminent quantum physicist of his time.

He tracked Bohm down after seeing a newspaper headline that he felt was speaking to him.[13] Bohm explained his scientific worldview to Jaworski in a manner that echoed Jungian notions of the collective unconscious: 'You cannot think of existence as local ... Yourself is actually the whole of mankind ... The entire past is enfolded in each one of us in a very subtle way ... We are all connected.'[14]

Jaworski and Bohm had further discussion about how the mind has powers beyond those we habitually use. In passing, Bohm strongly endorsed Jaworski's efforts, saying, 'You are on the verge of a creative movement. Just go with it.' He exhorted Jaworski to 'be alert, be self-aware, so that when opportunity presents itself you can actually rise to it.'[15] I'd describe that as an exhortation to combine synchronicity with *kairos*.

Following the meeting with Bohm, Jaworski was all the more energized to develop the American Leadership Forum focused on such ideas as connectedness with others and expanded notions of consciousness. He read all he could about synchronicity, tracing links from Jung's concept back to the ideas of the Ancient Greeks and Renaissance philosophers, as well as to Eastern spiritual traditions and paranormal phenomena.

Often Jaworski showed his preparedness to act on a seemingly improbable, but compelling, intuition. For example, he approached an attractive woman at an airport and explained that even though they'd never met, he felt he knew her from somewhere. His premonition that 'the future life was I going to have with her had already been told to me'[16] was seemingly confirmed when they later married. He learned his wife had dreamed she was going to meet a man during that interstate trip who'd be significant in her life, and was disappointed until her own premonition was belatedly confirmed by him approaching her at the boarding gate.

They married a year later. Jaworski detailed many examples of his wife's intuitive ability, including her prediction of their improbable house moves from Houston to London and Boston associated with his work, despite their having just built a large house in Houston with no intention of moving.

While reflecting on his life and leadership experience, Jaworski emphasized that things seemed to unfold most powerfully when he committed himself to what he felt was his life purpose, trusted in the playing out of his destiny, and allowed life's forces to move through him, without unduly attempting to control the process. In such a state of commitment and surrender, he tended to experience synchronicity in the form of 'predictable miracles'.[17] These included meeting the right people at the right time to help him achieve his seemingly improbable ends. Joseph Campbell refers to this as being assisted by 'invisible hands'.[18]

To help predictable miracles occur, Jaworski spoke of being in an open and interconnected state, waiting expectantly for the cubic centimetre of chance to present itself before acting 'with lightning speed and almost without conscious reasoning'.[19] I call this combining synchronicity with *kairos*.

Jaworski also described times when things didn't flow, misalignment with colleagues occurred and complications arose.[20] In retrospect this often seemed to have resulted from succumbing to the ego, or being concerned about failure and how one's actions might be perceived by others, rather than focusing on the larger calling. He recognized another potential trap: overactivity, becoming bogged down in detail and missing opportunities as a result of feeling pressed for time. On other occasions he may have stuck too closely to original plans rather than adapting to circumstances. When reacting in such ways he noted a much less frequent experience of synchronicity. I relate strongly to his advice.

An important archetypal theme that can help you to think about your life path is the 'hero's journey', a story of the stages of transformation in a person's life.[21] Joseph Campbell identifies this strand in many ancient myths, but it also surfaces in literature and the movies. A protagonist is called to adventure. He or she experiences a 'dark night of the soul' when facing a great challenge. The hero surmounts this, and then returns home after this 'initiation', bringing a boon to his people. Rather than being limited to extraordinary individuals, this theme has relevance to anyone's life in the context of personal transformation.

As elaborated by Robert Dilts,[22] the hero's journey begins with a sense of being in a wasteland, or living an inauthentic life. This may occur to someone at any stage of adult life – including after they've become established, and possessed of money, love and status. A feeling of not belonging, and of inner emptiness, causes the individual to break away from the familiar and to distance themselves from their usual supports. Anyone who resists such a call of the soul may endure symptoms of boredom, restlessness, alienation, depression or other forms of distress. Such dissatisfactions can prompt them in the end to pursue a more authentic or fuller life.

The hero's journey starts when we cross a threshold, taking a bold step in a new direction, outside our comfort zone. Along the way it can be important to have 'guardians', or mentors, to support us, especially if they have some experience of the challenges we are facing.

In our life's journey we often prevail not by fighting but through some form of surrender – the giving up of something old, followed by new choices consistent with our calling. The challenge isn't to kill the demon we face, but to transform it. I think of this as transforming a demon into our daimon.

As described by the psychologist Ernest Rossi, the hero's journey relates closely to a four-stage cycle of creative or transformative change.[23] These stages are often termed preparation, incubation, illumination and verification. In psychotherapy, the four-stage process of change might include a shift from initial wellbeing to a depression followed by a breaking out from old patterns to develop new patterns based on integrated new awareness. This cycle of change is also reflected in nature, perhaps most obviously in the four seasons of the year.

The Australian cartoonist Michael Leunig has offered what I consider to be the simplest and most evocative description of these four stages of change.[24] When trying to come up with an idea for a cartoon, he often finds it starts as a mess. As the struggle continues, he might have a sense of loss, perhaps thinking he can no longer create something worthwhile, despite past accomplishment at the task. Then there's an epiphany. As his creation comes to life, there's joy. Mess; loss; epiphany; joy. How memorably elegant that sequence is!

In a psychotherapy setting, I typically characterize the four stages of transformative change in people's lives along the following lines. First, they might be getting on with their lives in their usual way, and then something happens that challenges their equilibrium and makes them aware of a need for change. There may be a sense of dissatisfaction or desire for further enrichment.

The second stage, incubation, is a turning inward in response to the need for change, at times to the point of withdrawal. This is often painful, especially if the individual remains stuck in old patterns of responding. This stage is associated with high arousal and, at times, depression. In literature it may be referred to as the 'dark night of the soul'. At its most acute, I call it a 'little death'.

The third stage, illumination, involves breaking out of old patterns with new awareness, which offers an expanded range of possibilities for dealing with life's challenges. Sometimes there's a sudden realization, offering a perceived resolution to a problem or dilemma.

In the fourth and final stage, verification, the person draws on new awareness or insights by taking concerted action. They then check to see that this addresses the original challenge and continues to work for them in the longer term. These themes are universal, at times reassuringly so. Even the darkest times, perhaps especially the darkest of times, can lead to the most profound positive change, even if it feels like a kind of death at the time. Personal development will rarely be maximized if people face little challenge or discomfort.

I recognize these stages in my own experience of going through a severe depression, which greatly developed my understanding of mental health problems. This assisted my later work as a psychologist as much as any formal training I've undertaken. I invite you, the reader, to reflect on whether you've gone through such stages of change in your own life experience.

Having an understanding of this pattern of change can greatly help in times of crisis or challenge. It encourages hope and helps you recognize that much good can come out of even the darkest times. Joseph Campbell describes a good life as one hero's journey after another. The metaphor may prompt us to show courage and persistence in the way we might interpret and deal with crises in our lives.

In my view, the hero's journey involving the four stages of change is closely related to the phenomenon of synchronicity. Jung's close collaborator Marie-Louise von Franz pointed out that synchronistic experiences tend to occur at crucial stages of what Jung termed 'individuation', the process of becoming more fully ourselves, but could pass unnoticed if people had not learned to watch for such coincidences.[25] In other words, synchronicity is likely to occur more often at the transition to, or during, stage 3, an apparent illumination stage, as described in many examples here. It isn't so likely to occur at stage 2, when people often feel stuck and relatively lacking in direction. For those who have consolidated their personality development at an enlightened stage, as Jung and some others (including Deepak Chopra) seem to have done, this might be represented in frequent synchronistic experiences at stage 4. You could describe this as ticks from the universe on an ongoing basis, seemingly indicating that the individual has chosen a uniquely true and fulfilling life path for themselves.

The hero's journey, or the process of furthering one's development, doesn't always happen as dramatically as described here. However, we all face challenges in our lives and have issues to address. The themes associated with stages of change might show up in a more subtle way; but they will be there.

Doing a Life Review

In my view, significant life events to date that have helped to shape your trajectory, especially if they proved to be fortuitous or were accompanied by marked synchronicity, will help to illuminate the path of your destiny.

To identify a trajectory that might help your genius to emerge and thrive, it can help to extrapolate from key points on your life path so far.

Imagine your life to date in terms of 10 to 15 significant life-changing events that come to mind. Consider things that changed your course, especially if they resonated with you, at least in retrospect, as leading to a better or more fulfilling direction. Note the things that had a major sudden impact in shifting your life direction – the quantum leaps, so to speak. They might have even seemed like setbacks at the time. Or else they might have seemed obviously fortunate – as in a rare opportunity that came out of the blue. The list could even include a compelling insight that suddenly came to you, one you acted upon to advantage. You might also note some experiences that were more gradual, but nonetheless shifted your trajectory.

Underline, asterisk or otherwise highlight those experiences that were accompanied by strong synchronicity: they may direct you more truly towards your genius, or deeper purpose. A life review of this kind can give you a better sense of how fate seems to have nudged you in a certain direction. It can potentially illuminate your optimum path for the future.

PART TWO

Early Signals

5

Shifting Worldviews

Sometimes reading a book is simply entertainment; at other times it's a learning experience; and on rare occasions it's much more than that.

In 1983, aged 25, I attended a seminar by Dr John Travis, a medically trained teacher from Johns Hopkins University and co-founder of the 'Wellness Model'. This model proposed a framework for relating symptoms of physical and mental illness to lifestyle habits, attitudes and an underlying transpersonal or spiritual dimension. Dr Travis was wearing a long white flowing caftan. Behind him on a screen were projected feel-good images of what might have been Jonathan Livingston Seagull, soaring against white clouds – to reflect the joyous peacefulness on offer. I was deeply sceptical. I thought adults, especially well-educated ones who were older than me, were meant to be rational.

When I met with John after the seminar, he was very generous and gracious. He said that maybe he hadn't expressed himself well, but that much of what he was seeking to convey I could find in a book entitled *The Aquarian Conspiracy*. He talked about the scientists who were turning more and more to religion, in response to the mysterious worldview of quantum physics. That surprised me. I decided to read the book he'd suggested.

I'd always prided myself on being a competently rational and analytical thinker. You could say I was very 'left brain'. But *The Aquarian Conspiracy: Personal and Social Transformation in Our Time* (1980), by Marilyn Ferguson, changed my mindset forever.

Ferguson writes of paradigm shifts occurring in many fields, following on from the revelations of quantum physics. She then describes the potential for personal transformation – a paradigm shift in the mind. In the process, she highlights the benefits of intuitive and holistic perspectives beyond rational-analytic or linear modes of thinking. When I started reading *The Aquarian Conspiracy*, I approached it as a sceptic – at least at the conscious level. But when I experienced an apparent explosion of synchronicity in my everyday life, just after reading about it in the book, it wasn't only my 'right brain', or my intuitive processing, that told me that there was a pattern to be seen. My left brain, or analytical reasoning, registered that this was an uncanny set of circumstances that defied any rational explanation. My left brain told me that I'd better pay more attention to my right!

Here I'll attempt to convey what I gained from reading *The Aquarian Conspiracy* – the key ideas that shaped my perspective – and how I've applied those ideas in my working life and elsewhere to promote better mental health. Among them was the historical fact that broad social and cultural transformation was afoot well before the obviously momentous social changes of the 1960s, with the rise of feminism and the Vietnam War protest movement. Many over the prior century had foretold such changes.

A Shifting Worldview in Science

Marilyn Ferguson explained the extent to which modern science has shifted our understanding of the true nature of reality. Despite appearances and contrary to the usual way of thinking up to that point, it had been shown that the world was not made of solid 'stuff'. In fact, physical matter and the atoms that form it are ultimately more like a dance of energy than a solidly material presence in space. Space and time do not exist as such – they are an abstraction. That sounded weird for a start!

In a sense the world is like a hologram, an immaterial illusion. Our brains and our sensory organs through which we perceive our experience are also a hologram, which nonetheless creates an illusory sense of the world as being stable, tangible, visible and audible. Astronomers and physicists, including Einstein, described the universe as having an immaterial, but orderly, nature. Many leading Western scientists, such as David Bohm, argued that the underlying nature of matter emanates from a form of consciousness, echoing claims made over the centuries by Eastern mystics.

These are difficult concepts to get your head around. The required change in understanding seemed far more dramatic than that between seeing the world as flat and seeing it as round – that earlier paradigm shift, which in its time was difficult for many people to accept. This was conceptual change of a different order altogether. If the seeming solidity of a table that I could feel with a loudly audible knock of my knuckles was something of an illusion, then perhaps everything I apprehended through my senses was seriously open to question.

I started thinking about the implications of all this for my approach to my work and life in general. I might need to be a little more open to different opinions, however strange they may initially appear to be. Maybe that young fellow student in my first-year philosophy tutorial who claimed to be an idealist – suggesting that the world is made up of nothing but consciousness – was not the complete crackpot I'd taken him to be.

I'd previously considered myself to be open-minded, and a good listener. Certainly, I already held to a fundamental principle of psychology that we're affected not so much by the reality of any situation we face but by our view of that situation. It's abundantly clear that our interpretation of events can be highly subjective, highly individualistic.

All this prompted me to accept the essentially subjective nature of any individual's viewpoint. It also made me more prepared to suspend disbelief on all kinds of subjects. I was ready to look at the world in a different way. I was more likely to doubt the truth of my own perspective, and more hesitant to dismiss other people's views, regardless of how compelling my initial conclusions appeared to be.

Shifting Worldviews in Other Fields

The Aquarian Conspiracy went on to describe the extent of paradigm shift, or marked changes in worldview, that had been simultaneously occurring across the fields of health, business, education, politics and religion. For example, the health field was becoming more holistic in its outlook, more open to the idea of an integrated interaction between mind and body. There's an increasing acknowledgment that the workings of the mind, including social and emotional factors, have an impact on all illness, not just mental illness.[1]

Health problems shouldn't be viewed solely as negative outcomes, akin to mechanical problems in a vehicle, but are properly seen as potential pointers to areas of imbalance in one's life, in a way that can prompt constructive growth and transformation. There's increasing recognition of the patient's and clinician's intuition in appraising an individual's health.

In the education field, more holistic perspectives are reflected now in a number of ways, such as less authoritarian relationships between students and teachers, more emphasis on self-guided learning, and greater importance attached to creativity and experiential learning. In the workplace and business, there's a greater emphasis on finding a match between individuals and their work roles, often in a team context. Workplace relations have tended to become less authoritarian and more collaborative, and there's greater recognition of the impact of workplace environments.

In matters of faith there's less subservience in the West to religious authority. People increasingly explore spirituality outside formal religion, making their own choices. Often they critique the belief system they've been brought up in, subscribing instead to alternative faiths, or to *no* faith. Buddhism, in particular, has influenced the thinking of many Westerners, who understand what the Buddha said about the dangerous lure of worldly or emotional attachments, even if they don't meditate or pray.

In many of these areas we've witnessed a greater empowerment of the individual, more recognition of individual differences, an increasing acceptance of alternative views and a greater emphasis on the use of intuition as a guide. There's a strong interest in what the psychologist Abraham Maslow described as self-actualization, a process that involves going beyond satisfying your basic needs and seeking fulfilment by maximizing your potential.[2] Such notions appear to have foreshadowed the development of the 'Wellness Model' and the field of positive psychology.

Such evidence of widespread social change is encouraging. It supports the view that transformative change in one's own and other people's lives is not too much to hope for.

Types of Change

After outlining many areas where marked change had occurred, *The Aquarian Conspiracy* went on to describe the nature and processes of change itself.[3] Some forms of change are greater, more rapid or more stable than others. The three types of change are incremental change, pendulum change and paradigm change. I shall describe examples of how such change may appear in the therapy setting.

Incremental change refers to gradual, step-by-step change, altering your reactions or circumstances bit by bit. When we establish new habits, such as increasing our level of exercise, we often do so gradually over time. Such incremental change may ultimately prove highly beneficial, especially where the cumulative small changes add up to make a deeply rooted shift in behaviour, maintained by new habits. However, such change tends to be slow.

Pendulum change involves more sudden shifts in behaviour, sometimes from one extreme to the other. This is a less stable phenomenon. For example, someone could suddenly quit an addictive substance or remorsefully pledge to discontinue violent behaviour. However, if that person hasn't yet developed a range of strategies to manage future stressful circumstances, they're likely to resume their substance abuse or start acting aggressively again. In general, pendulum change may be rapid, but it's less likely to last than incremental change, as it may not be associated with an underlying change in attitudes or perspective.

Paradigm change is truly transformative. It's based on a genuine and profound change in perspective or worldview. A historical instance I've already mentioned is coming to see the world as being round, rather than flat. Another example is recognizing that the seeming solidity of the world is in fact an illusion. This takes a wholesale change of worldview. You can't change your view bit by bit to gradually experience a paradigm shift: it happens all of a sudden. Paradigm shifts are often discovered by an intuitive leap, perhaps while struggling to interpret unexpected and confounding observations. I experienced such a paradigm shift when I could no longer entertain the notion of coincidences being random.

By their nature, paradigm shifts can be difficult to make. We tend to be attached to long-held views by both emotion and habit. Furthermore, our old worldview might work well in many situations – or at least it used to, which is presumably why we held to it so strongly in the first place. Therapists often see clients whose patterns of behaviour are well past their use-by date, but the particular worldview underpinning that behaviour, such as the idea that it's safer to trust no one, might be totally understandable given the person's history, such as the repeated experience of childhood abuse.

Although a paradigm shift in thinking for an individual will typically take place very suddenly, it may take quite some time for such a shift to occur across a group, or field. For example, as described in Chapter 19, a shift in our common explanations for mental health problems is long overdue. Commonly, difficulties such as clinical depression are explained in psychiatry as being caused by a genetic predisposition leading to a biochemical imbalance in the brain that requires long-term medication as a primary treatment. This explanation is not only very simplistic, it's also pessimistic, and as a result might exacerbate the very problem that it's supposedly designed to alleviate. I believe that in the field of psychiatry generally there's a paradigm shift waiting to happen.

Paradigm change when experienced by an individual – for example, through psychological therapy, let's say – is transformative. There's a kind of epiphany. Many clients suffering from psychological trauma reactions benefit greatly from therapies that involve re-living past traumatic experiences to defuse their impact. At first, they might think that re-living such experiences is the last thing they'd want to do. However, particular therapy techniques can work dramatically well, partly by helping people re-experience the traumatic memory without the intensity of emotional pain. The person then realizes that their distress results from the way they remember an event, which they can influence, rather than the unalterable event itself.

A person overcoming post-traumatic stress commonly experiences additional transformative insights. For example, they might more fully appreciate, from their adult viewpoint, that the repeated abuse they experienced as a child was not their fault, despite the persistent guilt and shame that they'd always felt, partly as a result of the insidious ways the perpetrator had disowned responsibility. Another client might suddenly realize that a relative's tragic death might have been relatively instantaneous and painless, rather than having been experienced as a frozen moment of everlasting horror as, perhaps unconsciously, they'd envisaged. Or a client might come to fully appreciate that they'd done all they humanly could have done to avert another person's fatal accident, despite the terrible outcome and their intense wish to have been able to prevent it.

With severe depression, transformation may occur when the person first sees, from a suddenly changed perspective, that there really is light at the end of the tunnel, and that they've gained worthwhile awareness in the process of their recovery. With panic attacks or social anxiety, a client's personal goal of therapy might shift from trying to eliminate anxiety in feared situations to deliberately allowing some anxiety and managing it, so that the anxiety itself is no longer perceived as such a threat. When people deliberately face excessively feared situations rather than avoiding them, and find that they can put up with the uncomfortable feelings, the anxiety typically reduces. In the meantime, their sense of freedom and confidence is enhanced by a greater capacity to bear with the anxiety when it's present.

For excessive anger reactions, a person might come to recognize that it's not so much other people, or situations, that make them angry, but their own expectations. These can be related to rigid judgments made about others and perhaps overuse of a word like 'should'. Or perhaps they come to realize that they do have an inbuilt 'pause button' after all – in other words, that they're able to curb habitual reactions even when their emotions are starting to run away with them. Either way, they may come to experience an altogether different level of internal control, with improved relationships as a result.

Such moments of insight are commonly experienced as turning points in therapy, which I now associate with a shift from the second stage to the third stage of the creative cycle as described in the last chapter. They are best followed up by deliberate changes in behaviour to consolidate new habits. These might include reducing avoidance of previously feared situations, practising new ways of modulating your anxiety, actively reminding yourself that even the darkest of thoughts and feelings will pass, or consolidating more collaborative ways of dealing with conflict. Such efforts promote further recovery and enduring positive changes in patterns of behaviour and personality functioning, a hallmark of stage 4 of the creative cycle.

Other examples of transformative or paradigm change may result from a less stressful starting point, such as leaving work to pursue a passionate interest, an adventurous trip abroad or launching yourself into a new long-term relationship. However, for many people personal transformation might occur in the context of adverse circumstances – for example, in response to a severe crisis. Marilyn Ferguson describes a theory derived from chemistry that helps us to understand this further.

A Theory of Transformative Change

A Belgian chemist, Ilya Prigogene, won the 1977 Nobel Prize in chemistry for his theory of dissipative structures.[4] Prigogene described how this theory accounted for transformative change not only in chemistry in such areas as crystal formation, but also when applied to any living or 'open' system. An open system is a system that continually exchanges energy with its environment – the term applies to any living creature, but also to a traffic system, political system or even an insect colony. Closed systems, which involve inanimate objects such as a rock, involve no internal transformation of energy, or return of energy to the environment.

Prigogene explained how open systems are in an ongoing state of flux, because of the continual movement of energy involved. Parts of the system vary in what contact they have with other parts. Minor fluctuations within the system will have little impact on its overall structural integrity. However, more major or dramatic fluctuations can lead to sudden shifts, whereby the system reorganizes itself in a new way to make a new whole. This renewed organization will always be of a higher order and will demonstrate an even greater level of complexity. Flexibility begets further flexibility, so that the system continues to evolve. Weak links between the various parts, perhaps alongside strong links, make any system more flexible, albeit less stable.

My interpretation of this is that transformative change in any open system requires things to come apart before the system can be re-organized in a new way, typically at a higher order level of development. The example I commonly use with clients is that it's only after a road traffic system starts breaking down with too much congestion that innovations might be added, such as a new ring road around a city. All the old parts of the system are still in place – all the former streets are still there – but something new is added. The new adaptation may ease traffic for an extended period, but one day there'll probably need to be further innovation, such as improved public transport initiatives, to address renewed congestion problems.

I typically add that, from a psychological point of view, it seems that people often have to go through a period when they feel that they are 'coming apart' to some extent, in order to make the shift to the next stage of personal development. Not uncommonly, this follows a significant challenging event. All the past potential behaviours are still there, whether they seem to be or not, but something new might be added.

This helps to explain why people, or organizations, often undergo transformative change following periods of profound challenge or stress. I commonly suggest to clients who have experienced severe, or prolonged, distress that, provided their life gets back to a relative equilibrium, there's a likelihood that their personality functioning will be at a higher and more integrated level than before. When people come through a crisis or extremely challenging circumstances intact, it's often obvious that growth has occurred. Nelson Mandela is a clear example that comes to mind.

When clients seek psychotherapy in intense distress, I describe change processes in the following way. When we're severely depressed, or feel seriously stuck in some other way, there's something about our lives that isn't working for us. Something has to change. And sometimes the change required is dramatic. Sometimes we need to shift from where we are now to a quite different place.

I typically illustrate this with two hands by showing that to move from one configuration of interlocked fingers to another configuration, your hands and fingers have to first come apart to enable you make the shift. That symbolic coming apart can feel like a 'little death'. However, if we tolerate that coming apart, if we bear with the accompanying distress, then there's a promise: any way we get things back together will always be at a higher order level than before. The old ways are typically still available to us, but we have more at our disposal, so they may be superseded. That's the way that all living systems work.

These days, I'm able to tell clients the good news about how many others have come to manage that change successfully. I refer to the objective clinical research results obtained within our practice pointing to good recoveries of more than a thousand clients from such conditions as post-traumatic stress disorder and clinical depression. Sometimes, if they are severely depressed, I tell them of my own recovery, adding that I didn't believe it would happen despite witnessing the process in countless others beforehand. It's difficult to think straight when you're going through a little death.

Methods of Bringing about Paradigm Change

In *The Aquarian Conspiracy* Marilyn Ferguson described a range of situations and life experiences that might assist people to undergo transformational shifts.[5] The list includes creative activity, spiritual experiences, physically exhilarating activities such as mountain climbing, using psychedelic drugs, or critical challenges, such as life-threatening illness. She also described specific therapy interventions designed to help bring about transformative change, which she referred to as 'psychotechnologies'.[6] In the psychological and health field these may include such methods as hypnosis, meditation, biofeedback, body disciplines including yoga or martial arts, dream journalling, self-help groups and modern psychotherapies. She correctly anticipated that new psychotechnologies would continue to be discovered.

A main thesis of this book is that exploring synchronistic experiences in a focused way could be considered another form of psychotechnology. This is on account of its capacity to bring about transformative change – especially if you combine synchronicity with *kairos*, by acting in a mindful and timely way on any awareness gained from the synchronicity. In this way, synchronicity can be helpful as a life guide, as well as enhancing a sense of connectedness and developing intuitive awareness.

At this later stage of my career, I wish to convey the most useful lessons I've learned from my experience. This includes, in particular, a number of ideas that seem to be under-recognized, especially in mainstream mental health care. The notion of synchronicity rarely seems to be given credence in mainstream mental health settings. To many, it doesn't seem sufficiently rational.

As I describe in later chapters, I've unashamedly used synchronicity as a guide in my own life to make key life and business decisions. I believe it's served me well. It has guided my footsteps and given me insights into what it means to be human.

6

Something Is Happening

A Career Shaped by Coincidence

Before describing the explosion of synchronicity that came into my life after first reading about the phenomenon in *The Aquarian Conspiracy*, it's fitting to describe some of my earlier experiences of coincidence in my life and career path. That provides the context for what came later. I'd noticed the impact of coincidences on life decisions before, even as a young adult atheist who didn't attach any particular meaning to them – other than recognizing how they could change your life course.

My career in psychology started off with my receiving, aged 20, a cadetship – a form of psychology scholarship. That itself resulted from a serendipity, when a friend told me of an application for a mental health scholarship she was posting as we were on our way to play golf, and I subsequently posted an application for the scholarship myself. This led to a marked shift in my life direction. As mundane as the situation was, in retrospect it was a 'sliding doors' moment. Gaining the cadetship was a relief as I could quit my student pizza-making job. I accepted the offer despite my ambivalence about working with mentally disturbed people: I thought that after the two contracted years I could return to pursue academic interests in other areas, probably in social psychology.

However, after I became severely depressed for the first time I changed my view about working with people with mental health problems. I went down hard after a cluster of stresses, including: my mother being severely injured in a car accident, from which she was initially not expected to survive; splitting up with my long-standing girlfriend; and facing the toughest university exams I'd yet undertaken.

My efficiency and concentration in my studies were severely compromised. I believed I was at risk of failing. I catastrophized about the losses that could result to myself and my family, including hardship from paying back scholarship fees to date. I went downhill in a big way. That changed my view about working with people who were screwed in the head. I'd become one of them!

When working on an assignment, I'd start a first sentence of an essay, scribble it out and then repeat the process. This could go on for hours. It did go on for hours. I would then go for a walk around the block, pulling leaves from trees and tearing them into tiny bits, discarding the fragments on the ground as I walked. I averaged approximately three to four hours of sleep a night for several months, commonly woke during the night in a sweat, felt consumed by anxiety and a sense of failure, and harboured what seemed like never-ending suicidal thoughts.

The situation was made more difficult by the fact that my parents had separated. My mother had developed full-blown bipolar disorder, diagnosed soon after her near-fatal car accident some months earlier. My father left home, thinking that the attacks directed at him indicated that he was a significant part of the problem. Eventually my father and uncle recognized that my mother's behaviour was best understood as resulting from a serious mental illness. They intervened to arrange psychiatric assistance for my mother including hospitalization and medication. The situation settled, at least in that respect. My father eventually returned home.

In the meantime, I'd gone downhill in an even bigger way. I'd markedly reduced my social contacts. I remember my 21st birthday as one of the most depressing days of my life, despite playing golf with a friend and having a small celebration with my family. When, that day, I received a joint card from a number of university friends, wishing me a happy birthday and suggesting they were waiting for an invitation to celebrate with me, I felt no joy. I just felt exceedingly unworthy of their friendship, and guilty that I hadn't arranged to meet with them. I'd left it too late to do anything. I didn't have the energy anyway.

After that I kept going down, down, down. I suppose my sense of isolation and alienation was reflected in a note I'd started to write headed, 'To the human race'. That seems a bit melodramatic now. It nonetheless indicates something of how things seemed to me at the time. Through the note, which I never gave or sent anyone, I wished to record a kind of insight that I felt I'd gained about potentially descending into a more disturbed state of mind. I had a sense of my thoughts becoming more fluid. There was a temptation to give in to that.

I sensed that psychosis might represent a kind of choice. I felt an enormous temptation to drift into a different world where my feelings would be something other than what they were at the time. I had an increasing sense of foreboding. I was surprised by the extent to which I physically felt the impulse to suddenly turn the steering wheel while driving: I hadn't heard anyone speak of that before.

Somehow I got through the assignments. I was surprised to get high marks, because I wasn't functioning on that many cylinders. As planned before my relationship ended, I moved into a house with a friend and my now ex-girlfriend. That last aspect probably wasn't too smart. But I was gradually picking up, partly because I'd started seeing a therapist. When I'd first visited the community mental health centre to see a psychiatrist for assessment, I was utterly scared. I thought it was quite likely that I'd need to be hospitalized. That terrified me. I had little doubt that I'd need medication. I wasn't too keen on that either. I didn't even like taking aspirin.

I saw a young psychiatrist. He told me that he wasn't going to offer me medication. He didn't even mention hospitalization. Instead he suggested that I see a social worker. To this day I can't really remember anything else he said, but he seemed to have an air about him, as though he knew what he was doing. I was in a rather passive frame of mind, and I thought he'd listened well enough, so I went along with the idea of seeing the social worker.

Over time I made a gradual recovery. It wasn't easy. The first time I remember laughing in a four-month period was while watching a performance of Shakespeare's *As You Like It* with friends. I laughed a second time when my housemate (I only had one at the time, as my ex-girlfriend had moved out for some reason) intervened to stop me taking a carton of full beer bottles to put out with the rubbish. He exclaimed that he knew I'd been having a tough time, but I was really going to have to pull myself together if I was going to keep doing things as serious as that. Laughing together at the incident helped.

I saw the social worker for eight months. As our contact wore on, I thought she had a good job, a meaningful job. It crossed my mind that I wouldn't mind having her job, and could perhaps do it quite well one day. I remember the main things she said that made the most difference for me. I really felt their lasting impact. She decided what she needed to say, and expressed herself well.

Hinting at ways I'd responded dismissively towards her, she suggested that I was maybe clever enough to counter nearly everything she said, and perhaps to the extent I could really wreck my chances of recovery. She wove in the comment that our culture didn't have a way of marking a shift to manhood. I felt these things as a challenge, calling for a different level of maturity from me. I saw that some of the ways I'd been acting were darkly self-indulgent. I thought I might never recover from depression, but I didn't want to keep acting like that. From then on, whenever I recognized a negative thought, I at once distracted myself – for example, by immediately switching on the car radio and listening for specific musical instruments. I gradually got better.

During our final session I tried, with gratitude, to tell her how I believed she'd most helped me. I'm not sure how much she heard of what I said, as she was putting forward a different view. She explained that it was the cognitive-behavioural interventions we'd used that had made the difference, including the homework. I didn't have the heart to tell her that I'd never really done the homework. But I remain grateful to this day. She might have saved my life.

My career direction had shifted. The timing of events in all of this in some ways seemed uncanny. However, I didn't think of it in terms of synchronicity, a concept I hadn't yet encountered. I did, however, think that my illness and treatment were directing me on a new path in life.

I eventually made a full recovery – without drugs. That was a very valuable experience to have had, as a psychologist going to work in the mental health field. Somehow it made me more … optimistic. What had seemed dreadful proved to be a bonus. You could call it serendipity. The whole episode, including my recovery, would amount to a very significant piece in the jigsaw puzzle of my life.

An example of uncanny timing occurred as I was gradually recovering from depression. It was now May 1979, well into the fourth and final year of my undergraduate degree. I still didn't have a thesis topic, although almost all my fellow students had established theirs at least several months earlier.

As I saw it, completing my final year in the required time and retaining my cadetship depended on a long shot. I needed to find a lecturer willing to supervise me for my thesis who had rarely available 'captive' data that had already been collected, and would be prepared to make this available to me to analyse. That could save months. I approached a senior lecturer to ask if he had any captive data. He said that he could think of one possibility, but it would also require the unlikely agreement of another lecturer. He'd just started toying with a novel approach to psychometric personality assessment in recent days. He knew that the other lecturer had collected a large body of data that could be relevant to his idea.

He later told me that if I'd come to see him a couple of days earlier, he wouldn't have thought of the idea; and if I'd seen him a couple of days later, he would have already dropped the notion and wouldn't have been prepared to help me. Fortunately, when I approached the other lecturer straight after our conversation, he readily agreed to share his data. I was off and running.

At the time, I thought of this as a positive coincidence. Now I'd consider it to be an example of synchronicity paired with *kairos*.

The coincidence over my thesis was my first conscious inkling of how a person might have some influence over the fortuitous timing of events. It didn't mean that we literally cause good things to happen, and are at fault if they don't. It just seemed to mean that somehow good things seem to happen more often when you can get into a state of attunement; and if they do, or if opportunities arise, you're also more ready to respond, without even really having to try. I felt I was in that state after coming out of depression.

That seemed the case for other people as well. It's similar to Louis Pasteur's idea that chance favours the prepared mind. It was a kind of sense that if you change something in yourself so that you're open and ready for whatever happens, if you've let go of expectations or control but are still prepared to have a go, then positive outcomes are more likely to follow.

I've seen many situations involving friends, clients and others in which, with uncanny frequency, something very favourable follows a person's shift in attitude. For example, someone might seem almost desperate to find a romantic partner, but then progress to a greater acceptance of themselves and their circumstances. They appear to have more ease about themselves, not giving up but letting go, in a way that everyone else can see. And then ... something happens! They meet their partner – with whom they still seem happy decades later.

My own experience, after that one small foretaste, was something else – a 'hit you in the face' cascade of remarkable coincidences. The name of a new radio show that discussed themes similar to those in *The Aquarian Conspiracy* seemed to sum it up: 'Something Is Happening'. For example, one day I saw six clients, each of whom spontaneously reported synchronistic experiences.

A memorable example involved a socially isolated young woman whom I'd also seen the previous week. I'd then asked whether she'd ever heard of the expression, 'No man is an island'. She hadn't. However, at this later session she explained that her mother had recently taken up a creative writing course and had just been asked to submit an essay entitled 'No Man Is an Island'. The mother requested that her daughter, my client, write it for her. I was blown away! It sounded as though some prescient mentor from the universe was setting my client's homework.

I mentioned such experiences to Vicki, my colleague in the next-door office. That was a story in itself. Vicki was an experienced psychiatric nurse. She was the first person who'd told me there was no such thing as mere coincidence. She was well respected for her experience, her knowledge and her intuition. People greatly valued her insights, including her debriefings after she had observed a therapy group through a one-way screen.

Journalling

To gain more understanding about synchronistic experiences, and benefit from them fully, it can be helpful to record them in a journal. Whatever experience we invest in by recording it will tend to be enhanced. Carry a small notebook everywhere, and use it for impromptu notes or sketches about any uncanny coincidence, or any strongly numinous feelings you experience. Taking a photo with your smartphone is also worthwhile. Note anything particular that stands out about the context in which the experience occurred, including when and where things happened, and who you were with. Aim to have an objective record of key details, but also describe your strongest *subjective* impressions – in other words, 'notice what you notice'. Was the synchronicity mild, moderate or strong? On returning home, perhaps transfer your notes to a larger-format journal – one that gives you space to develop your thoughts about such experiences and note down the possible symbolism, over a period of time.

It was quite an experience to view a therapy group with Vicki from behind the screen. Curiously, neither myself nor anyone else seemed at all bothered by her occasionally pressing her fingers against her temple and declaring that she was going to send a telepathic message to the therapist because they'd missed something, or needed to change tack.

Vicki seemed to do this partly tongue-in-cheek, but part of her clearly believed in the sentiment. She suffered from a paranoid psychotic condition. All the staff knew this, yet few seemed to be bothered about it, and rightly so. Vicki knew herself well. As she explained to me once, every now and then she realized that things had got to a stage where she needed to take some time off work. With the assistance of appropriate psychiatric treatment, including her ongoing medication, she was fine.

I was impressed. I thought she was walking the walk. If our patients learned how to manage their condition as Vicki did, I reckon they would have been doing well. I usually thought that the things that she expressed, even in mock telepathy directed to a group therapist through a one-way screen, sounded sensible and wise.

It turned out that Vicki knew about *The Aquarian Conspiracy*. Indeed she knew a number of people who are referred to in the book, after working with them in Britain. Vicki was a wonderful informal mentor for me. She seemed to know a great deal about the science. Something struck me then. I'd come across an amazing book and was having a range of amazing experiences, and it was the woman in the very next office who seemed to know the most about all this out of all the people I knew – not only in Geelong, where I worked, but anywhere.

I didn't have to go to London or New York or Oxford or anywhere else to receive a sophisticated level of guidance. If I was receptive, what I needed was perhaps available in my own world, sometimes within a few metres. The universe provides.

Vicki was instrumental in the most synchronistic event I experienced at work around that time. Knowing of my interest in the science behind the spookiness, Vicki had lent me a cassette recording of Professor Karl Pribram, an influential brain scientist from Stanford University. On the tape he described a more holistic view of memory functioning than I'd encountered in my recent training in neuropsychology.

Not long after I'd received the tape, there was to be an extended meeting of all our psychiatric hospital staff to reflect on our ways of working. It was to be called 'Meeting of the Minds'. I sensed there was something very important about this forthcoming gathering. It was an opportunity to become involved in some genuine discussion about how we worked, to challenge the status quo, and to consider whether we should be talking about the implications of modern scientific developments. Topics we should air included the nature of open systems, the paradigm changes occurring outside our field, and the question of whether we should adopt a more holistic approach to mental health care. We could at the very least be considering a more integrated way of combining left-brain with right-brain thinking. I was primed.

I picked up the cassette tape and looked at it idly, while thinking about the potential offered by the meeting. For the first time I noticed the title of Karl Pribram's tape: 'Meeting of the Minds'. That said to me, 'Go for it!' I may have been one of the youngest staff at the hospital, but I felt I had something important to say. I made sure I said it. I spoke of the need for further paradigm change in the mental health field, allowing for broader and more intuitive ways of working, and going beyond a rigid focus on diagnostic classifications and medication. It seemed to go well.

At that time we had an open-minded clinical director who was generous in allowing differing views to be expressed, as they were at the meeting. It was only some time later that I realized how rare that could be in hospital settings, or in other organizations, for that matter. This experience encouraged me to be more outspoken in future about my views, regardless of how strange they might seem, or how much they might diverge from colleagues' perspectives. It cemented some of the insights I'd gained from *The Aquarian Conspiracy*.

Sadly, Vicki was forced to resign not long afterwards. My second-hand understanding is that she was forced to resign because of her significant psychiatric condition, regardless of how well she was managing it.

I didn't understand. In my view, Vicki stood out as a respected colleague, recognized for her active and effective contributions to patients and staff alike. She added great value to the organization. I've rarely known anyone to manage a significant psychiatric condition so openly and thoughtfully. Those were days when there was a definite stigma associated with mental illness, yet Vicki seemingly modelled a healthy acceptance. I never encountered any evidence of any patient being disadvantaged as a result of Vicki's interactions with them. When I think of Vicki being forced to leave, even now, I feel sad. I missed her.

Synchronistic events increasingly occurred with friends, house-mates and others around me. One evening I accompanied a friend to meet others at a local hotel bar. Someone started telling us about a humorous book they were reading called *The Hitchhiker's Guide to the Galaxy*. He described how the book amusingly supplied the answer to the question, what is the meaning of life, the universe, everything? For some reason I said the answer was '42'. That proved to be the answer given in the book. He assumed that I must have read it. I hadn't. To this day I don't know why I said it, but it just felt natural to answer the question like that.

My friend who witnessed this, to whom I'd recently described my amazing increase in synchronistic experiences, seemed as surprised as I was when my flippant response was confirmed. It could be argued that I must have heard the answer before, even in my sleep. I can't rule that out, but I doubt it.

My next recollection is more embarrassing. Two work colleagues, including a close friend, chose to have some fun at my expense on my birthday. They arranged for me to be paged throughout the hospital with a rudely changed Christian name, Chancres Mackey, to suggest I had a sexually transmitted disease. I later responded to a supposed client's phone message and found myself talking to someone from a local brothel. So when I next received a written referral to see an elderly lady with an unusual name whose primary complaint was buzzing sensations in the vagina, I promptly threw the referral in the bin. Enough was enough.

There are times when staff in a psychiatric hospital can tend to indulge in gossip – in-house gossip, that is, rather than outright breaches of confidentiality. A colleague came by and asked me if I'd heard of the referral of the woman with the problem with her vagina. It was obvious he was in on the act. I told him that I knew it was a set-up. It took him at least five minutes to convince me otherwise. I retrieved the crumpled, but legitimate, referral form from the waste paper basket, unfurled it and sheepishly passed it on to a female colleague. I was beyond taking the situation seriously. My playful tormentors had had nothing to do with this. I've never heard before or since of a similar referral. I put that one in the cosmic prankster category.

7

The Synchronistic Matchmaker

Flirting with Numerology

The timing of various events that led to my choice of clinical psychology as a field of work, or its choice of me, seemed like *serendipity*: chance factors that had a fortunate outcome. These events included: learning by accident about a psychology scholarship in mental health from a friend who posted an application for the same scholarship on our way to play golf; finding at the last minute a thesis supervisor who directed me to a clinical psychology project; and becoming depressed myself, which gave me a personal interest in a new area. But there was no doubt that my choice of life partner was based on *synchronicity*. I made a fully conscious decision to marry my wife based in part on the number six.

I had no idea what was going on with the number six when I was courting my wife. It's just that it came up a lot. I didn't even look up its meaning according to numerology until recently. The recurrence of the number itself was what struck me. And it was clear that this was mainly, or even exclusively, happening around my contact with my girlfriend, Sue.

The number six had already drawn my attention in various ways, despite my never having had any interest in numerology before. I had not even been particularly attentive to numbers. We holidayed interstate and booked a hotel room. Room 66. Elsewhere, we booked another hotel room. Room 66. Six tended to come in double form. While we were flying interstate, a fellow plane passenger shouted out the number six so loudly that it was comical – he must have had headphones on and was perhaps telling a friend where to tune the dial. It went on and on.

It reached a point where I simply took the number six, or 66, to represent our relationship. For it was in that context that these numbers seemed so often to occur. Our relationship deepened and I thought about taking the next step – popping the question.

But we were quite different in many ways. In Jungian terms I was very much the intuitive one, while Sue seemed to be much more at the practical, or 'sensation', end of the spectrum. In particular, I wondered whether Sue genuinely related to transpersonal or spiritual themes. If not, we would be a mismatch. By that stage, appreciating a deep order underlying the universe was fundamental to my evolving identity.

I was doing a one-year experiential group therapy course at the time, specializing in Gestalt therapy. It made you think about relationships even more deeply. This focused me even more on whether I should marry Sue, a deeply personal question. For some reason, a clear thought formed in my mind at one point – I don't know why – and it was this: within the next week I was likely to get an answer to the question that was preoccupying me. I didn't know where from, but I believed I'd notice an unmistakably clear sign.

Towards the end of that week, Sue drew something to my attention. She pointed to the box of matches we'd just used. The Redheads matchbox company had always previously used a picture of a red-headed woman on its covers. But this time the cover design was a playing card: the six of hearts! I was astonished. I wondered how I could have missed the six of hearts myself, since I had obviously seen the box.

It struck me that not only had Sue appreciated the synchronistic meaning of this, as a symbol of our loving connection, but she'd also shown that she could point out things that I missed – transpersonal or spiritual things. That did it for me. I was convinced. I took it that not only could Sue accept my spiritual side: she could actively contribute to its development. I had a conviction she was the right partner for me.

From then on I had no doubts. I related some of this story to my uncle and my brother-in-law after Sue's recent 50th birthday celebrations. Someone wanted to know why, at the party, there was someone dressed as the six of hearts playing card. Few friends knew the full story, but that particular friend came up with the idea in response to the party's fancy dress theme of everyone wearing something they especially related to Sue.

'It's good to know, my brother-in-law quipped, 'that your marriage is based on something rational!' My uncle immediately replied, 'It's probably worked as well as it has because it was not!' He was right. In the stresses and strains of work and study, raising children, and other pressures, there were times that cracks appeared. I know for a fact that nothing helped my conscious commitment to our marriage during trying times more than that six of hearts. There was something about it that made it an infallible guide for me.

There was another twist. Sue and I got engaged by what seemed to be a sheer fluke at 6pm on 6 June, which only added to my impression of the rightness of our union. I'd planned it to be the previous evening on our tropical island holiday, but the dress theme turned out to be 'island night'. The men, on such occasions, wore sarongs. I wasn't going to get engaged in a dress! The next day I planned to pop the question earlier, but Sue got stranded on a windsurfer with no wind, and this delayed her return to our room by an hour or two. My amusement didn't help, so it took another hour or so before the time seemed right. That pushed the time back, inadvertently to 6pm.

There were many times later when the number six, perhaps in its double form or other variants, such as 666, or 606, seemed to come up again and again. For example, on our 25th anniversary, when heading out on an interstate trip that felt like a second honeymoon, we ordered a coffee before boarding the plane. As Sue pointed out, our ticket for the café queue was number 66.

I never bothered to look up what the number six or its variants might mean until preparing to write this book. Some months ago, I did an online search for 'numerology', and the number six in particular, for the first time. The first site I came to referred to 'Sacred Scribes'.[1] Here I read that six relates to the Lovers card in the Tarot deck. Yes – that fits! It's associated to Venus, the goddess of love. Yes, that, of course, fits too. I went on to check the supposed meaning behind all ten digits, but only the number six turned out to be connected with love.

The description for six started by saying how it 'connects above and below' – with connotations of union, love and ability to use the imagination and intellect combined.[2] I related strongly to all that, whereas the descriptions of the other numbers didn't affect me in anything like the same way.

I looked up the number 66 on the same numerology site. 'Service, deep sensitivity, truth, order, economy, deep inner knowing, responsibility.' This just seemed like a condensed version of six. So I surfed for other websites, and found one on the 'numerology meaning of number 66', by Saravanakkumar.[3] He wrote that this is a 'double Venus' number, which also relates to Jupiter, making it extremely auspicious. Supposedly, it relates to 'success in relationships'. That's what I'd already taken it to mean, intuitively. I didn't feel that I'd missed too much by not having looked up the numerology in the first place.

I was glad, however, to have these positive interpretations, for I later learned that 66 also apparently related to Kali, the Hindu goddess of destruction – a literal reading of that didn't sound good! I then looked up 'Kali' online and learned that the name comes from *kala*, meaning 'black', 'time' and 'death' – qualities associated with her consort, known as Shiva, lord of death. Kali is the goddess of time and change. This made me think of the notion that something's 'time has come' – with intriguing echoes of the themes of synchronicity, *kairos* and the opportune moment.

I was becoming less sceptical by the minute. Kali, associated with 66, seemed related to that coming apart of systems described in the law of 'dissipative structures'. This idea, important in chemistry and physics, is about transformative change and growth – despite sounding like it means the complete opposite of that.

The Power of Numbers

The Greek thinker Pythagoras believed that 'the world is built on the power of numbers' and even viewed numbers as divine. Many know of his contribution to mathematics, but fewer are aware that his interest in number symbolism paved the way for later systems of numerology. Modern numerology operates by ascribing divinatory meanings to birth dates and, by translating letters to numbers, to an individual's name. From the point of view of synchronicity, recurring numbers may be interpreted in terms of their broadly accepted traditional meanings, although a personal significance sometimes seems to be the most relevant. I've known several clients who have reported their amazement at frequently encountering the number 11, perhaps in its repeated form, such as 11:11am on a digital clock. This is described as a 'master number' with special potency, like 22 and 33. Eleven is often described as being strongly related to intuition and psychic ability, which makes it intriguing that clients in a therapy setting seem spontaneously to raise it more frequently than other numbers.

The following associations were derived from research on various numerological websites. However, you may wish to explore potential associations as well, especially if you encounter a number with uncanny frequency, or in a numinous context. Many numbers can be symbolically related to positive or negative characteristics or situations, depending on the circumstances.

One
Pure energy, new beginnings, purity.
Two
Balance, duality, kindness.

Three
Magic, intuition, fertility.
Four
Stability, calmness, home.
Five
Movement, travel, unpredictability.
Six
Love, truth, sincerity.
Seven
Magic, mystery, imagination.
Eight
Enterprise, success, wealth.
Nine
Accomplishment, attainment, intellect.

A parallel would be the associations of the colour black in the Renaissance: it means not death in a morbid sense, but 'out with the old and in with the new'. I also learned that the repeated number 666 was not always considered negative, despite the connotations popularized in the Hollywood movie *The Omen*. In fact, it was often associated with encouragement to turn towards a spiritual rather than a materialistic view of life. It's even thought of as a sacred or holy number in some cultures.

I then checked out 606, which was more difficult. In the end I found a site called the 'Mystic Board', which sounded a bit New Agey for my liking. Nevertheless, I delved into it. The first entry I saw related to someone referring to waking up at 6:06am.[4] I was intrigued, as I'd experienced that often when setting out to write this book, including on the first day, and several others, in my initial phase of work. I took that to be an auspicious sign.

A couple of months later I was reading a section in Roderick Main's *Revelations of Chance* that talked about synchronicity directly helping an individual to find his or her vocation, or partner. A footnote referred to a relevant book chapter entitled 'Significant Meetings and the Synchronistic Matchmaker' – the first time I'd seen or heard that expression. Fittingly, this happened to be footnote number 66.[5] I saw that as another tick.

I again encountered the cosmic prankster a few hours after concluding a first draft of this current chapter. I went to a friend's house for a monthly gathering of our movie club. Our host had unexpectedly created a short film spoof, obscurely related to the main feature, *The Shining*. His spoof was based on bizarre numerology references, through which someone or something unknown was directing messages to our movie group.

It was pointed out in this short film that *The Shining* was listed on page 666 in the book *1001 Movies You Must See Before You Die*. The spoof ended with the punchline that people who read such meanings into numbers are 'losers with too much time on their hands'. I later emailed my host and fellow members, expressing feigned offence at being categorized in such a way – given that I'd just written a book chapter endorsing the validity of numerology. I explained that I felt especially aggrieved, given that key anecdotes in my writing related to the repeated number six. As I already knew, my friend who'd made the spoof had no idea that I'd written on such a theme. I was actually thankful, of course, for the extra anecdote.

Recently I saw a headline referring to synchronicity in a newspaper article about the retirement of a famous Australian newsreader. In reflecting on his career, Mal Walden spelt out many coincidences occurring on 6 June, including his commencement of several radio jobs and his television news role on that date.[6] That's why he chose 6 June to retire. I wonder whether Mal Walden knows that 6 June is also the date of Jung's death, something I learned only recently while reading *Jung the Mystic* by Gary Lachman. Given my affinity with Jung's work, I consider that to be a particularly spooky coincidence.

The Tarot

In additon to the I Ching (see p.16) and numerology there's another structured system that relates to synchronicity and has a strong underpinning of philosophy around spiritual themes and personal transformation: the Tarot. As with the I Ching, this is more than a fortune-telling tool: it's a profound system of symbolism, rich in psychological wisdom.

For a Tarot reading, cards are taken from a shuffled deck, turned over and laid out in a particular pattern. The 21 Major Arcana cards in Tarot provide a sophisticated illustration of stages on the hero's journey, an archetypal story of stages of transformation in a person's life.[7]

Beginning the journey is the naïve Fool. Early cards include the Empress and Emperor, referring to a relationship with mother and father figures. The Lovers card reflects the development of free will. The Chariot is about leaving home. The Hermit relates to a wise old man, and the guidance that shows us the way. The Wheel of Fortune can represent a chaotic time when we're at a standstill. The Justice card signifies the impact of past traumas, which can nonetheless be transcended. The Hanged Man can represent a time when we're at a standstill, being tried. The Death card represents the dark night of the soul. The Devil relates to how we keep ourselves stuck in our current circumstances through guilt or co-dependency or the like. The Tower involves a breaking down of our personality in order to rebuild it in a healthy way. The Star relates to our hopes and the manifestation of our dreams. The Sun represents a soul reborn. Judgment involves moving forward into wholeness. The World represents wholeness at the end of the journey – enlightenment, if you like.

I've consulted Tarot readers on three occasions. Following encouragement from my mentor, Ross, I saw a Tarot reader just after I handed in my Master's thesis. Without knowing that I was a student, or any other details for that matter, the reader immediately spoke of a dilemma I faced. He told me that a university dean (it was actually a professor) was encouraging me to go on with further studies. He highlighted that I was torn between going ahead and discontinuing the rigorous demands of study in the interests of life balance and satisfaction.

How did he figure that out? He was right. It concentrated my mind and helped me to make a more conscious decision. Later, two different Tarot readers also referred to details in my life with uncanny accuracy.

8

Revealing Dreams

Watch Out for the Shark!

Dreams, like synchronistic experiences, can be strikingly enigmatic. But what do they mean, if anything? Jung and his followers, including myself, believe that dreams can provide us with personalized guidance about ourselves and the course our lives are taking, as though from a deeper or more profound source than our usual modes of thinking. However, the guidance typically comes in the form of a symbolic language that may take some studious effort to decode. Actively considering how a dream's symbolism may relate to our current life circumstances is a creative project that enhances our self-awareness. In my experience, Jungian principles of dream interpretation are the most useful also for making sense of synchronistic experience. This chapter describes some of the techniques I've found most helpful in trying to find meanings in my own and others' dreams.

I'm standing in front of a substantial university building. Facing me are two people in conversation, one of whom is an academic: he works there and I don't. I'm there to pick someone up. Looking over his shoulder, I see a very strange sight. An oversized ewe gives birth to a very large sac, which then bursts open. Two ugly, oversized lambs emerge and at once get to their feet. They are surprisingly sure-footed. A word immediately flashes through my mind – 'viable'.

These days, when interpreting a dream, I often spin off associations very quickly. I particularly look out for the most idiosyncratic elements of the dream: the features that somehow resonate. In this instance, for some reason, I immediately think of the two lambs as representing my two spontaneous and unscheduled attempts to write an introduction for this book, approximately four months after I'd first decided to write. I at once get a strong feeling of affirmation: my initial attempts might not be at all elegant, but they are viable. They were a long time, perhaps too long, in gestation. To see their viability, I have to look beyond the academic facing me. I might need to watch out for my perfectionistic tendencies, and remember that I'm not writing primarily for an academic audience.

The sense of affirmation resulting from this dream's resonating message helped me to rise to my writing challenge. I consider the dream to have been designed personally and specifically for me. I see it as a letter from the gods.

I recall another memorable dream from many years ago, one I call 'the fearful flight with primitive men', which occurred after the great flowering of synchronistic experiences I've already described. I dreamed that I was standing up, but wobbling precariously, on a narrow flying plank. There were native men in front of and behind me on the plank, most confidently balanced, despite flying at speed over a landscape many hundreds of metres below. At first I was very scared. However, surprisingly soon I found that, like the men, I could balance on the plank as it curved on its arcs through the sky. The dream helped me to commit more to trusting in my intuition, an innate form of processing I associated with native peoples.

I always take the trouble to consider possible interpretations to my dreams, not least because I see them as having practical utility. The secret is to arrive at an interpretation that resonates. I initially based my dream interpretations on what I learned from Peter O'Connor's books, *Understanding Jung, Understanding Yourself* and *Dreams*,[1] before studying Jung's writings, which I initially found less accessible.

One of the main practical principles I follow is that every element of a dream can relate in some way to yourself – to what's happening in your life at the time, to your hopes and fears about the future, or perhaps to events in the past that are still affecting you. If you approach a dream with these possibilities in mind, an association will probably suggest itself. If that association resonates strongly, or feels intuitively right, you can be relatively confident of your interpretation.

Jung might have agreed with Freud's famous description of dreams as 'the royal road to the unconscious' and his claim that analysing dreams could lead to greater self understanding, but he disagreed with Freud's view that the symbolic language of dreams was mainly designed to disguise unacceptable impulses and urges from conscious awareness. By contrast, Jung believed dream symbolism was designed to reveal rather than conceal. For him, dream stories were often like parables, or metaphorical statements, describing a deeper truth about ourselves than we were consciously aware of.

In particular, Jung suggested that dreams typically have a compensatory quality, pointing to something in us that's out of balance, such as disowned negative aspects of our personality. He gave the example of a woman who was known for her arrogant self-importance. She dreamed of attending an important social occasion, one no doubt fitting for her self-perceived status, where the congenial hostess directed her to where she belonged – in a cowshed! In time, the vivid dream symbolism helped her to see a valid point in the harsh joke.[2]

Jung gave an even more striking example of a colleague with a passion for dangerous mountain climbing who repeatedly teased Jung over his claims that dreams were meaningful. One day the man sceptically related an 'idiotic' dream in which he kept climbing up from a mountain summit into empty air in an ecstatic state. Jung explicitly warned him that this dream perhaps foreshadowed his death in a mountain accident if he didn't show due care. The man failed to heed the warning and stepped off a mountain-side six months later, killing not only himself but also his friend below him. In this case, the man paid with his life for not appreciating that dreams can reveal hidden and disruptive aspects of one's personality.[3]

Some dreams more obviously include archetypal imagery, such as that of Jung's patient, a young man, who dreamed of picking an apple from a tree before looking around cautiously to check that no one had seen him.[4] Jung noted how the dream's meaning could be 'amplified' by relating it to the archetypal theme of plucking forbidden fruit, occasioning a 'fall' in the stories of many cultures, including the loss of innocence in the Biblical Garden of Eden. (Jung defined 'amplification' as the 'elaboration and clarification of a dream-image by means of directed association', including parallels from mythology, folklore, ethnology and religion.)[5]

The night before this dream, the young man had had a rendez-vous with his housemaid, with whom he'd recently started a love affair. Consciously, he claimed to find nothing wrong with his amorous behaviour, as many of his friends had acted in a similar manner. By contrast, his behaviour in the dream suggested a degree of disowned guilt.

An important symbolic figure in many dreams is the 'Shadow', typically of the same gender as the dreamer, and commonly representing a disowned aspect of ourselves or something we don't openly acknowledge.[6] For example, Peter O'Connor writes of a male client suffering from depression and numerous psychosomatic symptoms: he dreamed of being in a dark corridor of a warehouse and encountering three bikers who coldly stabbed an old man with a screwdriver before passing the body on to him.[7] He allowed the body to fall and ran away. When considering how the figures in the dream might relate to himself, he recognized that the bikers' behaviour could reflect his own anger and aggressive impulses which he'd suppressed all through his life: a self-sacrificing man, he was always trying to be agreeable to others. Dreams involving Shadow figures can serve a purpose in helping us to accept ourselves more fully, with all our faults.

Now I'll summarize the most helpful principles I've found for dream interpretation, many of which also relate to interpreting synchronicity. Look out for anything in the dream (or synchronistic experience) that stands out as novel, idiosyncratic or strange, since this is likely to be pointing to something new that's developing in our lives. Or as I put it, 'notice what you notice'. As Jung suggested, ask

Dream Figures

Despite the subjective nature of dream interpretation, Jung offered a number of helpful clues that might point to possible meanings. One approach was to consider carefully the various types of figures who appeared in dreams.

The Persona: Jung used the term 'persona' to reflect the public face we present to the world, which could also function protectively, or defensively, as a mask. In dreams your persona can be reflected in the type of clothing you wear. For example, dreaming of someone in a clown suit might reflect an unconscious fear that you've been making a fool of yourself. Dreaming of being naked, but without other people noticing, could reflect a sense of vulnerability or self-exposure. Being in uniform might represent a kind of rigidity in the way you present yourself to others.

The Shadow: This figure in dreams represents a darker or less acceptable side to your nature – a side that's possibly disowned. The Shadow figure is commonly of the same gender as the dreamer. One example of the Shadow as it might show in a dream would be someone who is highly critical of others, which might reflect our own tendency to judge. Any appearance of the Shadow archetype can help us to recover disowned aspects of ourselves to become more whole, and perhaps prompt us to think about how we'd prefer to act in future.

Anima and Animus: Some dreams include a particular type of archetypal figure that relates to balance in our personalities. When a man's dream includes a shadowy female figure, this might relate to the Anima archetype, representing the female, or Yin, element of the male psyche. The female figure in the dream might then represent something about the man's less developed feminine side. For example, if an overly competitive and emotionally distant man dreams about a malnourished woman, this might reflect how he has yet to develop his 'feminine' side, which would be more in touch with his and others' feelings, enabling a more meaningful connection with others. Similarly, a woman might dream of a male figure, related to her Animus, or the masculine image within her psyche. These types of dreams are more common around mid-life, at 40 or so years of age, when such issues tend to come more to the fore.

what is the purpose of the dream (or synchronicity)? What is it trying to tell you? Avoid any standardized 'cookbook' interpretation of the dream's symbols, since the key thing is what strikes you as being especially relevant *to you*. Consider whether the symbolic language of the dream suggests something to you about your subjective state, an inner truth that might go beyond what you could discern through intellect alone. Notice the mood of the dream. Ask yourself what the dream might relate to in the context of your current life circumstances, beliefs and values: does it in some way connect your inner and outer life experience? Try 'amplifying' the meaning of any apparent symbols, following Jung's method – a process that will be enhanced if you learn more about myths, folk tales and archetypes.

Bear in mind that the symbols in the dream can have different layers of meaning. For example, if you're in a vehicle, which may say something about your relative progress in an important area of your life, consider why it might be a car as opposed to a train or a plane? Are you travelling alone, or impeded by obstacles, or is your journey risky?

If, in your attempt at dream interpretation, nothing immediately comes to mind, but the dream feels especially numinous, you might 'file it away', allowing time for possible associations or meanings to form in the back of your mind. Sometimes the truth of a dream is only revealed later, as when Jung repeatedly experienced fearful dreams of large sections of Europe freezing over – only later did he learn that they probably related to the outbreak of World War I months later.[8]

At this point I want to describe two specific dreams that guided my life path when I was 30. It wasn't until later that I fully understood them, but even at the time I could see their bearing on the choices I faced. Both dreams seemed to relate to challenging circumstances in my professional life. I'd been working in the local psychiatric hospital for about ten years, and had been the senior psychologist for the last five. There were some things in the workplace I felt angry about, though perhaps without recognizing the true strength of these feelings at the time.

There had been a lingering unresolved conflict at the hospital over several years, which external regional managers had been unable to address effectively, despite the fact they'd been asked to help in a crisis. There was an extremely strained relationship between a hospital executive member and his staff, many of whom felt mistreated and bullied. His approach was rigid and autocratic.

The time for confronting this executive about his behaviour was long overdue. I decided to speak up in a forthcoming management review meeting involving all staff members. I knew that many would welcome this, but didn't know how much support they'd express at the time. I felt my career was potentially on the line in challenging someone who was objectively in a more powerful position than myself.

I had two dreams around this period. In one I was in a large public swimming pool. There were few others around, and almost none apart from me in the water. I sensed that there was a shark in the swimming pool heading in my direction. It was coming for me. I needed to get out quickly. I swam desperately towards the side of the pool, as quickly as I could. As I swam I noticed a fit lifeguard.

He was a young man, a few years older than me, who was running to help me get out in time. He reached me and pulled me out just as the shark was about to bite.

I interpreted the figures in the dream as relating to aspects of myself. It immediately came to me that the shark might represent my own, not wholly acknowledged anger. I interpreted the pool as the emotions in which I was immersed, as I knew that water commonly relates to emotions. The lifeguard seemed to represent a more mature version of myself. I believed I'd gained a useful insight. I needed to draw upon a more mature side of myself to contain and manage my anger. Otherwise that powerful feeling could be harmful and self-defeating. I had the capacity to achieve this, but I needed to proceed with great care.

In the second dream, I was standing on the edge of the Sydney Harbour Bridge. I felt scared, as I knew that I had to jump into the water off the side facing the Opera House and swim towards Sydney Cove, near Circular Quay. The water didn't seem as far below me as it would have been in real life, but it was it was a long and frightening drop nonetheless. Yet somehow I knew that I'd survive it. Before I jumped I noticed a large hemispherical structure, made of metal scaffolding, in the middle of Sydney Cove, a few hundred metres from Circular Quay. I would need to swim to that hemispherical structure to reach safety.

I don't actually remember jumping, but I remember being in the water. I swam and made my way towards the structure. As I got nearer, I became aware of an old man in a small boat heading towards the rear part of the scaffolding. I reached the scaffolding and started to pull myself up on it. I was exhausted, but sensed that I was going to be all right. The elderly man was arriving at the structure around the same time, and I sensed that he'd rescue me. The light was murky and the waves were choppy. I felt helpless: without the man and the structure, I'd be in serious danger.

I took the bridge to represent a transition stage in my life. I had some sense of awareness that I'd need to take a dramatically different path – I couldn't just keep going in the same direction as before. However, what really struck me in this dream was the half-spherical structure in the water. I commonly thought of a sphere as representing the self. So I took the scaffolding hemisphere to represent a relatively immature and newly developing self – unfinished, but still significant. I interpreted the jump into the waves in darkness as the leap of faith I needed. Naturally, I'd be buffeted by strong and challenging emotions. The old man represented wisdom I might need to rely on – from a character who was more remote from me than the young lifeguard in the earlier dream. This suggested I might need some external help, in addition to enlarging my perspective to find further wisdom within.

The dreams helped me manage my feelings while dealing with a gruelling period at work marked by extreme conflict. Like synchronicity, they gave guidance as though from a more profound source. When going through darker times, I tend to be guided more by dreams than by synchronicity, which I typically experience when feeling more whole, or in a positive frame of mind. It was good to have a warning from my unconscious about the need to be vigilant in dealing with the conflict. Perhaps I could have heeded this message even more fully, but it did cause me to moderate my behaviour. Sometimes a dream, like a synchronistic experience, does nothing more than put you on your guard. And that can be a precious gift.

Types of Dreams

In his essay on 'General Aspects of Dream Psychology' in *Dreams*, Jung described several types of dreams, albeit with some overlapping characteristics.

Reaction dreams: These result from past trauma – an example would be nightmares following a bad war experience or severe assault. The dream is like a reproduction of the original traumatic experience, albeit with distorted elements. Jung likened these dreams to a lesion of the nervous system and explained that typically they wouldn't be eased by dream analysis. Today such dreams are recognized as a symptom of such trauma-related conditions as post-traumatic stress disorder.

Prospective dreams: These might anticipate the future in some way, involving planning for a future event or perhaps suggesting a solution to an existing problem. Jung suggested that such dreams might at times suggest solutions superior to our conscious reasoning, because they're able to draw on a combination of subliminal thoughts, feelings and perceptions, or what we might call implicit processing, based on intuition. Jung warned against treating prospective dreams as infallible predictions.

Telepathic dreams: These relate to the uncanny foreseeing of specific events, such as Jung's dreams anticipating someone's death as described in Chapter 3. Whereas they often relate to strongly emotional themes, they can also foresee seemingly unimportant occurrences, such as the arrival of a letter.

Archetypal dreams: These are commonly 'big' or especially numinous dreams, which are more likely to be remembered indefinitely. They typically involve archetypal symbols, sometimes ones the dreamer couldn't realistically have been exposed to, such as mythical and religious symbols and motifs. For example, Jung described how a ten-year-old girl had a series of dreams containing numerous references to mythical and religious symbols and motifs that she wouldn't have encountered in everyday life, such as a horned serpent, angels in hell and four separate gods. Sadly, Jung accurately predicted that the dreams, which involved repeated themes of destruction and restoration, pointed to the child's early death.[9]

Compensatory dreams: In general, Jung considered that most dreams had a compensatory quality, pointing to aspects of life that weren't available to the dreamer's everyday awareness. For example, a dream might portray a grandiose person in a more humble light, or a falsely modest person as having ambitious aspirations. If you looked up too much to a father figure, you might dream of that person portrayed in a more fallible light, prompting you to trust more in your own judgment.

9

A Wider World

Blessings and Mishaps

During the gruelling episode of troubled hospital politics, described in the preceding chapter, I was able to look forward to some serious stress relief: I'd already planned to take eight months off work the following year, on long service leave, to travel the world with my wife. Years later, especially when reading my travel diaries, I more fully appreciated how this period influenced my views on life and mental health.

Travelling overseas for an extended period is an education in its own right, with guaranteed novelty and challenge, combined with the freedom to explore. But some of the reading I did while travelling, as described in this chapter, shaped my evolving worldview as much as any other experiences.

After a comparatively joyless year, 1988, I relished changing my role to that of a backpacking tourist. Among other things, I eagerly anticipated encountering some long-standing professional heroes at a conference in Oxford, UK, before visiting Findhorn, a spiritual community in northern Scotland.

Given that I'm a person prone to introspection, many of my diary entries of the trip relate to inner experience as much as the wonderful sights I saw. Synchronicity can help with personal growth, but there's no substitute for having novel experiences and reflecting on them. The best way to think of it is as a source of useful pointers, potentially underscoring the meaningfulness of an experience. Synchronicity isn't so much a life experience in its own right as a prism through which to see yourself more truly.

Much of my learning on that trip was unexpected, and related to the nature of travel itself. It was not all as idyllic as I might have anticipated. We were struck by the ups and downs of travel, the blessings and mishaps. A car breakdown on a lightly travelled road on the way back from Gallipoli would be followed by a cup of tea and a spectacular view of a sparkling Aegean sea, shared with a sympathetic park ranger. Repeated brake failure on one-lane roads in the barren landscape of the far north of Scotland would be followed by a fortuitous mechanical repair and a breathtaking sunset drive around misty Loch Ness. The prospect of another night sleeping in the car would prompt an optimistic wish that we might find a youth hostel right on the lake around the next corner – and, remarkably, that's exactly what happened!

A theme emerged around the challenges of travel: an alternation of good and bad times, which increasingly seemed like a metaphor for life itself. Things rarely seemed dreadful for more than a few hours at a stretch.

There were many other things we learned from this period of travelling. I'd always thought that American culture seemed superficial. A Hawaiian weekend newspaper I picked up on the first day had some of the most sophisticated articles on schizophrenia and community interventions that I'd ever encountered. I saw a TV interview with Joseph Campbell, an expert on myth whom I hadn't previously encountered, talking about marriage. His comments were so profound that I've used them for marital therapy ever since.

Campbell's ideas included seeing a relationship as something of a higher order than the individuals themselves. Enlarged by each partner's giving, the relationship gives back greatly in return. A key to this is to recognize that when you made a sacrifice, it was a sacrifice not so much to the other person as to the bond between you. Campbell added, with appealing simplicity, that you can tell whom to marry by following your heart. This reminded me of the matchbox with the six of hearts on it. Another wider theme he highlighted was 'Follow your bliss'. As I wrote in my diary at the time, 'Synchronicity is a key for me.' By that stage I'd noticed that my most blissful states in life were often accompanied by coincidences I was convinced were more than just coincidences.

During this trip, the most striking synchronicity I experienced was at Findhorn, a spiritual community in northern Scotland. Sue and I visited for an 'Experience Week', an introductory course, with 25 participants from around the world. It was an experiential group with classes on themes of personal development, spirituality and work activity.

During our initial exploration of the main building and environs, we came to a flat grassed area on the side of a hill, where I was astonished to see a large, hemispherical scaffolding-like structure, exactly the same shape as that of the hemispherical scaffolding form in my dream about a fearful jump off the Sydney Harbour Bridge. The unmistakable connection took my breath away. It was big enough to walk inside and covered a circular mandala on the ground below it, an archetypal symbol of wholeness.

This was the first genuinely powerful experience of synchronicity that I'd noted in the seven weeks of travelling up to that point. It intrigued me that it occurred on the first day of arriving at a spiritual community. But there was one thing about the structure that most stood out as different from the one in my dream. Apart from its being made of wood rather than metal, it seemed 'more stable and substantial, less rudimentary', as I noted in my diary. I took this to be 'a reconnection with my spiritual development, and an encouragement that I had come further' – given that what I took to be the symbolic representation of my self seemed more fully developed.

As the days passed, there was something about the group interaction at Findhorn that I found frustrating. When people joined in large, structured group discussions I detected an air of overblown positivity. People seemed to alter their manner of expressing themselves, censoring any critical comments they'd tentatively or openly expressed elsewhere. This was partly why I preferred one-to-one conversations. As I noted at the time, if groups could express themselves more openly, I'd perhaps come to prefer them, for the feeling of being part of something larger.

I experienced synchronicity around such musings the next day, when group members took turns in reading passages aloud from a book written by a certain 'John', who was 'channelled' by someone else. I'd adjusted to a certain level of weirdness by now, so this did not seem altogether strange. The section I read out was about how people had learned good ways of relating as individuals, but not so much in groups. In a way that echoed my diary entries of the day before, the text said there was potential for people to go much further in developing ways of relating collectively. I noted that this was likely to be a relevant theme throughout my life.

It's only recently, while reviewing my travel diary, that I more fully recognized the long-term impact of my reflections about groups that week. Ever since then, I've had an abiding interest in practising in group settings, including founding a large group psychology practice, developing group interventions and programmes, and conducting peer group supervision sessions.

I experienced further synchronicity at Findhorn after some other things began to grate, despite the apparently positive culture of the place. There was considerable jargon, such as calling the group leaders 'focalizers', and describing a warm-up ritual for the groups as an 'attunement'. I sensed some hypocrisy, including what appeared to be an increasing discrepancy between what people said in public and in private. There seemed to be signs of hierarchy, including the markedly reverent tones with which people referred to the founder, Eileen Caddy.

I spoke about all this to some of the others, including a young Swedish woman, Maria, who shared many of my critical observations. As I noted in my diary, we agreed there was a degree of denial in the Findhorn community as a result of the place 'expecting itself to be a utopia'.

The Experience Week was drawing to a close. I felt I needed to say something about some of these things that bothered me. In one of the first groups after arriving at Findhorn each participant was invited to select an angel that would supposedly guide their visit. I'd selected the 'Angel of Truth'.

Things were shaping up for me to let the Angel of Truth off the leash. My preparedness to do so was spookily bolstered after I finally got around to changing our car aerial, which had broken, all the while thinking about my conversation with Maria about Findhorn's utopian aspirations. Shortly afterwards, Sue and I went for a drive. When we switched on the newly fixed radio, it was tuned by chance into an interview: someone was saying that people should beware of the 'megalomania' that goes with places that try to be a 'utopia'. Such a place may end up becoming restrictive or subtly controlling, even if motivated by genuine ideals. In trying to be too good, it could develop its shadow side. Wow! I call that strong synchronicity.

Serendipity – More Than a 'Happy Accident'

When might fortuitous coincidental outcomes, or 'serendipity', be more than just a happy accident? Such circumstances might include meeting new people, or coming across enlightening information, or getting a lucky break (perhaps following a mishap) that clearly changes your fortunes for the better.

Some researchers at University College London have explored this theme for several years with the aim of harnessing its power. They identify three defining features of serendipity: unexpected circumstances; an 'Aha!' moment; and a valuable outcome. Dr Stephann Makri and his colleagues suggest that we can increase our chances of experiencing serendipity in the following ways:[1]

- creating mental space by changing our environment, even by going for a walk
- varying our daily routine and looking out to meet new people

- being observant – keeping our eyes and ears open
- seeking novelty and relaxing boundaries – for example, trying out new foods, places and ideas
- looking for patterns while also making links to our past experience
- aiming to capitalize on the unexpected.

It may be easier to follow these suggestions while enjoying the novelty and freedom of travel, but we can apply the same principles in our everyday settings if we focus on the two things that people who experience more serendipity were found by the UCL researchers to often have in common:

- having the wisdom to realize when an opportunity is being presented to you
- seizing the opportunity and taking action – this connects with my previous observations about synchronicity and *kairos* (eg, see p.24).

I took that as a tick from the universe to speak up. When I did so, I found it more challenging than I had expected. Tears poured as I spoke. But I think people realized that what I said was heartfelt. Most liked my comment that when I got to Findhorn I thought it was the next best thing after Disneyland. Perhaps they weren't as reverent about Findhorn as I'd thought. Even some people who disagreed with me told me they respected me for saying what I believed. I felt that speaking up was worth it. I usually do, even when it's been difficult.

Some time later we were travelling to the Greek islands. On the ferry I met a young woman who'd previously read the book I was reading at the time, *Zen and the Art of Motorcycle Maintenance* by Robert Pirsig. She said that virtually all the books she'd read of a philosophical and spiritual nature emphasized one thing: the oneness of all things. I agreed.

Pirsig's book made me think about my tendency to intellectualize things, and also my egoism. I reflected on the idea that those qualities are often culturally shaped, and rewarded in our education system. I became more aware of how I tended to become overexcited by how interesting things seemed to be, rather than focusing on relating to others, or to my surroundings, more fully. That seemed to relate to Pirsig's theme of tapping into the quality of experience – the Tao.

As I was reading Pirsig on the Ancient Greeks, a coin fell out of my pocket. On the face of the coin was Democritus. It seemed synchronistic. I later learned that Democritus is a key figure in the history and philosophy of science who contributed to a rationalistic scientific perspective. I suspect all those years ago, when the coin fell from my pocket, I'd become much more ready to let go of Democritus.

Pirsig highlighted our cultural bias towards rational thinking, rather than intuition. This view was echoed in Joseph Campbell's book *Myths to Live By*, which I read soon afterwards. Rational thinking has been overvalued, I'd argue, as a guide for conducting our lives. We've so often ignored the 'truth' of myth as a guide to behaviour: accumulated human wisdom over many centuries deserves greater credence.

These reflections took me further, leading me to question mechanical models of health care. If someone has a 'breakdown', the word implies that, like a broken-down machine, they might at best recover to their former condition of efficiency. But in fact disequilibrium can be the setting from which creative growth can come. The negative image of the mentally unwell is unwarranted. It's a lot easier for people to move on from psychological turmoil if they see it as containing seeds of hope for a fuller development, helping them end up ahead of where they were before. I noted these ideas in my travel diary.

Two later diary entries seemed to have a particular resonance. I'd been reading *Teachings of Gurdjieff: A Pupil's Journal* by C.S. Nott. Gurdjieff seemed to highlight the importance of taking action, rather than just gaining greater insights. I noted that in order to learn,

I must change what I do. I felt this was an important message for the mutual development of mind, body and spirit. Some resolutions spontaneously started to form. I came to the conclusion that I'd really love to have an ongoing mentor.

I lamented that few psychologists I encountered seemed particularly interested in philosophy or transpersonal issues. It was important too, in my opinion, to become more involved in community-based activities. I also recorded a 'need to experience more suffering', suggesting to myself that 'that is a focal point around which I can learn more'. I forgot that I'd written this latter entry until reviewing my travel diaries when preparing to write this book. Be careful what you wish for.

On the peaceful Thai island of Kho Phangan, enjoying beautiful sunsets on our final evenings before returning home, I noted one of the final thoughts in my diary: 'I don't want to play too safe in life. I want to take a few risks, but for the right reasons. I would like guidance on options "from above" so to speak.'

We returned home, and within days I was back at work at the hospital. I felt that my perspective was uncommonly sharp and fresh. But things were not good. Many of my colleagues appeared utterly demoralized. This seemed especially true of those from the 'allied health' disciplines of psychology, social work and occupational therapy. These disciplines seemed to have become swallowed in a generic case management system in which specialized roles were stripped of professional authority and autonomy.

Dispirited colleagues told me of their dissatisfaction at work. Bullying was rampant. People's doors were mostly shut, where previously they had been open, encouraging colleagues to drop in. The culture was toxic. It felt like a wasteland.

I never found my feet on my return. I couldn't understand it. It was taking a disturbingly long time to adjust after my travels. I increasingly doubted myself. Many who remembered the role I'd previously assumed in speaking up about management problems at the hospital wanted me to take on a similar role; others were working to ensure this never happened.

All I really wanted to do was to find my feet and leave the hospital. I'd made that decision before my return. But I never found my feet. Before I had any real clue as to what was going on, I was descending into a kind of malaise. I found I had no certainties any more. It took me a while to realize I was becoming depressed.

What next emerged was without doubt my worst ever experience. Yet I don't believe I could have learned more about the nature of mental health problems in any other way.

10

Hell on Earth

Into the Abyss

Sometimes things are so bad you can't imagine anything good ever coming from them. Being hospitalized with severe depression would typically be one of those times. But through that living hell and my recovery, I learned some of the most valuable lessons, certainly for my work life but also for my life generally. Over and above anything else, my learning from this experience later set me on a path to promote 'positive psychiatry'. This is my deepest personal story of crisis and transformation.

I can remember a time when I'd lost all sense of purpose. No wonder I wished I was dead. There wasn't much synchronicity then. I suppose that fits. In my experience, synchronicity is a sign that you're on the right track. I wasn't.

It was getting dark. Actually it had been getting dark for a while, but it was getting a whole lot darker a whole lot quicker – and that was taking me by surprise. My colleagues at the psychiatric hospital obviously didn't realize how lost I'd become within myself. They were responding to the old me that they saw – which I suppose is no surprise, as I would have looked pretty much the same on the outside.

They didn't notice the greater number of mistakes I was making, which is probably no surprise as many of the mistakes were perhaps rather subtle. But I noticed them. They seemed major to me.

One particular mistake led me to unravel completely. I looked in my top drawer at work, mid-morning, and noticed that I'd brought the wrong keys with me that day. I was shattered! I felt I'd completely lost it. It was like being sucked into a vortex of sorts. My life was a mess.

I went for a walk. I rarely left the building in work time, apart from lunch or a work errand. This time I just needed to get out. I walked towards the waterfront. For some reason I thought of my recently deceased grandfather. He was someone I'd felt very close to, even though I didn't see him much. He was a warm and gentle man. He worked as a pharmacist on a casual basis even in his early 80s, when he also started teaching Sunday school.

My grandfather was lost to me now. Even in spirit. Looking up at the clouds, I tried to connect with him, but to no avail. I remember that when I walked out of the building it was one minute to noon. I had a compelling sense that something different had to happen – something had to shift in me by noon to pull myself out of this. Otherwise, I anticipated a cascade of negative experiences. In retrospect, I suppose I was further gone than I realized. But my downward spiral was certainly very rapid in that last week or two. A half hour had passed. Nothing was different. Nothing had shifted. I was doomed.

I walked around the waterfront and into the city mall, a shell of my former self. I knew where I was, but I'd never felt more lost. Things were coming to a head. These things don't just affect yourself. This was causing massive strain on my wife. I was sleeping little. I'd get up and pace around the house. Something had to change. But nothing was changing. Except that I couldn't go back to work.

Around that nearly lowest point, perhaps something did change – though it was subtle. I woke up during the night with a brief image flashing through my mind, one that gave me a fleeting sense of peace: a glimpse through the rear window of a friend's house to the lush greenery outside. I sensed that it was important to ring my wise friend, Ross. Next morning I did so. Ross answered 'Hello' with his usual gently rising intonation. It was a great relief to hear that. It didn't take him long to pick up on the seriousness of the situation.

After some time he calmly said that he thought we should consider the possibility of hospital. This was something I'd already thought of, with fear. Ross also spoke to Sue. After the phone call I sat on the couch with Sue. The subject of hospital came up. I remember weeping on the couch, prolifically, like a baby. But despite my distress, there was at least a part of me that felt some release – a letting go of sorts. As I wept, with Sue crying alongside me, I decided – if you could call it a decision, given that I didn't even have the will to live – that I would go to hospital. This was the biggest 'little death' I'd ever been through.

As Sue drove over the Westgate Bridge, into Melbourne, there were ominous dark clouds beyond the crest, further accentuating the feeling of foreboding. I began mentally rehearsing how I could make my escape: simply jump out when the car was moving or wait for the less immediate, but no doubt less painful, option of waiting for some opportune traffic lights. None of this would have been obvious from the outside.

It was perhaps years later that I recognized the irony. I remember that during my first year working as a psychologist in Geelong, when the in-patient ward was first opened, I fantasized about being admitted to the ward to see what it was like. This, however, would have been merely a fiction: to go in as a genuine patient would be a different experience altogether.

I have only a vague recollection of the interview preceding my admission. It was several months before I learned from Sue that I'd been admitted at 6pm on 6 June – exactly six years after we'd got engaged. If I'd recognized the synchronicity at the time, it would have felt spooky – assuming I could have felt anything much at all. And perhaps it would have given me a clue that something worthwhile might eventually come out of this after all.

But I did feel something different from despair that first night, at least for a short while. There was a brief period, maybe up to half an hour, of a strange calm – perhaps in the eye of the storm. I was talking to a young woman who, like myself, had just been admitted. She was surprised, I think, when she learned my occupation. In this brief pocket of time, something just came out of me. I told her about that same old process, the need for a coming apart so that things could get back together in a new way. I moved my hands and fingers with the same gestures I always used to represent that. I elaborated a little further ... pretty much in my usual way.

'Can I come and see you?' she unexpectedly asked, despite already being in treatment with someone else. I was taken aback by her question. I didn't want to screw up another person's life – for example, by giving them misleading hope – when I was doing a pretty bad job of my own. I still feel some guilt about how I distanced myself from her from that point. She seemed somewhat bewildered by that. I think she felt we'd made a meaningful connection at a time when there were few meaningful connections to be made.

Later that evening there was a revelation that intrigued me through my despair. When the staff became much less visible, the patients became more lucid. I was shocked to hear their confidently expressed and assertive appraisals of particular medical staff – which doctors they'd recommend and which they wouldn't. They didn't mince their words. At this hour, they seemed much less passive and alienated. But such observations of anything outside myself were fairly short-lived. I was too far gone. I ruminated incessantly.

At an early lunch with other patients, one asked me the commonplace question, 'How long are you in here for?' 'About a week,' I replied, not really out of any sense of optimism, but only because the alternatives seemed too dreadful. 'That's what they all say!' she responded. She predicted six weeks – an uncommonly long admission elsewhere, but seemingly the norm in this private hospital. My heart sank, if it had scope to sink any further. I recognized that, regardless of otherwise attractive appearances, she was one to avoid.

During the first night in hospital, I awoke with a startled feeling: nothing different there. But this time it felt much worse. I got out of bed and looked in the mirror. Previously I'd felt a deep dread, but immediately it became a raw, intense horror. An alien creature with hot red eyes looked back at me. I made no allowance for being loaded up with a strong combination of pills. I had some very dark premonitions, feeling there was nothing at all left of my former healthy self. From being a senior psychologist in a psychiatric hospital to being a patient in one. It was like being sucked down a very dark vortex. I was completely immersed in the dark night of the soul. All was lost.

I tried to kill myself by inducing a heart attack. I figured that if I just tried hard enough, and willed a massive increase in my heart rate, I could cease to be in a way that would leave no outward marks or mess. My heart rate did indeed go up. I counted it getting up to about 220 beats a minute. I had an unholy ringing in my ears that became impossibly loud. I thought it just might work. It didn't.

I later went to the nurses' station. I explained matter-of-factly that I thought I'd just had a heart attack. Shortly afterwards they took some measurements. They reckoned I was physically OK. I remained sceptical.

When I was about to be admitted, I had one other specific concern. I'd recently been asked to see an in-patient who had unusual drop attacks, during which he'd suddenly drop to the floor. We were badly understaffed and I couldn't get to see him for more than one or two brief meetings, including once with his wife. I knew he'd been admitted later to the same private hospital that I was about to enter. I explained my predicament to the admissions officer. He reassured me there'd be no likelihood of our encountering each other, as we were in two different wards on the same floor.

It turned out that all that separated these wards were two long, open corridors. Ironically, this other fellow and I were the only two 'pacers' in the building – him from his ward and me from mine. I quickly became skilled at gauging his whereabouts and keeping one corridor's length behind him. I didn't know how long it would take for me to be uncovered. In the early days I believed I'd perhaps been admitted as a punishment for not having got to see him more often – that's how I thought at the time.

One day I was playing Monopoly. I was in my tracksuit pants – seated, and surrounded by others. I saw him walk around the corner with his wife. There was no escape. They walked towards our group, perhaps thankful for any minor diversion. Oh no! Contact was inevitable. They reached us and halted. I was facing them. Then there it was: the look of vacant recognition. A barely perceptible shift to a quarter-smile. I was stripped bare. It was official: my little death was complete.

When, early on, I saw a psychiatrist, he asked me about my personal history. I found myself talking about my earliest memories as a preschooler in Fiji. There was something curiously soothing about that. Talking about Fiji and other parts of my earlier life connected me a little more with some past good in myself. I later resolved to never take for granted the potential healing benefit of taking a person's history.

The psychiatrist prescribed me a range of pills – the highest dose of antidepressants prescribable. I hated this. The first time I raised them to my mouth, and swallowed them one by one, I thought to myself that I was taking in my own death. Talk about a reverse placebo effect! Nobody asked me what I thought about taking the pills – certainly not the psychiatrist or any other staff.

I remember attending an art group. I did a painting. I was shocked to see how it formed into a band of jarringly juxtaposed bright reddish wavy lines, joined together to form a colossal wave – seemingly about to crash. It almost looked volcanic. I suppose that's how I felt inside.

There were very brief pockets of relative calm. I remember talking to a man a little older than myself who happened to be a friend of my brother. We asked each other what brought us to hospital. It turned out that he had panic attacks. I was stunned that he'd been admitted merely for this, especially given that he didn't seem to have any clue as to why he was hospitalized, or what therapy procedures he might undergo. I asked whether he was using standard anxiety management strategies for panic attacks, including deliberate exposure to his panic symptoms. He noted my surprise when he made it clear he hadn't a clue what I was talking about. I learned from my brother some time later that his friend had promptly discharged himself after our conversation.

Even as I started getting more used to being in hospital after a while, it seemed that some of my friends didn't. I saw the look

Autobiographical Therapy

Writing in some detail about painful past experiences can be highly beneficial in processing the emotions associated with them. This includes deeply personal experiences such as the loss of a loved one, a distressing failure, experience of abuse, a relationship break-up or workplace conflict.

A number of researchers, among them James Pennebaker of the University of Texas, have described strategies to help people benefit from such writing, including improved mood, physical health and social adjustment. It might be best to write about events or situations you feel you can currently handle.

It can help to set aside 20 minutes or so on several consecutive days, or once a week for several weeks, to write about a distressing situation that has had most impact on your life. Write continuously about your deepest emotions and thoughts about the situation and how it affected you. You might also consider what, if anything, you've gained from the experience. You could perhaps describe how you might aim to manage such a predicament if it arose again. Write about just one topic, or different topics each day. There's no need to show your work to anyone.

This kind of self-expression especially helps if you find that, over time, you can give a more organized or coherent account of the situation, have less need to try to suppress thoughts or feelings about it, and have gained further insight into it.

of horror in a good friend's eyes when he saw how different I looked. (People's eyes often become an ungodly red within hours of admission, owing to medication.)

My wife, Sue, visited me frequently. When one day my friend Ian came to visit, he told me: 'You've got to look after number one.' I had always thought that a selfish expression, but he didn't mean it that way. It helped. Authenticity goes a long way in such situations. Ian had been good enough to come in and just be himself, nervous though he was. Another visitor gave me a book, *Chaos*. This was clearly well intended, but I felt seriously challenged when I saw the title. It sounded like a book about my inner world.

Every day I could look across the street and see a café called 'Somewhere Else'. That, of all places, is where I wanted to be. In all honesty I genuinely believed I'd never reach somewhere else. But if I did, I'd celebrate by paying that café a visit. One day I did, with Sue. It was the sweetest anticlimax I've ever experienced.

And then there was a healing of sorts – a mini-turning point, later in that first week. A young student nurse was allocated to spend some time with me. We went into a small room near the nurses' station where there was a piano and an exercise bike. She played the piano while I rode the bike – hard. I still thought I might die from a heart attack, but this time, as she gently played the piano, there was a question mark over the prospect. I would leave it to chance.

I pedalled and pedalled, frenetically. Then I got tired. I slowed down. I didn't think I was going to have a heart attack after all. From that point I was a little more … hopeful. Just a bit. It felt like the most curative experience so far in that hospital. I could tell that student nurse had a good spirit. Her presence had a peaceful yet somehow uplifting impact, which made a difference.

Being in a private hospital was very expensive, and we had limited private insurance. It was time to move, but I was in no way ready to return home. The decision was made that I would go to a public psychiatric hospital. There was an unexpectedly poignant farewell when I left the clinic. I'd shared a room with a young man with prominent tattoos. We seemed to be from different sides of the tracks. Despite barely speaking to each other for the entire week, there was some unmistakable affinity between us. Just before I left our room, we looked at each other. He came over, we both opened up our arms, and we gave each other a big hug. And we both really meant it.

Within a day or two of switching to the public hospital, I was starting to feel noticeably better – a bit more alive. It greatly helped that I met an architect of similar age to myself. We got on well. We could even joke. We wondered aloud on a film outing how crazy people were meant to act while travelling on a bus. We made a few noises along with flapping hand gestures. It felt good to be able to make a joke – even a lame one.

In the ward we often chatted with two middle-aged housewives. They were much younger than most other in-patients, apart from several teenage girls with anorexia. At times the four of us laughed. We seemed to feel more normal in each other's presence. One day we somehow got a netball and threw it around a patient lounge area. The younger woman was very skilled, with terrific control of the ball and a superb throw. We all saw her differently. For a few minutes, she was a skilled sportswoman.

I was sad to hear later that this incident was raised when medical staff were speculating whether I might have any manic tendencies. My spirits were certainly higher during that game, perhaps more than any other time in hospital. I suppose there was some small risk we could have broken something. But not much. It seemed a pity that a rare bit of healing magic could be reduced to a potential symptom.

Again I was struck by the patients confidently asserting their views when staff were not around. They were brutally honest in their appraisals of the various leaders' performance in therapy groups.

A number of friends continued to visit, including a psychologist friend, Rod. He urged me to remember the experience I was going through. I doubted I'd want to: it was just raw pain. But at some level I think I did resolve, or at least allow myself, to take in more of my experience. In time I started to feel as though there were strands forming a net at my back, created through contact with friends and family (and that piano-playing student nurse), preventing me from falling further.

Amazingly, after about a week in the public hospital, I felt ready to leave. I said my farewells to a fellow patient who said she could tell I was one who was never going to be coming back. This was affirming. I felt so normal when I left that I went straight to a five-day psychology conference. I remember taking the antidepressant medication in the university toilets, feeling furtive about it, and wondering how shocked my conference colleagues would be if they knew where I'd spent the last two weeks.

The following weekend Sue and I went to stay in Daylesford, a 90-minute drive inland from Geelong, normally a wonderfully peaceful town with lake walks and spa baths. This time the peace was broken. I awoke in the middle of the night with the image of two work colleagues in mind. I immediately thought of them as lifeless 'survivors' in a draining hospital system. I didn't think *I* could do that: just survive. But that was what seemed to be called for. I fell rapidly into a deep black hole. I was suicidal again. Dead inside.

I was readmitted to the public hospital. This time the other patients seemed to be almost uniformly old. There was only one patient I related to: a psychiatric nurse. As coincidence would have it, we found ourselves on the same psychiatric hospital team a couple of years later. I'd confidently say we were among the highest-functioning people on the team. If only our colleagues knew that we'd once been fellow patients on a psychiatric ward! We never talked about our mutual hospital experience when we worked together. We didn't even hint at it. It was probably too soon afterwards.

One day I was feeling particularly defeated. I'd fought as hard as I could. It had been relentless. I resolved that if nothing happened in the next five minutes I'd make a radical decision. I didn't know how, but I'd find a way to put an end to my suffering. Within a minute or two the phone rang. It was a close friend making one of her infrequent but always sincere and supportive calls. It was good timing. I've thought ever since that if it weren't for that phone call I might not be here. That call made it possible to resolve to continue. It was hard for me to dismiss the timing: even in my darkness I believed it was synchronistic.

PART THREE

Tuning into the Universe

11

Return to the Light

The Self Regained

I don't feel I gained much from the main psychiatrist I saw in the public hospital. He basically summed matters up by suggesting that when council workers are leaning on their shovels, and perhaps look like they are being lazy, they might just be pacing themselves. It seemed that he was suggesting that I could pace myself better, and that my main issue might be a form of burnout. That seemed a bit simplistic.

On one occasion, a psychiatric registrar who'd arranged to see me offered the opinion that I didn't really belong in hospital. He seemed to have no particular therapy that could help me, but I do believe that his genuineness and honesty made a slight difference. Sometimes slight differences add up.

Somehow, little by little, I gradually picked up. I could notice more of what was going on around me. It seemed to me that there were some staff members, about 10 per cent of the total, in whose company I felt a slight boost in mood. They were from a range of ages and disciplines. On the other hand, there were a few staff who seemed controlling or competitive, and after interacting with these people I felt worse. It generally wasn't difficult to avoid them.

Friends continued to visit. One friend took me to a nearby park and we chatted. When he drove me back, he told me that staff had told him he could only take me out on condition that he personally brought me back into the ward, since I was a suicide risk. But he dropped me off at the front of the hospital and drove off. He'd shown good judgment: I now felt more normal.

I was experiencing only incremental improvement, but that was something to be thankful for. My departure date was fixed for around four weeks after my second admission. It helped that I solved the cryptic crossword on my last day in hospital. That seemed like a good sign. It had always been an achievement in the past, even for my former normal self.

Just before leaving hospital, I started seeing a psychologist who was slightly younger than myself. He was clearly very genuine and authentic in his manner. I could tell that he related to me, in various ways, including sympathizing with my experiences of hospital politics. He was skilled at flexibly applying the cognitive-behavioural therapy (CBT) with which I was so familiar. He somehow helped me to acknowledge some of my past strengths in a way that made me feel they might still be present. I arranged to see him regularly after I was discharged. I also committed to seeing a private psychiatrist. One day the psychiatrist looked me straight in the eye and said, 'You don't think you'll ever get well, do you?' This caught my attention despite my thinking that he was stating the obvious. What was most striking was his confidence: 'You *will* get well. I *guarantee* it!' Somehow, something got through. It made a difference. Also, he likened hospital politics to a snake pit, and this too was somehow affirming as well, as it acknowledged the challenges I'd faced.

I combined seeing films at the Kino cinema, my favourite movie theatre in Melbourne ('Kinotherapy', I called it to myself), with seeing the psychologist. The regular contact with him helped to keep me afloat on what felt like a swirling dark sea of pain. He seemed young, but also animated and engaged as well. I thought of him as a lifebuoy – my mind often played on words around that time.

I received a letter from my uncle, a psychiatrist. It was as well meaning as any of the support I received; but I felt more despondent afterwards. The letter documented a substantial family history of depression. My uncle probably thought he'd given me a reason to not feel guilty. I felt I'd been given a reason to feel more helpless.

One afternoon I accompanied my father-in-law on a drive around his farm. I was spending a few days with him as he visited local farmers as a stock agent. He's a man of great warmth and generous spirit. Something must have rubbed off. As we drove past the farm dam I suddenly realized that I'd gone for a few seconds without a suicidal thought. That was another mini-breakthrough.

Then something happened that led to a major breakthrough. I received a letter from a friend, a psychiatric nurse. He urged me to see a particular therapist he knew, a man named Max. He said that I was a spiritual man and needed to see someone who could work at that level. I didn't feel like seeing another therapist: I was already seeing a psychologist and psychiatrist. But my friend's heartfelt and generous encouragement was something I couldn't ignore.

I saw Max twice, for an hour and a half each time. Max had run an Australasian psychodrama school for many years. He had studied with Moreno, the founder of psychodrama, for six years. Max was a wizard. On the first occasion, he just let me speak; and speak I did, a great deal.

One of the first things he said to me was, 'Well, I don't think that it's tragic!' What? Not tragic? I was shocked. I might have lost everything! Yet somehow he seemed to be utterly attuned to my situation. Later in the session he gave me feedback about how he saw me as a person and the situation I was in. He used words that I thought would have accurately described how I used to be. But he'd only known me for an hour. This gave me hope that any past good in me was not all gone.

Talking about my gruelling professional experiences, he suggested that I'd gone where angels fear to tread. I felt that at some level he approved, despite questioning my actions. I'd been dealing with powerful forces that I'd underestimated, perhaps foolishly so. It was easy to take any feedback from Max. It was so obvious that he cared, even when he was blunt. He was deft at knowing how much someone could take.

The second time I saw Max was a true turning point. I'm not sure what he covered in the first hour, but in the third half hour we did a two-chair exercise. Back and forth I went between one chair and the other. This separated out two aspects of myself that I was shocked to experience in their most distilled form. On the one side: plaintive, defenceless, all but defeated, with an emerging hint of indignation at the injustice of it all. On the other: a harsh and vicious judge, disgusted, ferociously intense, relentlessly rejecting and aggressive. I had a thick branch in my hand that I was ruthlessly flailing at myself.

At the end of the session Max said seven magic words. I didn't realize they were magic at the time, but they were. He said, 'I think you have an imperfect solution.' I'm not sure that I made much of that at the time, but I certainly felt relief when he said it.

I then left Max's rooms and was in the car park, about to open the car door. At the exact time the key went into the lock, it struck me. It was a feeling rather than a thought: I suddenly realized that I'd let go of the branch. It was an important moment. I understood why Max's words about an imperfect solution resonated so strongly in me. I knew that I was dealing with the challenge of my own perfectionism, among other things – that much was plain. So … an imperfect solution! How elegant! Surely an optimal recovery from a perfectionism-influenced depression would be an imperfect one. My recovery up to that point was so slow, so pathetic, so public, so … imperfect. If I could accept that in myself, then I felt in future I could accept anything.

I started to doubt whether in fact this *was* an imperfect solution, because it seemed an exceptionally good one to me. Now I even had a rationale. I love rationales – they make a complex world simpler. And I find they often work.

I continued to see the psychologist and psychiatrist, and told them about the epiphany with Max. Their reactions were markedly different. The psychiatrist explained how it all came down to biology: there were variations in brain chemistry that occurred independently of our experiences. He clearly believed my brain chemistry had just fortuitously shifted, after months on the same medication – it was just by chance this happened after my meeting with Max.

The psychologist's reaction was more understanding. He saw me all the way through to a full recovery – and briefly beyond. I ran into him about 20 years later at a national conference. By that time he was a recognized world leader in a specialized field. He explained on that occasion that after hearing what I'd said about the session with Max he'd introduced the two-chair technique into the formal training of his students. I was most impressed.

Things continued to pick up. I still had several months of accumulated sick leave left to me, since I'd had very few sick days in my first ten years of work. I would recover as well as I could and then return to work. Maybe things would turn out, or maybe they wouldn't – at that stage, I no longer felt so invested in a specific outcome.

I was alive again. I enjoyed my Kinotherapy. One day I sent a friend a postcard after seeing a movie. This made it start to feel like a holiday.

After I returned to work, people left me alone for the most part. That was good. It was a gentle return. Happily, to anyone who might have taken issue with me, I was seen as no threat. At least that is how it felt. I liked it that way.

I was heartened by my early therapy sessions with clients. I hadn't lost my craft, I was glad to know. I didn't advertise where I'd been – any such disclosure would come well down the track. But I was struck by the deeper level at which patients on the ward seemed to confide to me. I suspect they told me more than they told most of my colleagues, even outside sessions.

A number of clients looked quizzically at me at times as I commented on their experience in a way that somehow seemed to resonate more than they expected. They sometimes said they wondered how I seemed to know so much about what they were going through. Without realizing it, I was reading people more deeply and perhaps more accurately. This was effortless on my part.

Two years later I returned to postgraduate study. It was a wonderfully stimulating Master's course in clinical psychology with many accomplished fellow students, most of similar age to myself. I learned an enormous amount. But I still consider that I learned even more as a clinician from that six-month period of depression and recovery.

It took me two years to get off all medication. One day I was playing doubles tennis and belted down an ace. My tennis partner, a doctor friend, then made a quip, 'You're off the Prothiaden, aren't you?!' He was right. I'd gone off the last of the medication in the past week or so. His comment made it feel like a mini-celebration. As much as I may have needed it, the medication had played havoc with my sporting ability. Now I could feel even more my usual self.

One day soon after, I was driving home from my father's pharmacy, and tears just poured and poured down my face. I thought of the drawn-out period I'd gone through. With a bittersweet ache I uttered the words, 'It's just been so hard!' Sometimes grief from prolonged mental distress comes out at a certain point in recovery. When you start to see your struggles in the past tense, you can be more ready to grieve what was lost, or what it cost you.

After my recovery, barely a day would go by when I didn't appreciate being able to enjoy normal life. There were several years afterwards when I worked 60-hour weeks, juggling hospital work, study and establishing a private practice. In the meantime, I fathered three children. Despite substantial life demands and challenges, nothing ever seemed remotely as difficult as getting through a single day during that period of darkness. It was almost impossible to take normal life for granted. I was freed from preoccupation. I could be spontaneous.

I left the hospital in Geelong where I'd always worked until then, and took up a senior position at a hospital for war veterans in Melbourne where I helped develop a nationally recognized programme for post-traumatic stress. I became a specialist in treating trauma reactions, and started presenting research at national and international conferences. It was satisfying to finish my public hospital career on a high note. Then I shifted to full-time private practice, where I loved the autonomy, and the opportunity to use my skills to the fullest.

There were many busy, very productive years ahead. My practice grew. Our family grew. We moved to a house near some parks for the children to play in and a bay to kayak in. Joy, and synchronicity, returned.

The first obvious synchronicity occurred when my wife pointed out something I'd not noticed – that I'd been admitted to hospital on 6 June. Not only that but I recalled I'd been admitted around 6pm. This was the exact time and date I'd become engaged six years earlier – prompting me to feel there was a deeper, archetypal significance to these contrasting subjective experiences of being in heaven and hell on earth. On reflection, both contribute, albeit in quite different ways, to one's purpose and meaning in life. This synchronicity prompted me to look for what I might gain most deeply from having gone through such a painful experience, viewing it as somehow 'meant to be'.

In the years afterwards, when our practice grew (my wife joined me as practice manager), there were a number of synchronistic, or at least serendipitous, experiences in the purchase of work buildings. The first practice building we owned was purchased after a last-minute client cancellation allowed me to attend a nearby auction of a house I'd admired but had no conscious intention of purchasing. When no other bidders attended, the opportunity seemed auspicious to start negotiations that ultimately led to our buying the building.

Years later, when we wished to expand, an opportunity came up to buy our former doctor's premises, a few doors along from our first building. When we purchased it, we learned that the title was unexpectedly in the name of a Sue Mackey, which was the name of my wife, the new owner. This remarkable coincidence made our acquisition of the building feel auspicious.

A few years earlier I'd seen my former doctor in the room that I now consult from. I'd received some results from an extensive medical check-up. When the results turned out to be all favourable, I suddenly realized that I hadn't expected that: I'd been unwittingly harbouring a sense of a foreshortened future, a not uncommon trauma-related symptom, from the period when I'd been suicidal some 15 years earlier. It seemed synchronistic to be working now in the very room in which I'd received positive news that seemed to gift me extra time to do the things I enjoy and find meaningful. That's curiously motivating, in a manner that's hard to convey in words.

We also learned that the premises next to our first work building, which we still own, was one of two from which Tom Bowen practised. Bowen was the originator in the 1950s of the Bowen Technique, a holistic physical therapy for injuries and pain relief that's still widely used around the world. This led me to believe that truly innovative therapy approaches could emanate from humble beginnings, something that continues to encourage me in my development of 'positive psychiatry'.

Other synchronistic experiences relating to my period of hell on earth included fortuitously encountering the psychologist who'd helped me recover from severe depression at a recent therapy conference in Lima, Peru, where I was invited by another colleague to present at the same session. He subsequently invited me to join the local scientific committee he was chairing to prepare for the World Congress in Behavioural and Cognitive Therapies in Melbourne in 2016. Having such a different relationship with him, under such different circumstances, seems to underscore the extent to which the dark night of the soul can be transcended, and indeed that outcomes gained from going through that experience can be thoroughly worthwhile.

I take these fortuitous events and connections to be more than just chance. I interpret them as apparent ticks, and free kicks, from the universe, indicating that the unfolding of certain events is 'meant to be'. Some might consider me superstitious for holding this view. By contrast, what I know for a fact is that my belief in these experiences as synchronistic rather than merely coincidental is highly motivating and energizing. And increasingly I meet others, including clients, whose synchronistic experiences, and their feelings about them, echo mine.

I shall describe one further poignant example of synchronicity, which occurred while writing here about my experience of being hospitalized for depression, a task I initially found daunting. As I started to write, the thought popped into my mind that at the time I'd felt no compassion for myself at all. On the first page, just as I was starting to express how gruelling the experience was, a small patch of light started to form right next to the sentence I was writing. It seemed to be formed by sunlight passing through a tiny gap in my left hand, which was resting against my temple. To my utter surprise it became more and more defined and brightly illuminated as I wrote. Within a minute it had gradually formed a clearly defined and brightly illuminated heart shape. This seemed like a striking sign of compassion from the universe. My task then became substantially easier. The experience helped the words to flow.

Psychotherapy and Counselling

Therapy or counselling can at times be most beneficial, and not only when you're struggling with mental health problems, such as depression. I've described my own experience of seeking therapy in earlier chapters. I did so again in 2012 from a position of relative wellbeing. I sought the opportunity to meet again with Max Clayton, the therapist who'd so greatly helped me overcome a severe depression all those years ago. I saw him once a month on about eight occasions to pursue personal, relationship and transpersonal growth.

Decreased stigma in exploring mental health issues is leading a wider range of people to seek various forms of counselling. This is reflected by a considerable growth in life coaching.

Positive psychology explicitly offers interventions that are relevant for people regardless of their level of wellbeing. Anything that promotes self-awareness, or being well attuned to your thoughts, feelings, intuitions and relationships, is likely to be helpful in your exploration of a worthwhile life path.

12

Wisdom on Tap

Learning from a Mentor

When you encounter mystical experiences, and seek to integrate them into your life and spiritual development, it's invaluable to have a guide who has experienced such things before. It's from my friend Ross, above all others, that I learned the most about synchronicity.

The term 'mentor' may seem almost quaint these days. I've been fortunate to have had some exceptional mentors, from within as well as outside my profession. Regular meetings with a mentor can assist transformative growth without your having to go through a crisis. Ross did, as I've mentioned, help me through a crisis too, including helping me to accept the unacceptable when I went into hospital. He greatly assisted my recovery afterwards. We've met for lunch on a semi-regular basis for the last 25 years.

Ross, who continues to keep very busy in retirement, always seems to be thinking about other people. He's very readily prepared to help others, especially those in distress. Ross continues to add finishing touches to the house he built. It's substantial, yet understated, and is a work in progress, just like himself.

Ross doesn't have a mobile phone, but keeps in touch. He talks about everyday things in a way that seems down-to-earth and high-minded at one and the same time. When we walk to a café for one of our long lunches every couple of months, I notice the beauty of our surroundings so much more, simply by noticing how much he appreciates what's all around. He's full of curiosity and wisdom in equal measure.

When we meet, it's sometimes on one of the rear decks of his house at Lorne, a prominent coastal town on the wonderfully scenic Great Ocean Road. From the deck you can look down through gum trees to the beach far below, with surfers, families and distant bathers enjoying the sun. The place seems rather magical. Once, when visiting with my wife and children, we were lolling on the grass below when along came an echidna, or spiny anteater. You don't see them very often – they are shy creatures. When I talk with Ross, the peace of our conversation is punctuated by the splashes of birds in the bird bath a few metres away. They seem as unselfconscious as the echidna.

Ross has told me many remarkable and eye-opening stories, including some about his experiences with clairvoyants. A London clairvoyant once made some uncanny predictions about his next job upon his return to Australia – he'd been in London for about 18 months. She told him that he'd have a job involving large sheets of paper with figures in four corners, which related to insurance. He'd live three miles from his work, and catch public transport that, confusingly, didn't seem to involve a bus or a train. He'd move from the fourth to the fifth floor after a year at the job, with a large salary increase.

On returning to Melbourne after three years away, Ross did find a job as predicted. It involved managing the newsprint for a large Melbourne newspaper. He felt that he had no knowledge or ability for such a job, but he applied and was accepted. His role involved providing regular financial reports to the board. Initially he had to estimate the figures, owing to the complicated, archaic methods they used there. Then, over two to three months, he devised an innovative system which involved recording figures in the four corners of a pro-forma on large sheets of paper. The bottom left figure related to insurance, a major component of the daily reckoning.

Ross's methods and system were efficient and reliable, and allowed for any inaccuracies to be honestly accounted for. He conducted a stocktake that was recognized in the annual report as the most accurate in the history of the company. As predicted, he was living three miles from his workplace. His transport was a tram, apart from occasional days when he walked. He was promoted after a year with a generous salary increase and moved from the fourth to the fifth floor.

It's difficult to dismiss this example of clairvoyance using the common argument that the predictions are so ambiguous or non-specific that it's easy for any gullible person to read truth into them. He suggests that, as in any field, clairvoyants vary in their ability, good ones being rare.

I recently checked some facts in a few stories Ross told me that had had the most impact in changing my worldview, and they were perfectly accurate. As strange as the stories are, I trust Ross. He speaks the truth. I feel uplifted after our every meeting. The feeling lingers. That's another kind of truth he speaks.

One of Ross's favourite expressions is 'Accept that whatever is, is.' It came from his aunt, a painter, a seeker of truth herself. I met her just once and have never forgotten her wisdom. She was lauded for her work when she was finally persuaded by prominent artists to exhibit in her 80s. The exhibitions sold out. To my untrained eye, her artwork on Ross's walls has an uncommonly archetypal quality. For example, one watercolour is an abstract image of a Madonna-like woman and child painted in flowing strokes on upside-down newspaper. It hints at the sublime beyond the mundane and seems to ask, 'What's important, what's truly newsworthy?'

One of Ross's most memorable synchronistic stories involved his aunt. Ross needed her signature on a legal document by a particular date. He'd tried to call his aunt for several days beforehand, but was unable to contact her. He eventually decided to drive the two and a half hours to her home in a bayside suburb of Melbourne in the hope of meeting her. After reaching Melbourne city, many kilometres short of his destination, his intuition suddenly told him to 'turn left here'. He did so. Approximately one kilometre farther on, he saw his aunt's car parked on the other side of the road. It was rare for either of them to be in that area, let alone at the same time. She was astonished to see him there. They talked. She signed the document.

Ross, perhaps surprisingly, sees nothing strange in such coincidences. He was matter-of-fact about this one. It led to the signing of the document – a practical means to an important goal. It simply lent credence to his belief that intuition doesn't lead us astray, but appears to be infallible.

When I first heard of this incident, I was struck by how such a seemingly non-rational thought process could assist in achieving an end. It went beyond noticing an uncanny coincidence after the fact. To Ross at least, there was something predictable about the event. He knew from experience that his intuition was worth acting upon. He has many such stories.

A second anecdote seems even more remarkable, at least from a rationalistic perspective. One winter evening many years ago, Ross was invited to a dinner party by a friend who wished to introduce him to some other friends. As a female guest stretched out in front of the fire, he thought to himself, 'I've seen those legs before.'

Prompted by recognition of the woman's rather angular face, he recalled having a clear image of her as a fellow ship's passenger on the P. & O. vessel *Himalaya*, which sailed from London in the winter of 1950, more than 20 years previously. Ross was then 11 years old. Now he remembered her as the striking figure who repeatedly walked around the deck of the ship, arm in arm with a dark-haired man, a doctor, who disembarked with her in Colombo, Ceylon.

The woman confirmed all these details and remarked what a good memory he had, especially given his age at the time. Somewhat puzzled, she asked him how he knew that her former husband, whom she'd met on the ship before Ross saw them walking together, was a doctor. Ross replied that he didn't know how, he just knew. In further discussion they agreed what a beautiful ship it was. Ross recalled how spectacular it was on deck on the evening they sailed, with the ice on the rigging – there had just been an uncommonly severe blizzard in the UK. This shocked the lady. She enquired which sailing he was on. 'December the sixth, of course,' he replied. But she'd set sail in summer, six months earlier: Ross must have seen her across a gulf of time. They just looked at each other. Despite the chronological discrepancy, Ross was able to describe the pattern and colours of the checked skirt she'd worn while walking on the deck. She confirmed Ross's description, saying it was her favourite skirt at the time: she'd worn it almost every day. Somehow Ross seemed to have tuned into a special experience she was having: 'You know, that was the happiest time of my life. I always felt I left my soul on that ship!'

Although Ross was at first taken aback by all this, at another level it struck him as perfectly natural. It seemed like a manifestation of 'continuity beyond manifest existence', as he put it. He added that he and his new friend have since talked about that experience on a number of occasions.

Ross briefly introduced me to her after a chance encounter during one of our lunchtime meetings. Years later, the day before she moved to another state, they encountered each other in the car park of a local supermarket that was not his usual one. They'd unsuccessfully tried to contact each other for some weeks before she left. Ross was walking back to his car, thinking of her, when he saw her get out of the car beside his.

These two stories raise questions about what synchronistic events or encounters might mean. Observing people on a ship six months after they'd actually disembarked from it shows that our usual conceptions of space and time don't always apply.

The next story is more delicate, and I shall omit some significant details in the hope of not causing anyone unnecessary discomfort or distress. It involves an encounter of a very different kind – one so unusual that Ross made detailed handwritten notes of it at the time, which he showed me years later.

Ross was once driving on an interstate highway. He wondered what had led him to spontaneously take that route, as he'd virtually promised himself that he'd never drive that way, owing to its association with painful family memories. At one point, he was redirected by road works to travel to the other side of the road. At that moment, he was engulfed by an extraordinary sensation that he described as entering his being – physically, mentally, totally.

Ross felt his usual self during this experience, but the sensation was undeniable. It began with strong bodily feelings starting from his toes upwards, and was soon followed by powerful positive emotions, including 'delight, ease, wellbeing, happiness, calm, peace and stillness'. The sense of completeness was indescribable. At first he thought that perhaps his mother had died and was telling him all was well. But he dismissed this just as quickly when he had the spontaneous thought, 'Not mother'.

Then two words kept intruding on his thoughts, over and over: 'Youthfulness accompanying'. He felt a presence that was 'around me and within me … separate from me, yet invading my being … but not excluding my being and its individuality'. He then had the spontaneous thought, 'Look for an ambulance!' and then later, 'Look for the hospital, look for the hospital!' The sensations and messages stopped as soon as he drove past a regional hospital.

Some days later, Ross learned some details from a friend about a car accident some years earlier in which a young man they knew had suffered fatal injuries. Ross did not immediately make the connection at the time, but shortly afterwards realized that the sensations and messages he'd experienced a few days earlier had commenced at the location of the young man's accident, and ceased in sight of the hospital where the young man had apparently died, after being taken there by ambulance. This seemed even more remarkable as Ross's purpose for driving on that highway at that time was directly related to the man's death years earlier, for reasons I shall not elaborate upon.

Ross described then having a sudden flash of awareness, thinking to himself, 'But didn't you realize that that was him [the young man] in the car indicating everything was OK? Of course!'

At a more everyday level, I'm reminded of someone else's view on synchronicity – Helen's, from my local health food store. Some context is required. I've developed a habit of occasionally asking relative strangers a couple of impertinent questions. One question is: do they experience synchronicity, defined as an uncanny timing of events that seem to go beyond pure chance? The second is, if so, what do they make of it?

Find Yourself a Mentor

Having a mentor – a wise or knowledgeable person we can trust – is invaluable for developing skills or understanding in any area of life. If you have a mentor who can listen and talk with you openly about private and personal (including spiritual or transpersonal experiences), so much the better. If you have a mentor who has experienced synchronicity, and is ready and willing to discuss such experiences with you, that's perhaps the greatest preparation of all.

Bear in mind the following points before selecting and approaching your mentor:

- you need not be of similar age: both younger and older people can bring you a refreshing change of perspective
- a difference in gender can help you see things differently too
- choose someone who can speak patiently and clearly – whether an extravert or introvert
- opt for someone with breadth of experience and openness to new ideas – so that they have something to gain as well as you
- don't be offended if they say no – after all, this is quite a commitment
- if not a mentor, you might seek out peers, or 'spiritual friends', who are interested, as you are, to discuss transpersonal experiences
- if you can think of an especially helpful mentor, at any time from your distant past to the present, you might consider writing them a gratitude letter: this positive psychology intervention involves expressing your heartfelt thanks to someone important to you and explaining how they have influenced your life direction for the better.

I asked these questions of Helen as she was weighing my muesli. After saying yes to the first question, she went on to say that it's about 'things connecting when they are meant to ... and people connecting when they are meant to'. She added: 'It's a learning planet!'

After finishing serving me, Helen said she believed there normally was a rightness to the timing of what happens, whether sad or happy. But terribly sad situations such as a young person dying in a car accident were more problematic. She admitted sincerely, 'I don't know what that's about.' She then added, rather mysteriously, 'Non-attachment – going to a good place.' Somehow, I felt that strongly echoed Ross's sentiments when he'd told me the otherwise very sad tale of the young man's accident, something that Helen didn't know I'd written about just a few days previously.

Personally, I've never had contact with a spirit to my knowledge, although I do recall an incident that occurred about an hour after learning my grandfather had died. I was flying a kite with my young son and wife on her parents' farm. A black bird came and hovered for seconds within a metre of the kite. I had never seen anything like that before. My wife and I had the same thought: that it was somehow related to my grandfather's spirit.

One of Ross's most thought-provoking observations was that there's a 'continuity beyond the manifest world ... and individuality within the continuity'. He added that if there's anything to learn from such experiences as my sighting of the black bird, then that will occur naturally. Perhaps, as Ross suggests, 'the learning will be at a rate one can absorb and understand'.

Regarding such experiences, Ross summed up as follows: 'I see each incident as a privilege. Each serves to reinforce what I hold to be true. There's a continuity beyond this manifest world. I see these incidents, each one as a different example from the other of reinforcing what I believe in.' He continued: 'It seems so plain to me and always has. It's never been a mystery to me. The mystery is why so few people seem to have these experiences, and so few are aware of continuity.'

'The ego and intuition are separate and opposite. You must put it, the ego, aside. The intuitive doesn't lead [us] astray. It seems infallible. Failure comes when ego intervenes. Intuitive awareness is spontaneous, is immediate. There's no lead-in. No thought. No pondering. Intuition doesn't require questions – it just says, "That's it!"'

Ross commonly ends our conversations, as he did on this occasion, with a brief reflective silence followed by an admission: 'I don't know.' He doesn't look for explanations for synchronistic experiences, preferring to 'go with the experience'. He believes it's in the nature of synchronicity to be inexplicable.

In Ross's view, as in mine, synchronistic experiences confirm that your intuitive thinking is on the right track. On one occasion an extraordinary coincidence saved his life. He'd been walking beside a highway in Queensland and had decided to sleep at the side of the road, beneath a bush. He'd got himself comfortable when it started to rain. He suddenly had a strong urge to move to the other side of the road. He was somewhat reluctant to do so, as the other side was damp and windy and the ground was rougher than this dry, sheltered spot he'd settled in. However, he thought he'd better move. Only minutes later, a passing car ran off the road through the bush where he'd been sheltering, and then back onto the road again.

Despite not being a builder, Ross originally built a house which in its location, colouring and design corresponded with striking similarity to the prophecy of the London clairvoyant who'd accurately predicted his future job. What puzzled him greatly was his reason for being there: he'd acted solely on intuition. He recalls an Australian Tarot reader telling him, 'You're meant to be there, the house is for a reason. You just don't get it, do you?! People are there to sit and talk, or others just to sit there.' Ross acknowledges that many visitors emphasize how much they like being there, or how helpful it's been for them, although he still remains surprised by their expressions of appreciation. Even primary school children and teenagers say they're just happy to be at his house, sitting with him and talking.

I've been one of many people who've sat with Ross on the rear deck of his home and talked, and at times just sat, over the past

20 years or so. I find the atmosphere to be one of almost inexplicable peace and acceptance. I always leave feeling relatively happy and whole. I've long been at the receiving end of his guidance and, at times, his wise support. I'm sure I have more of an idea of what the Tarot reader meant than Ross does.

I like the informal and creative way in which Ross follows his daimon – at least, that's how I think of it. To me, at least, Ross is a modern-day shaman.

Despite year after year of learning from Ross through our occasional extended lunches, which often turned into whole afternoons, I never thought I would ever experience such profound synchronicity as he described. But 15 years later I was proven wrong.

13

A Confession

Hypomanic Wellness

How could an enlightened state of mind be confused with psychosis? One person may view someone they meet as showing advanced development in their thinking; another may perceive them to be crazy. This suggests that there's much yet to learn about the human mind. I believe synchronicity is a window into such conundrums. I also believe we'll often gain more by exploring the things that confound us than those we already understand fairly well.

In his book *Synchronicity: The Art of Coincidence, Choice and Unlocking Your Mind*, Dr Kirby Surprise points out that psychologists and psychiatrists sometimes misdiagnose synchronistic experiences as a sign of thought disorder, or psychosis.[1] Dr Surprise, a counselling psychologist, reports having seen many clients who have been recommended medication, or hospitalization, after reporting synchronistic experiences.[2]

Dr Surprise differentiates *satori*, an enlightened state sometimes associated with synchronicity, from a psychosis, with which it's sometimes confused.[3] *Satori* is the experience of a collective consciousness, or unified awareness, transcending the illusion we have of being a separate 'self', detached from others and the world around us. The term expresses our feeling that we're part of a universal consciousness. All cultures appear to have an equivalent term for such a concept, as Dr Surprise notes – and yes, that *is* his real name!

The following three chapters continue my personal story, specifically in relation to these themes. They illustrate a belief I hold

Satori – A Spiritual and Mystical Experience

Satori may be described as a powerful, ecstatic experience, involving the dissolution of ego boundaries, associated with feeling part of a unitary, undivided or collective consciousness. It's typically blissful – and brief. It can be confused with psychosis owing to the altered perception of reality with which it's associated.

It's a spiritual experience: it involves expanded or extra-ordinary awareness and has personal meaning for the individual in coming to grips with issues of existence. It's also mystical, as defined by William James (see p.33) – being ineffable, noetic, transient and seeming to relate to something beyond our own will. It involves intuitive as opposed to rational thought processes.

Other terms that refer to transcendental insight, or the capacity to see a truer or more comprehensive reality, include *joriki, kensho* (Zen) and *bardo* (Tibetan Buddhism).

These experiences might all be described as 'liminal' states, which anthropologists have recognized in cultures that conduct ecstatic rituals. During such states, the usual ways of thinking about time, space and physical laws such as causality are transcended.

that what may seem to some to be a form of psychosis, sometimes defined as using irrational means to attain irrational goals, might instead be considered an enlightened way to be effective in attaining one's *rational* goals. I find this story a difficult one to tell, and not just because of its personal nature. It deals with circumstances around my mother's death. Over and above that, it involves friends and family members, none of whom I wish to hurt or offend. It's a story that has motivated me to write this book, and simultaneously tempted me to shelve it. I believe that what I have to say is relevant to our approaches to mental health care. It helps illustrate how we need to go beyond a reductionist medical model to understand matters of the mind.

It's only recently that I've acquired a suitable language to speak of these things in a way that might make more sense to others, apart from those who have had similar experiences. The events described belong to the time in my life when I most fully recognized the benefit of combining synchronicity with *kairos*. I discovered first-hand the power of supra-rational thinking.

In 2005 I conducted one of my regular weekly group supervision sessions with five psychologist colleagues. Something about this one was different. I found myself saying certain things, without having any idea why I did so. I suspect that this was not just surprising to me. I told my colleagues that under major stress and chronic time pressures, I'd allowed myself on rare occasions to go into a 'hypomanic-like' mode of functioning. This meant I had more energy, was more productive and required less sleep.

Another benefit was to promote maximum creativity. Some of my best ideas had come from such a place. I was reminded of my friend Ross telling me one day that he'd heard of a number of scientists in America who met to support each other in harnessing the manic tendencies that had been diagnosed in them. This helped to focus their professional efforts with greater productivity and creativity.

It isn't easy to put into words what I mean by a 'hypomanic-like' mode. I was never assessed as having manic tendencies, even though this was briefly considered when I was hospitalized for depression 15 years earlier. However, I did believe that, in the past, I might have developed a subtly different state of mind when facing uncommonly heavy and persistent demands – for example, during intense periods of taking university examinations. This seemed to involve a gradual speeding up of thought and action, with a reduced need for sleep. It facilitated more divergent thinking, such as more readily making associations or rapidly seeing links between different ideas.

In truth, my use of the term 'hypomanic' was somewhat tongue-in-cheek. I didn't think I was referring to a form of illness. However,

I did wonder whether I shared some associated genes with my mother, who'd been treated for a long-standing bipolar disorder. On several occasions over the years she'd been taken off medication on a trial basis and had relapsed each time, quickly developing manic symptoms. I thought it was possible I had a similar biological potential, through some shared genes, for similar changes in brain chemistry – but to a lesser degree, with positive effects in my case.

I wondered whether this might enable me to draw on some of the benefits of hypomanic tendencies through more subtle changes in brain chemistry than a manic condition, perhaps enabling me to manage with less sleep and increase my output, but without succumbing to an actual illness.

In other words, I intuitively sensed that it might be possible to experience a 'hypomanic wellness', as opposed to a hypomanic illness. If an illness were partly defined by experiencing costs in terms of negative emotional, financial, occupational or relationship consequences of a certain state, then surely a state of mind that conferred benefits in these areas could be considered a form of wellness. That seemed to me to be a matter of simple logic.

At home that evening, I actively contemplated why I might have made this 'confession' to my colleagues. Then it struck me. I'd probably said it because I'd never have to use that strategy ever again. I didn't anticipate ever again facing such major challenges that I'd need to become hypomanic to resolve them. Things at work were likely to be more settled for a long time. We'd recently established a large, and seemingly stable, staff base. I felt a sense of quiet celebration as I had this thought.

My sense of assurance was short-lived. Within a few days, I learned that my mother had an advanced form of cancer in several parts of her body. She was emphatic that she wanted no drastic medical intervention. Things were going to take their course. At the same time we unexpectedly lost a staff member in especially difficult circumstances, which caused a sudden increase in workload. Whereas just a few days beforehand it seemed that I'd never have to draw on a potentially advantageous, yet depleting, mode of thinking,

I faced circumstances where I might be tempted to call on that hypomanic process again.

Given my mother's extremely serious predicament, I needed to deal with a temporary spike in work demands quickly and efficiently, so that later I'd able to take more time off work to spend with her in hospital. It was uppermost in my mind that I wanted to help my mother die well. Beyond this, there were a number of other complex and challenging family circumstances around that time which it wouldn't be appropriate to detail here. Some related to tasks and challenges associated with my role as executor of my mother's will. I needed something out of the ordinary to assist me.

I was now seriously tempted to test whether it was possible to mindfully draw on the tempered use of hypomanic symptoms to deliberate advantage. I thought of this as 'doing a Daedalus', after the Greek mythical hero who fashioned wings affixed with wax to successfully fly away and escape captivity from King Minos. This was in contrast to the fate of Icarus, his son: Icarus fell to earth and died after flying too close to the sun, which melted the wax by which his own wings were attached. I couldn't help wondering whether Daedalus's bold success has tended to be forgotten in the light of his son's demise. I wanted to do a Daedalus rather than an Icarus.

I considered several strategies to mitigate the risk of going into an unduly unbalanced mental state. They included evaluating how efficiently I was performing various tasks, confiding in trusted others about how I seemed to be faring, and being guided by intuition – and in particular by synchronicity, or 'ticks from the universe'.

There was yet another rationale for going into that hypomanic-like, creative thinking mode. Early after her admission for palliative care, I saw my mother lying on what then struck me as, perhaps literally, her deathbed. A thought popped into my mind. She'd often suggested something to me over the years that sounded like a crazy wish. She'd repeatedly said to me with apparent relish, just as her maternal grandmother had said to her, that one day somebody in our family would be famous. I'd always been dismissive of such comments, which seemed both superstitious and status-seeking.

But now I felt for the first time that I somehow wanted to give my mother what she wished for – or at least to pretend to.

As she lay back on the bed, propped up against pillows, I looked into her face and said, 'You know, Mum, how you always said that someone in our family would be famous – Mum … I think it's me!' My mother looked me straight in the eye and said immediately, yet calmly, 'You've got it!' So far so good. I sensed she was pleased. But I was relieved that she didn't get carried away. She just stayed calm and matter-of-fact, and we quickly got onto something else.

However, I didn't forget this. In fact, it was at the forefront of my mind every time I visited my mother, often daily, from that point onward, over a period of weeks. But it called for some kind of back-up, some kind of fleshing out, to maintain any credibility, especially as my mother now seemed to be fading fast. I decided to tell her some stories on her deathbed – to fit with the theme. It would pass the time, for one thing, and I wanted to spend as much time with her as I could.

Soon afterwards, I told her that I'd often experienced strong synchronicity. My mother simply replied, 'That's God speaking to you – you deserve it!' That seemed very affirming. I thought her response was an eloquent way of conveying that she too believed there were benevolent forces and a harmonious order in the universe, even if things might not always seem that way.

With regard to the stories, I thought that some of the thinking I'd done over the years might just might fit the bill. 'Oh Mum,' I threw into the conversation, 'I think I might have come up with a theory that could revolutionize mental health care.' 'That's interesting,' she replied genuinely, clearly wanting to hear more. 'It's called Positive Psychiatry,' I said. 'It's like Positive Psychology in that it's optimistic, but it focuses more on biological factors.'

From then on I told my mother more and more stories. I figured I could get away with anything – the grander the better, in fact. Neither of us had much incentive to play it down. There wasn't much to lose. There isn't anything that helps to spin a story more than divergent thinking. There isn't anything, at least in my experience, that helps you to think more divergently than deliberately and gradually entering a hypomanic-like thinking process. In the meantime, I thought I might come up with some creative ideas that – who knows? – might last me the rest of my career. So I was going to let it run.

I spun fanciful stories about how we could change our brains, about how we could have internal control over whether our brain receptors were open or closed, and *which ones* were open or closed. We could control the production of neurotransmitters through an act of will; we could also discontinue their production at will. Something started to resonate within me. After all, had I not done that with the hypomanic process that I had confessed having used to my colleagues in the group supervision session? Indeed, wasn't I doing that now? On and on I went. The more divergent the better.

My mother continued to lie back and listen, occasionally nodding and declaring approvingly, 'That's interesting.' I kept on going. And then something strange unfolded. The more time went on, the more I sensed that some of these ideas were not half bad. That was the biggest surprise of all. I was starting to convince myself, whereas I'd started out only trying to convince my mother.

I might have looked relaxed enough. But I was focused. It wouldn't be for long. It didn't seem to be too much to ask – of myself at least. Day after day my sister sat with us as well. Perhaps she was just gifted at keeping a straight face – and looking relaxed about it at the same time. But she seemed accepting of all of this, which made it easier to continue.

It was not that my mother was obviously fading fast, but to me there were ominous signs she hadn't long left. My uncle seemed to have the same conviction, and not through any instinctive pessimism on his part. My thinking, as I told the stories, was becoming more disinhibited in its creativity. In my shifting mental state, I came to sense that something was about to happen to reveal the likely nature and timing of my mother's impending passing. I soon experienced a powerful synchronistic event that fitted with this theme.

One day I was jogging my usual route along the Geelong waterfront. I was musing that there was much more going on in life than met the eye. As I ran, I thought I'd put some of my divergent ideas further to the test. I believed more people were experiencing synchronicity than were letting on. I would just approach someone, and ask them straight out about it. I predicted that my hunch would soon be unmistakably confirmed.

Soon after having this thought, I saw a fellow aged around 60 walking toward me. I easily recognized him as someone I regularly passed on a morning jog. We'd often exchanged a nodding glance, but had never spoken. He was conveniently stopped as he performed some stretches. I slowed to a walk and approached him directly.

I said something to the effect of, 'I know this might seem strange, but there was this fellow a long time ago called Carl Jung, who spoke of numinous forces or strange experiences. One of those experiences is synchronicity, which means a very uncanny timing of events that seems to go beyond pure chance. Do you mind me asking you whether you've experienced anything like that?'

The man paused, and scratched his chin slowly, taking a quick sideways glance or two at my face. He wasn't immediately dismissing me – which was something of a relief! Then he looked up and said with a deliberate tone, 'Ten years ago there was a department store that opened in Melbourne, called Daimaru. I said it would last ten years. It did. Ten years – not nine, not eleven, but ten.'

After a brief pause, he added that some years earlier his father was ill. People had advised him that his father would need long-term nursing accommodation. However, he had the conviction, for some reason, that his father would survive only another three weeks. And that's what happened.

Just before I left my new acquaintance, Ron, he made a further remark, apparently quite unselfconsciously. 'My wife and I have an expression,' he offered: 'the Lord's timing.' What an elegant expression for synchronicity, I thought. It seemed that my hypothesis, that the first person I approached would have experienced synchronicity, was spot on.

I felt no doubt from that point that my mother would survive only three weeks more. Although one or two others pointed out that there was no medical reason to presume this, and it was contrary to medical expectations, I continued to feel just as strong a conviction that they were wrong. It simply felt like an awareness.

Around the same time another synchronistic event occurred that led to an equally strong numinous feeling. I was in the lift in the hospital foyer, waiting for it to rise to the level of my mother's ward, when the lift doors started to close, but then suddenly stopped about 30 centimetres apart. There was a pause for several seconds before they opened up again. For some inexplicable reason, the word 'portal' popped into my mind. Then the doors started to close a second time – and the same thing happened. Others in the lift reacted with visible surprise. When the doors started to close a third time, this time they closed fully and the lift ascended. I didn't understand why, but I felt there was something prophetic in the 'portal' closing three times. This stayed in my mind for a while.

Soon afterwards, my mother gave me some very heartening news. Medical staff had found that she had a problem with an occluded 'portal vein', yet told her that they could perform an operation that would relieve the pressure. Something resonated in me when she said that. It was good that they could operate, though I didn't know what a portal vein was. However, I had an idea as to what would happen.

Over subsequent weeks my mother told me of her relief from the first, and later from the second, operation. They reversed two occlusions in her portal vein. There was no reversing of the third occlusion. My mother died three weeks after my encounter with Ron, give or take a day or two.

14

Doing a Daedalus

Throughout my mother's time in hospital I continued to allow my thoughts to become more creative and loose, regaling her with new theories about the mind that I'd supposedly been developing ... and eventually beginning to see unexpected merit in them.

My musings about a potential 'hypomanic wellness' were illuminated further by seeing two current films. One, a documentary, was called *What the Bleep Do We Know?*[1] It was based on interviews with scientists and thinkers on the subjects of spirituality, philosophy, brain science and quantum mechanics. In particular, it covered themes related to brain chemistry and the way that neural connections can change in response to particular experiences.

I was particularly intrigued by the work of Masaru Emoto with crystals, showing that water crystals could reportedly be influenced in their structure and aesthetic appearance according to their exposure to particular words, symbols and music.[2] As Emoto described, this potentially had major implications for human functioning, given that our bodies are largely comprised of water.

Another film I saw was the newly released re-make of *Charlie and the Chocolate Factory*[3] starring Johnny Depp. I was struck by the extent to which this seemed a metaphor for how the brain worked. The factory, I felt, represented the brain, while chocolate in its various forms symbolized neurotransmitters. The ingredients in the chocolate recipes introduced at the factory might represent the different neurotransmitters people might emit according to their own genes and brain chemistry. I suspected that the genes I partially shared with my mother, who had a manic-depressive condition, might enable me to produce the neurotransmitters to induce a 'hypomanic wellness'.

I interpreted the Oompa-Loompas as being analogous to mechanical processes by which the neurotransmitters were produced. Willy Wonka's quest to find a person of integrity to run the factory pointed to our need, when given the opportunity to exercise something as wonderful as the human brain and consciousness, to do so with integrity and virtue.

My 'experiment' in hypomanic thinking could be risky. However, I felt that the challenges I faced were beyond what I could manage in my usual ways. Furthermore, I had an extremely strong intuitive sense that the 'planets had aligned' to encourage me to plunge into divergent thinking. I saw many potential advantages of 'doing a Daedalus', some of which I cannot fully elaborate on here as they relate to complex and personal family circumstances. Suffice it to say they included getting on the wavelength of someone close to me with difficult mental issues.

Apart from regularly checking in with people I trusted, including several psychologist friends and colleagues, my main safeguard would be to continue to draw on the experience of synchronicity. Synchronicity had long seemed to be a most helpful guide in my decision-making. I couldn't recall regretting any decision I'd made on that basis. If I ceased experiencing synchronicity at any point, or failed to achieve goals that I'd set, I would shut down the process.

I'd never experienced such an extended series of remarkably synchronistic events before in my life; nor have I ever done so again. I was initially encouraged by my mother's own comments that synchronicity was 'God speaking to you', and also by my encounter with Ron, who referred to 'the Lord's timing', as I described in the previous chapter. Mostly, though, I was encouraged by the repeated synchronistic experiences themselves.

There were numerous examples of uncanny timing around the completion of events. For example, once on a train journey to Melbourne, I had a premonition that the song I was listening to on my iPod would stop the very second the train came to a halt, in about two minutes' time – and that's exactly what happened. I was reading Jung's book on synchronicity at the time, which I'd recently seen displayed at a favourite bookstore.

I discovered that Peter O'Connor, the psychotherapist from whom I'd learned so much about Jung, worked on the floor above my mother's long-standing general practitioner. On another occasion I had a sudden compelling thought that I should walk into a music store and purchase the top-selling album. It was *See the Sun* by Pete Murray.[4] My numinous feeling while purchasing it made more sense several weeks later, as I'll describe.

Words would pop into my mind, and then resonate with an event that occurred soon afterwards. One example was the word 'portal', as I've mentioned (p.152). On another occasion I was lying in bed one morning contemplating the challenges I faced. I asked myself, 'Am I going to be a worrier or a warrior?', remembering a passage in Castaneda's *Journey to Ixtlan* where Don Juan urges a student warrior to be always ready for a cubic centimetre of chance. I then got up and went downstairs, shocked to see my son's souvenir samurai sword on the stairs – the only time I'd known it not to be left concealed in its usual safe place.

One afternoon, I'd been on a tram returning from visiting my mother in hospital when for the first time I became tearful in public. I alighted at the next stop, entered a nearby building's foyer to help settle myself away from public view and tried to call a friend on my mobile, but she didn't answer. I felt disheartened, but within seconds my brother rang me. The timing of that call reinforced my sense of connection with and support from him.

I then noticed a statue in the foyer that looked like a forked tree trunk, which immediately brought to my mind the phrase, 'split log'. Later that day, the notion of 'doing a Daedalus' came to mind, after which I looked up Daedalus in the *Encyclopaedia Britannica* and in other books in my home library. One passage I read included a specific reference to a split log – I think in connection with Daedalus's craftsmanship. I felt fortified and validated at some deep level by such repeated resonant experiences.

A number of songs I heard seemed to carry particularly poignant and personal meanings for my current circumstances. I saw them as synchronistic messages to inspire me during challenging times.

In particular, I noted the lyrics of three songs by the band Pearl Jam.[5] I interpreted certain phrases from three songs, 'Off He Goes', 'Man of the Hour' and 'Wishlist', as referring to the process of inducing a hypomanic wellness in order to deal with a major challenge.

For example, 'Off He Goes' mentions a man on a motorbike in high winds, always riding too fast. He's been taking on too much, and having thoughts that are too big for him. Yet he ends up smiling and strong, despite the singer's concerns. To me, that sounded like a metaphor for someone in a hypomanic state who settles better and more quickly than others might expect. I took this as an encouraging sign that what looked to others like a form of mental illness was in fact not illness at all. However, I also took the end of the song as a warning, because the man was going off again. I'd need to rely on my checks and balances.

In 'Man of the Hour' I took the song title to relate to having to rise to an uncommonly challenging situation. I took the image of doors being open now as a reference to the doors of perception into a quantum world, a state of mind from which I could see more directly into a truer, but little recognized, nature of reality.

Echoing the lyrics to 'Wishlist', I felt an urge to be like a bomb exploding: I wanted to go off in a way that constituted a sacrifice while somehow still living on. This meant going through the hypomanic process, which entailed some personal risk, and, I hoped, later reversing it without medication, so that I recovered well for the indefinite future. This could lead to a more optimistic prospect, for a vast number of people, of influencing their brain chemistry and enhancing their mental health. This is how I interpreted the wish in the song to be the evidence, the grounds for 50 million hands raised towards the sky. I wished I was the messenger, bringing nothing but good news – the upbeat message of not only positive psychology but also positive psychiatry to all those struggling with mental illness.

In other words, I thought if my experiment was successful (that is, if I were to prove myself able to switch on a certain type of hypomanic reaction to good effect and then switch it off again), this could be inspiring for those with mental health problems. I wanted to demonstrate that changes in brain chemistry usually associated with mental illness could be more susceptible to conscious influence, and more reversible, than previously thought. I intuitively sensed that this had something to do with a different type of perception than usual, which was somehow related to quantum mechanics, without understanding how. The ultimate result might be to encourage more optimistic views of how we could mindfully influence our brain functioning, including the activity of our neurotransmitters, to help facilitate a more balanced brain chemistry.

I mused as the weeks progressed that, whereas others had split the atom, I'd 'split the self'. Part of me could relate to everyday reality in exactly the same way as usual; but I was having ever more frequent synchronistic experiences, and another part of me was simultaneously interpreting their symbolism as though reading the subtitles of a movie. At times my synchronistic associations seemed to occur in a stream, as with my interpretations while watching *Charlie and the Chocolate Factory* or listening to Pearl Jam songs.

I felt I was putting into practice the capacity to 'create my day' by anticipating positive outcomes for the tasks I was attempting – a strategy described in *What the Bleep Do We Know?* Things often seemed to be running like clockwork. For example, at an earlier stage of 'doing a Daedalus', I needed to complete two medico-legal reports for clients who'd been injured in their workplaces. I completed dictation of these reports in approximately a quarter of the time that I'd usually take to do so. It seemed that my thoughts were quicker and more fluent than usual as I dictated them. I'd also managed a markedly increased caseload for a few weeks, enabling myself later to take several weeks off work.

Rather than acting impulsively, as would typically be the case if someone were having a hypomanic episode, I felt I was performing well my legal responsibilities associated with the executor role in relation to my mother's affairs. Also, there were some significant potential challenges related to complicated family circumstances that I felt I was negotiating well.

I wished to document the different mind states I was experiencing, preferably in an objective way. I took photographs of things that drew my attention. These increasingly included things like book covers, newspaper headlines and household objects that I felt might reflect some symbolic meaning, even if I didn't know what that might be at the time.

As a further means of documenting my mental state, and perhaps to hold myself in check, I raised the issue at a group supervision session before taking some weeks off work. I began the session by distributing a photocopy of the diagnostic criteria for a hypomanic episode according to the *Diagnostic and Statistical Manual of Mental Disorders (DSM)*.[6] I went through the criteria for a hypomanic episode, one by one, with my colleagues, readily acknowledging that I was meeting several of them, at least in a technical sense, while discounting others.

There was no disputing, for example, that I was functioning with a decreased need for sleep. I was also showing more intense, goal-directed activity, at work in particular. I felt that my thoughts had sped up. Indeed, these were some of the reasons for my choosing to switch into that mode in the first place. I didn't think I was meeting another diagnostic criterion of being distractable, as I believed I could concentrate well; and I didn't see my thoughts as being drawn to irrelevant stimuli. I was generally attuned to synchronicity, seeing meaningful connections where others might have seen randomness.

I believed in the end that whether my reactions technically met the criteria for a hypomanic episode came down to whether I got an extra tick for a single remaining symptom: grandiosity. To check this, I gave my colleagues a real chance of addressing the question accurately. I told them that I thought I'd developed a theory that could revolutionize mental health approaches in the Western world.

At that stage I thought my colleagues would have added another diagnostic tick without much further ado! I was a little surprised when they didn't – at least not as a group, and not openly.

Just one person spoke up. Calmly and thoughtfully, she said she thought I might indeed have come up with such a theory, in what I'd referred to on numerous occasions as 'Positive Psychiatry'. I was surprised and reassured. Perhaps I'd underestimated how much I'd expressed my divergent thinking in the past?

Nonetheless, as the weeks passed, some of my friends became concerned about my mental state. One friend said straight out, 'Chris, you're psychotic – you need medication!' I took no offence at this, knowing she was motivated by genuine concern. I also recognized that she was expressing what might be considered a standard psychiatric opinion. Time would tell how things turned out.

I was continuing to experience frequent synchronicity. I felt intuitively that I was on the right track. In the meantime, I continued to tell my mother stories.

At one point, a medical friend attempted to convince me to cancel a scheduled public talk I was due to give, concerned it might reveal that my state of mind was disturbed. The talk went well – despite my making references at some length to my intuitions about *Charlie and the Chocolate Factory*.

Some seemed less inclined to judge my behaviour as an expression of mental illness. For example, my brother said, 'Your crown chakra's opening up!' He seemed to be genuinely suggesting my experience could be a form of enlightenment. Later he went on to say that such an experience commonly required a considerable degree of work afterwards to integrate any understanding gained. I was encouraged by this additional comment that he thought I might be someone capable of doing that.

My brother-in-law gave me a gentle warning that I needed to be careful about my mental state – he lent me a book, *Shaman: The Wounded Healer*,[7] while urging me, 'Healer, heal thyself!' Around the same time, I bought a painting from him depicting a Pegasus figure. I identified with the winged horse image and felt a numinous connection with it while doing a Daedalus. I hung the picture above my work computer for inspiration.

At another point I felt I'd developed some intuitive insights in relation to an aboriginal dot painting that I'd long owned. Adopting the typical aboriginal symbolism, the painting depicted a person as a U-shape, with a stick and a circle on either side of the U. I took the stick to represent the physical body and the circle to represent the self, or thoughts and feelings. The U-shape, the central symbol, I saw as representing the person's soul, or spirit. I also saw the U-shape as a kind of receptor. This seemed to be a transpersonal reference to the person receiving waves of signals from the universe, depicted by continuously streaming lines, or waves, of dots. To me that was what synchronicity felt like: repeated streams of information from the universe, received by your spirit.

The painting also depicted some large dendritic (branched) shapes. These might traditionally be taken to represent something like bush potatoes. However, to me they looked like dendritic connections in the brain. I felt the painting symbolically related to brain science, with the dendritic shapes and waves of dots showing how somehow the brain received 'messages from the universe'. I wasn't sure exactly how, but I thought there were some kinds of receptors we didn't yet know about which processed numinous experience. I thought the aboriginal painters had intuited these.

I decided to discuss my observations with a local journalist with whom I was slightly acquainted. I lugged the large framed painting into the newspaper offices. He patiently listened to my story for the best part of an hour. He later told me that what interested him most was how much I seemed to get out of one painting. As I was carrying the picture back to the car, an elderly pedestrian approached me to say she liked it. We chatted about it for a few minutes. I later learned she was the mother of a friend. A number of friends, it turned out, thought I might harm my career by doing such things as taking a painting into the local newspaper offices, not to mention speaking about strange things to random people in the street.

A further incident, which seemed especially synchronistic and fortuitous to me, prompted another friend's concern. We'd purchased a new work building the previous year, and had been struggling for many months to find a builder to renovate it. This was becoming a distracting and costly problem. There was a builder I favoured for the quality of his work. However, I'd experienced some conflict with him two years earlier in connection with another property when a planned sale didn't go ahead. Perhaps it would be wiser to avoid further dealings with him. However, I'd felt a particular affinity with this builder, Len. This resulted from past conversations when I'd felt we were on the same wavelength. There was some strong synchronicity around our past interactions.

I intuitively envisaged a pattern falling into place, somewhat like a missing piece of a jigsaw. I thought I might be able to negotiate a favourable arrangement with Len for him to renovate our new property. I rang him – I hadn't encountered him since our dealings two years earlier – to ask if he'd be interested in meeting with me. There was a brief pause when he answered the phone, but he soon volunteered that in recent days he'd thought of me. I saw that as synchronistic – a good sign! He readily agreed to meet with me when he returned from a building job in Queensland a few days later.

On the afternoon I was due to meet Len, a psychologist friend visited. I saw that as synchronistic too, especially as she happened to be an expert on bipolar disorder and hypomanic states. I told her I was about to meet the builder and thought it might turn out well. I explained that I'd been experiencing a number of fortuitous events associated with synchronicity, and felt that things were running in my favour. I saw this as an experiment in 'applying quantum mechanics to business advantage'.

I told my friend her visit was particularly fortuitous, because she was a scientist at heart, and she could therefore objectively witness the outcome. She seemed quite concerned for me, and urged me not to get my hopes up. I could see her point, but I'd been guided by synchronicity and intended to act on it.

When we met, Len said he'd been thinking just a couple of days beforehand that he'd like to build something for me. That was why he'd responded so positively. I took that to be a big tick from the universe. I came home about an hour and a half later – it took longer than I'd thought. I guessed my friend, who was staying overnight, might have feared that I'd disappeared into nearby Corio Bay after a crushing disappointment. I explained that the builder had offered to start the project within a few weeks and would complete it at cost price.

Soon I gathered that my psychologist friend was not reassured about my judgment or mental health. I believed the positive outcome had spoken for itself. But later it seemed clear that my friend was interpreting my behaviour as the product of a mental disorder. I was then struck by a remarkable event. During our conversation, each of us clearly having different views about the soundness of my thinking, the wooden backrest of my friend's chair suddenly snapped right through with a loud crack. I was gobsmacked! I'd never seen or heard of anything like that happening before. The wooden backrest seemed quite solid, and my friend was slightly built. It felt strongly to me there were numinous forces at work.

The thought that immediately went through my mind was that the breaking frame of my friend's chair was symbolic of a flaw in the framework of her thinking about my mental state. It was only years later that I learned there was a term for this. Jung once described how, during a visit to Freud's house, they'd disagreed about the existence of paranormal phenomena. At that point, they heard a very loud crack from a nearby bookcase, which stunned them both. Jung called it a 'catalytic exteriorization phenomenon'.[8]

I went to visit my friend Ross some time later. I noticed that he too seemed quite concerned about my mental state. We discussed one of his aunt's paintings. He claimed it was simply a woman brushing her hair. I could see that, but I was particularly taken with the archetypal sweeping forms and raw energy in the painting. I felt he must also be readily able to see that but, as I remarked to him, I thought he wasn't admitting to this, presumably because he wanted to emphasize a perspective that could help to ground me.

I took more and more photos of household objects, even if I couldn't see any particular relevance in them at the time. Other things I photographed had an obvious symbolic meaning for me, such as a samurai sword and a broken chair.

The last time I saw my mother before she died, I was conscious of feeling a particularly strong and special connection with her. I knew that most likely I wouldn't see her alive again. She hadn't seemed conscious throughout my visit. At one point I squeezed her hand especially strongly to say goodbye. I felt a slight squeeze back.

Around that time, perhaps even that day, I caught the train home from the hospital and was particularly struck by a story in the newspaper. It was about someone who'd deliberately infected himself with a certain pathogen, and then reversed it. I thought that was strongly synchronistic. That's what I felt I was doing, but with a mental rather than a physical process. I hadn't reversed it yet, but felt certain that I would.

The day after my mother died, my brother and sister and I met in our childhood family home, in circumstances I'd arranged as executor of the will. I believed there were potential challenges in this situation that could affect our relationships for years to come. However, the night before the meeting I'd intuitively envisaged a kind of ritualized procedure we could go through, which might be helpful in dealing with such an emotionally charged situation. Some clear images spontaneously formed in my mind as to how things might unfold. I felt strongly heartened. For the first time in a long while, I slept well that night.

As I headed off on the one-hour trip to Melbourne next morning, I felt confident – despite my wife's concerns about my state of mind and the way things would turn out. The next few hours unfolded pretty much as I'd imagined. My siblings and I expressed shared values, which would help the process of dealing with my mother's estate proceed smoothly. I felt affirmed and supported in my role as executor. There were strong indications that our sibling relationships could extend even more positively into the future than before. This was not necessarily the expected result: I was much relieved. We shared stories and even laughed about a range of events, including some of my recent behaviour.

For example, I described one incident whose timing was such that no doubt my wife feared I'd completely lost my sanity. One morning she unexpectedly returned from work to find me naked on the stairs with a samurai sword in my hands. It was a relief to describe this experience to my siblings to uproarious laughter.

As I drove back home from the meeting with my brother and sister, I felt that the bold and intuitive approach I'd taken had proved to be gratifyingly successful. Over and above that, I felt that I'd helped my mother to die well. Apart from the stories I spun at her bedside, we'd had many conversations reflecting a deeper connection than we'd enjoyed for decades. She'd elicited from me a more creative and intuitive way of responding to the world. I also felt much closer to my brother after recognizing the strength of his propensity to think in a transpersonal fashion. I recalled that he and my mother had at times talked about the 'music of the spheres', which had previously meant little to me. I also sensed that I'd developed further understanding of the mind that I could draw on for the rest of my career.

However, in the day or so after my mother died there had been two additional major challenges to face. One involved several friends' continued concern about my mental state. A number of my closest friends in particular felt a need to intervene. I'd just returned from meeting with my brother and sister. As a transition before returning home, I'd walked a circuit of the nearby botanical gardens while playing 'Man of the Hour' on my iPod, in what felt like a quietly affirming ritual. I presumed this would be the last time I played it before I discontinued 'doing a Daedalus'. The song finished at the exact moment I completed the circuit, just as I'd anticipated.

I returned home and explained to my wife how well I thought things had gone earlier that day, hoping she'd be reassured. I knew my recent behaviour had been unsettling to her to the point of her considering asking friends to intervene. I told her I didn't wish to go out to a larger group gathering that evening as planned. I felt it was time to wind down. In the early evening, my psychologist friend rang to see how I was. While on the phone, I heard the front door open and several voices at the entrance. I hung up and went into the next room to meet some friends who'd just arrived – I'd suspected something like this might happen.

I decided to take a bold approach – a number of situations had turned out better this way. I decided to openly tell my friends of many of the symbolic strands that had been running through my mind of late. I mentioned things such as a great-grandfather who'd gone missing, generational patterns in bees, synchronistic experiences and an assortment of other ideas. At one point I detected a look of combined horror and disgust. Perhaps I'd chosen the wrong strategy!

My friends clearly remained worried about my state of mind. One said she feared I might be suicidal, based on something I'd said about car accidents. I recalled a comment I'd made days earlier to another friend about a newspaper picture of an upended vehicle. I'd intended to refer to this image as symbolic of a process of transformation, whereby one's view of the world is turned on its head. Rather than feeling suicidal, I tried to convey that I felt blessed in life generally, regardless of the current challenging times and the loss of my mother. My friends listened to me for about an hour. Afterwards one stated, seemingly on behalf of all of them, 'Chris, you're psychotic!' They seemed insistent that I see a psychiatrist for treatment, suggesting I might need immediate medication. They said they'd informally arranged for this to happen, later that evening.

The only way I could deter my friends from going through with this plan was to assure them that if I didn't return to sleeping well, and if I didn't in general get back to normal within the next few days, I would indeed see a psychiatrist. But I wouldn't see the one they suggested. I instead offered to see another psychiatrist, whom they knew had been openly critical of my work. My friends seemed to accept my proposed alternative, which was a relief to me. I wanted the opportunity to complete my experiment.

That night I slept very well, as I suspected I would. Things were going well in some ways, despite my well-intentioned friends interfering in my plans. One further challenge remained, however, to justify 'doing a Daedalus'. How would I 'turn off' the hypomanic state that I'd utilized, and how could I do this quickly? The answer came intuitively.

15

Seeing the Sun

I can't exactly recall how my idea for coming out of a hypomanic state came to mind, but it was spontaneous. It seemed to just happen. I'd slept well for a couple of nights already, but I didn't feel I was completely back to normal yet.

One morning, lying in bed after my wife had left for work, I noticed an imminent sunrise through a gap in the curtains of our bedroom window. I felt a strong intuitive urge to focus on the sun as it rose. While doing so, I felt it would be good to concentrate intently on the thought of pulling myself fully back into my more usual self. I felt the urge to focus more on everyday things outside myself, and to let go more of intuitive musings. Such musings had seemingly done their job. I sensed that I should look intently at the sun as it rose to provide a clear focus on outer reality. This idea was seemingly prompted by the title of the CD I'd recently bought, *See the Sun*.[1] I now felt I understood why I'd had the compelling urge to go into a nearby music store to check out the number one album, and the numinous feeling its cover and title gave me: it was directing me what to do.

I was going to suspend any deliberate thinking, and just focus on the sun rising through the now fully open curtains: this might help me feel more fully integrated and grounded within my own skin. I also wanted to record the experience to lend further objectivity to my observations, so I took a series of photographs throughout. I intently looked at the sun as it rose. I focused on the sunrise from an initial faint glow to a bright morning sun, over half an hour or so.

By the end of this process I felt more grounded, and more consistently connected with an everyday perspective on the world.

I felt less inclined to muse on internal thoughts, focusing more directly on my senses. Later that day I was aware of having almost fully returned to 'normal', so to speak – not that I'd felt particularly abnormal beforehand. I slept well over the following nights.

Over coming days I took further photographs to reflect my more usual view of the world. These included more shots of people, or broad views, in contrast to the more disjointed series of close-up photos I'd taken of disparate objects. The photo sequence seemed to document the transition in my thinking back to a more usual mode. A feeling of numinosity nonetheless continued, associated with the whole experience of the previous two months.

It was just a few days later that we attended my mother's funeral. I was heartened by the minister's spontaneous affirmation that we were one of the most organized families he had dealt with. I felt well supported by, and connected with, a wide circle of friends and family. They responded warmly to several eulogies, including my own. Friends and family mingled well at the wake. Even to those who'd recently considered me to be psychotic, I suspect I seemed 'recovered'.

I was somewhat surprised that my friends who'd recently told me they thought I was psychotic and needed medication didn't ask me how I'd apparently returned to normal so soon, especially without any psychiatric intervention or medication. I had no doubt that they'd be relieved that things had turned out that way. But it seemed that what took place had not fitted in with their worldview, and so it was largely ignored. They seemed to think that there was no significant ongoing risk or concern, so things could be left as they were.

I felt that there was something incomplete in not processing the experience further, including having more discussion with these friends. However, I thought this might be too uncomfortable, especially for some of them, for quite some time.

My friend Ross was exceptional in volunteering that he believed any push for me to receive psychiatric help would have been misguided. Nonetheless he had been concerned himself about my mental state, which suggested that my actions hadn't appeared well integrated to others, regardless of how well I felt I'd managed my difficult circumstances.

Things from that point seemed to progress fairly smoothly. Within days of my mother's funeral, I delivered a presentation as an invited speaker on a panel, and felt that I'd spoken, if anything, more creatively than usual. The spontaneous feedback was as favourable as any I'd previously received, despite some friends having expressed fears about my offering another public talk around that time. I soon returned to work, where my clinical sessions progressed well. I continued to perform the tasks of an executor in a seemingly productive way. The more time passed, the more it seemed that others thought everything had returned to normal.

Subjectively, I felt that I'd deliberately called on the power of supra-rational thinking at a time of uncommon challenge, when I needed to summon energies that were much more powerful than usual. Yet the experience was so out of the ordinary that I had a serious need to make sense of what had happened. I would have preferred this to involve some consensual understanding with others. There was nothing in anything I'd heard or read that helped me to make sense of what I'd experienced. My frequent experience of synchronicity and the compelling intuitive feelings I was using as a guide seemed to defy any conventional understanding.

What I experienced didn't seem to be attributable to an unusually strong grief reaction. In other challenging situations involving significant distress and grief I haven't reacted in ways that were remotely hypomanic.

If my unconventional behaviour had resulted from psychotic illness, why did it seem so effective in many ways? And how did it resolve so readily without medication? If, on the other hand, I'd been acting according to a creatively effective, or even somewhat enlightened, approach, as I felt at the time, then what processes were involved in this?

Intuitively, I felt I knew a lot about what had happened – I'd somehow switched on a certain type of brain chemistry that overlapped with hypomanic processes, and this had assisted my thinking, mood and intuition. I'd switched it off afterwards when there was no further need for it. I had a sense of how to do this without ever having heard anything about such a process before. I'd been guided by synchronicity, a form of mystical or transpersonal experience. It had come in the form of compelling intuitive insights reinforced by symbolic messages in movies, songs, titles and newspaper and radio references – or at least, that's how it felt. But how did that tie in with science and logic?

It was many years later, while writing this book, that I learned about more objective ways of separating such seemingly transpersonal experiences from psychosis. John Rowan's book *The Transpersonal: Spirituality in Psychotherapy and Counselling* introduced me to Ken Wilber's psycho-spiritual model.[2] Here I read about Wilber's explanation of an enlightenment process in terms of several trans-egoic stages, as I've described in Chapter 2. This included insights about how people often baulk at having further psychic or mystical experiences – out of fear.

However, many people across a wide range of cultures, perhaps all cultures, share a belief in mystical experiences. This includes many scientists. Quantum physics has revealed the extent to which the physical world doesn't conform to traditional notions of reality, regardless of appearances. It suggests that the true nature of reality may have more in common with the teachings of Eastern mystics than with our more typically materialistic worldview. Psychologists such as Carl Jung, William James and Abraham Maslow have suggested that dismissing psychic or mystical experiences can limit our personal growth, our progress on the path to individual destiny.

Consistent with a psycho-spiritual model, I believe that around the time my mother died I had a *satori* experience, accompanied by frequent synchronicity.

However, as many have warned, people having such experiences can be at risk of psychic inflation.[3] Looking back, I think I'd fallen into that trap. I'd experienced such an explosion of synchronistic experiences that I felt I'd happened upon an almost unique and secret way of exploiting synchronicity. As time went on, I increasingly felt a sense of specialness associated with that feeling. I now see that as reflecting a degree of grandiosity in my interpretation of my experience. The fact that even my mentor, Ross, was obviously concerned about my state of mind around that time suggested that my perspective had not been well balanced.

There were also clear signs that I was fixated at times on 'illuminations',[4] regardless of whether my experience of synchronicity represented authentic transpersonal awareness. The seemingly chaotic series of photos I took points to a relative lack of integration of my experience, going well beyond responding to encouraging 'ticks from the universe'. Understandably, my apparent fixation on seemingly random objects was unnerving to a number of people around me.

However, in conventional health settings I believe there's significant potential risk in being too ready to 'medicalize' a person's reactions, interpreting them in terms of psychopathology. It was surely no accident that the several friends who directly suggested to me that I was psychotic were all trained in, or otherwise strongly influenced by, a medical model.

John Rowan highlights the importance of someone not being hospitalized while negotiating a trans-egoic stage of development, regardless of complications.[5] At such stages of development, there can be a higher level of awareness, combined with regressed or more primitive forms of consciousness, such as intrusive and disjointed archetypal thoughts or images. Although such experiences had long been recognized by a wide range of cultures, potentially worthwhile or valid spiritual experience could easily be missed, or misunderstood.

When in spiritual crisis, it may be important for a person to receive help from someone who understands and respects the process, preferably through having gone through it themselves. There would probably be few such practitioners in mainstream mental health systems. Rowan suggests that many who enter a mental health system at such a stage risk getting stuck in hospital without a satisfactory resolution.

Being treated according to a medical model for psychosis could be especially invalidating for a person who might otherwise be seen as conducting a legitimate spiritual quest. It could limit them with a simplistic label and compromise their functioning.

In differentiating mental illness from aspects of spiritual emergence, the field of transpersonal psychology seems relevant. John Rowan refers to a series of useful questions that can help differentiate between transpersonal and psychotic experience.[6] They were originally suggested by David Lukoff, a clinical psychologist and transpersonal therapist who experienced a spiritual crisis of his own in his early 20s, which overlapped with psychotic symptoms.

Firstly, does the person suffer from a mental health problem consistent with usual psychiatric classification, such as a psychotic condition? Secondly, do their reactions involve mystical or transpersonal experience, even if in the context of a crisis? Thirdly, is a positive outcome likely? And finally, is there a likelihood of harm to the person or others?

Looking at these questions in relation to my own situation, I'd agree my reactions were consistent with the definition of a hypomanic episode, especially at later stages of my 'experiment'. Some would say this was strongly the case, whereas other clinicians with whom I've discussed the matter still dispute whether the label applies. With regard to the second question, the circumstances certainly overlapped with transpersonal experience, as indicated by my long-standing transpersonal beliefs at the time, as well as objective indications of frequent and strong synchronicity.

Were positive outcomes likely? My response to the situation seemed to contribute to positive outcomes, including a range of practical benefits. Was there a likelihood of harm to myself, or others? I'd suggest not, despite a remark I made being misinterpreted as reflecting suicidal tendencies. Part of the challenge to others seemed to relate to their difficulty in accepting mystical experience.

Complex spiritual issues are slowly becoming more recognized in mental health circles. David Lukoff proposed the use of the term 'mystical experience with psychotic features', to pinpoint the phenomenon, and to mitigate against unnecessary medical treatment, including hospitalization.[7] I can see how such a description could fit my experience.

Straight after 'doing a Daedalus', I planned to do two things to process my experience further. First, I would attend in two months' time the Evolution of Psychotherapy conference in Anaheim, California, a gathering of the world's most creative and influential psychotherapists from a full range of therapy schools. This would help me review my recent experience from a psychological and scientifically based point of view. Secondly, I'd return to Findhorn, the place where I'd most closely identified with numinous spiritual experience, including incidents of synchronicity, 15 years earlier. This would help me explore a transpersonal perspective that might help me to further integrate my experiences.

In the meantime, one other opportunity attracted my interest. I saw that an Australasian conference on bipolar disorders was fortuitously and conveniently arranged in Melbourne, only a month or so after my 'doing a Daedalus'. This too might help me to process what had happened to me in the light of recent psychiatric understanding.

One session at the Melbourne conference stood out above all. The speaker described how a man he knew had been advised by an indigenous healer to treat his manic tendencies by looking into the sun. I was greatly struck by this prescription being so similar to the one I'd intuitively given myself. Sadly, however, this person had burnt his retina to the point of blindness by acting on that advice. I sat in the audience as a professional attendee thinking, 'No, don't look into the sun during the day – you'll burn your retina out!' Clearly it could only work if you looked at the sun at dawn (as in my case) or perhaps at dusk, as depicted on the cover of Pete Murray's *See the Sun* CD. Of course, I didn't mention this to anyone. I didn't think it would do any good for my reputation!

During this bipolar disorders conference I felt there was an extremely heavy emphasis on medication as the core treatment. This was despite an international leader informing me that he believed that psychotherapy would loom large in the treatment of bipolar disorder in 20 years' time. His tone sounded prophetic. 'Why wait 20 years?' I thought to myself.

As I walked to the conference on the last day, a Sunday morning with empty city streets, a sudden thought popped into my mind: I lamented the seeming lack of consideration at the conference of a transpersonal or spiritual dimension to people's experience. There seemed little scope to acknowledge such a phenomenon as synchronicity and recognize its potential relevance to mental health. At that exact moment I heard a passing car toot. I looked across and felt instantly affirmed. 'That's better!' I thought. It was my sister driving alongside. It was a most unexpected encounter. We met up. It was very rare for either of us to be in that area, let alone at the same time.

16

Signposts to Enlightenment

From Anaheim to Findhorn

The Evolution of Psychotherapy conference is held in the United States every four to five years, commonly in Anaheim, California. It's unmatched as an opportunity to learn about innovations in therapy. The teaching faculty involves 30 of the most prominent leaders from the full range of therapy schools, including cognitive-behavioural therapy, family therapy and hypnosis. Some of the pioneering leaders were octogenarians or even older, but seemingly as creative as ever.

I was there at the conference to learn whatever I could, but I was particularly interested in recent findings in brain science. I had questions and hunches about the workings of the mind that persisted strongly following my experiences a few months earlier. I was excited by the prospect of meeting Martin Seligman for the first time, the foremost leader in the positive psychology field.

I was also looking forward to seeing Dr Ernest Rossi, a psychologist and expert in hypnosis, whose work had inspired me but whom I'd never met. If I'd previously gained a sense that we may have a more profound influence over our brain chemistry and functioning than typically acknowledged in the mental health field, my perspective was about to be expanded much further!

Dr Rossi and another inspiring presenter, Daniel Siegel, a psychiatrist and neurologist, both explained the evidence for neuroplasticity. This is our capacity to develop new neural pathways, including new neurons, or brain cells, and new synapses, or connections between brain cells, throughout our entire lifespan.

Rossi and Siegel both described how we aren't only capable of changing our brain software, so to speak, by altering behaviours and habits, but we can literally rewire ourselves in a manner that changes our hardware as well! Therefore, we're continually creating and recreating the structure of our brain and mental processes at many levels. We can alter not only our minds, but also the functioning of our genes. Any influence between our genes and mental functioning is two-way. The key issue is not so much what genes we have, but the relative level of activation of those genes, a process known as 'gene expression'. Gene activity can be switched on or off. This hinted at potential mechanisms behind 'doing a Daedalus'.

Rossi further highlighted how these processes related to the 'novelty-*numinosum*-neurogenesis' effect. The term *numinosum* relates to a sense of fascination, mystery or wonderment. Rossi explained that the novel experiences that have the greatest impact on neurogenesis, the creation of new brain cells and of connections between them, are those that are the most numinous – that inspire the greatest sense of fascination or awe. Such experiences switch on genes that create new proteins, which form the new brain cells and neural pathways.

This seemed to highlight the relevance of synchronicity. I felt, for the first time, that I was hearing something at a scientific conference that directly related to my recent experience. By definition, synchronicity is numinous! By definition it also involves *meaningful* coincidence, drawing on a person's intuition to evoke its perceived personal meaning. This seemed to provide a rationale for drawing on synchronicity as a psychotechnology.[1] Meaningful synchronistic experience, in being novel and numinous by its very nature, can switch on certain genes and promote new brain connections. It can enliven us, and help us make creative interpretations of our experience, perhaps bolstered by the positive emotions that typically accompany it.

This could expand our understanding of the human potential to influence our functioning beyond the parameters of heredity. Nature and nurture are much more fused, and interactional, than previously thought. This might allow for a more optimistic outlook as to our potential biological flexibility, and our capacity for self-renewal, than anything suggested at the recent conference I'd attended on bipolar disorders.

There were other inspirational leaders at the conference. The late James Hillman, the Jungian psychotherapist, spoke with great depth about transpersonal themes related to one's daimon, or destiny.

Thomas Szasz referred to themes from his famous book, *The Myth of Mental Illness*, that seemed just as relevant decades later.[2] He pointed to an excessive tendency to label people as having a mental illness when their views conflict with one's own – for example, in situations of political conflict.

I thought of my friends who'd recently labelled me as being psychotic. I also recalled an incident many years earlier when I'd mentioned to a psychiatrist colleague that I'd attended a public talk by Dr Szasz in Geelong the previous evening. 'He's mad!' responded the psychiatrist, neatly proving Szasz's point that those with divergent or challenging views are often too readily dismissed as psychotic.

At the conference I met several people who seemed much more open-minded about transpersonal experiences than usual. I found the opportunity to discuss some of my own experience of a 'hypomanic-like' process, and synchronicity, without feeling judged. Several presenters highlighted transpersonal or spiritual themes in their work, while still displaying a scientific rigour. It felt like a breath of fresh air. I felt further primed to visit Findhorn to explore the extent to which my experience of 'doing a Daedalus' related to spiritual themes.

Many residential programmes at Findhorn are conducted at Cluny House, a stately building on the outskirts of Forres, overlooking a golf course. The evening before my two-week course I visited the dining hall and enjoyed a stimulating conversation about transpersonal themes with two residents. I felt that I'd come to the right place. I rarely had such conversations in mainstream psychology settings.

Soon after arriving at Findhorn I went to explore the gardens. I was disappointed to note that the hemispherical scaffolding structure was missing – the one so similar to the structure in the dream I'd had that I'd taken to symbolize my level of self-development (see p.105). I'd intuitively noted in my diary all those years earlier that I believed I would encounter further symbolic representations of my level of development in the future. It therefore seemed uncanny when I encountered a somewhat similar scaffolding sculpture in a different part of the garden. This time it was fully spherical, albeit smaller. That seemed to fit. I did indeed feel more whole now; more rounded. That experience gave me a numinous feeling at the start of a two-week intensive group course.

The course I attended trained you to be a facilitator of the 'Transformation Game'.[3] This is a board game, intended to help participants pursue their life path by processing issues related to their physical, emotional, mental and spiritual development. It encourages you to reflect on potential personal setbacks and insights.

There were frequent references in the game to facing challenges while being at one's 'growing edge'. From what I'd recently learned about brain science, it seemed that this expression might have been more than mere metaphor. I thought that the novelty and challenge of the game might facilitate neuroplasticity, forming new synapses and neurons to create a literal 'growing edge' in our brains.

I decided from the beginning to push myself to be open in expressing some of my unconventional beliefs, including my views on synchronicity. It seemed a safe place to do so. It was 6 June, the same date on which I'd become engaged and had later been admitted to a psychiatric hospital. Believing that date to resonate with my deeper life story, I declared to the group that it was my 'spiritual birthday', whatever that meant. Another participant, Anne, responded that it was her actual birthday. I suspect that this interchange led us to develop a much quicker and more meaningful personal connection than we otherwise might have made.

It didn't take long for Anne to describe to me experiences and beliefs beyond those I'd previously heard people divulge. These included beliefs about past lives and otherworldly encounters with a ghost, or spirit. She nonetheless appeared to be thoughtful and intelligent, and I wasn't surprised to hear that her father was a physics professor.

Others revealed more about their transpersonal experiences to me – reminding me of the time when a number of clients had started divulging to me that they'd been sexually abused. I wondered what might prompt such openness. Then I realized that something must have changed within myself, if others were showing greater trust that I'd be receptive. Perhaps we take on new information that challenges our current worldview at a rate we can handle: when we're open to hear more about sexual abuse, or mystical experiences, or other taboo topics, we might come across a greater incidence of such events.

Some other participants described convincing examples of having psychic abilities. For example, one woman claimed to have accurately intuited the location of a sunken vessel that took authorities a long time to find after vainly searching in a quite different location. She understandably chose not to inform authorities of her hunch, as she didn't expect to be believed. I found such stories illuminating: at the time I didn't know that even the US army had used 'psychic spies' with some success.[4] I couldn't help but wonder whether we might have vastly more resources at our disposal than we tend to use, because they don't fit the rationalistic perspective emphasized in our culture.

I encountered a burst of synchronistic experiences at Findhorn, dramatically more intense and frequent than usual. As these experiences escalated in frequency and numinosity over the two-week period, I noticed my energy levels increase and a greater openness in me to fluid or divergent thinking. Early in my stay, the course leader said I reminded her of Tigger, the character from Winnie the Pooh. Apparently, I came across as bouncing, energetic, and with a kind of innocence.

At a later stage of the course, as my energy levels rose further and my focus on symbolic interpretations of events became even stronger, my experience seemed to overlap with the hypomanic-like process I'd experienced while 'doing a Daedalus'.

One morning I had a series of particularly numinous synchronistic experiences while going for a long run. Even as they occurred, I thought of them as being linked around the theme of our potential capacity to influence our own brain chemistry and functioning. I ran from Cluny House to the outskirts of Forres, passing farmland on the way. Early on I ran by a shallow stream with a depression in the rock bed that continually filled up and spilled over with water. For some reason, the thought popped into my mind that the depression in the rock was symbolic of a brain receptor being repeatedly replenished with a particular neurotransmitter. It struck me that our brain functioning is affected in part by how much of a particular endogenous neurotransmitter we're producing at any particular time.

Later I found myself running towards open farmland. For some reason I gained a strong sense that something numinous was about to happen. This sense increased as I ran past a farmhouse called 'Middlefield', which I immediately took as meaning that I was about to enter the middle of the quantum field, whatever that meant.

Soon afterwards I passed a sign for a van hire business with a picture of a horse-drawn chariot flying through the air and the inscription, 'Apollo – your chariot awaits'. This felt numinous. I viewed the speedy flying chariot as a metaphor for 'doing a Daedalus'.

I then ran alongside a field, half covered with a recently planted crop and half with a more advanced crop. For some reason, I immediately thought that the crop management here was a metaphor for how every cell in our body replaces itself every six years. I thought this symbolized our potential for the continual biological growth and renewal of the physical structure of our brains, including brain receptors, which pointed to their potential flexibility of operation beyond what was generally acknowledged.

I then passed a field where approximately half the cows were standing and half were lying down. It immediately popped into my mind that this could be a metaphor for brain receptors sometimes being active, or open, in responding to neurotransmitters, but at other times being inactive, or closed. I recalled having specifically and deliberately imagined such a mechanism in a conscious attempt to influence my own brain chemistry while 'doing a Daedalus'.

It's hard to describe the numinous intensity of what I then noticed. I was struck by the extraordinary brightness of the sun's rays fanning down in vast angled shafts of light from the clouds above. It almost seemed more like an animated movie than real. I felt this intense, numinous experience as strongly validating the notion I'd just then held in my mind – that one day it would be found that we could influence our brain chemistry, not only by the amount of neurotransmitters that we produce, but also by some internal control over whether our brain receptors are open or closed. If this were true, potentially we could have much more internal control of our brain processes than previously thought. Perhaps people would learn to switch on a hypomanic process with conscious control, and then switch it off again, at will. This seemed to fit.

I then started heading back towards Findhorn. Soon afterwards, I was amazed when I saw something I hadn't noticed before outside the van hire business – a two-metre-long turquoise number '6' painted in the middle of the road. I'd long associated six with synchronicity – it was a 'tick from the universe'. I'd also used the colour turquoise to symbolize synchronicity, after having read of this association in the 'spiral dynamics' model as applied to private psychology practices.[5] This is the reason our practice website is based on a turquoise colour scheme. To me the turquoise number six represented very strong synchronicity. I interpreted this as further supporting some of the intuitive insights I was entertaining about brain chemistry.

I later ran past a school where I noticed a shaft of light striking a single lower window of a school building, 50 metres or so inside the school grounds. I had a compelling feeling to go and look in the window. After jogging there, I peered inside. Centrally placed on a window ledge, brightly illuminated by the sun, was a toy figure of Tigger! It had the smaller character, Roo, resting on its shoulder.

I was struck by the coming together of my compelling impulse to run to the window, my nickname of Tigger, and, to a lesser

The Spiral Dynamics Model

The spiral dynamics model, developed by Don Beck and Chris Cowan, describes different stages in the development of an organization, or organizational culture.[6] Lynn Grodzki has adapted this model for small professional businesses, and especially private psychotherapy and counselling practices.[7] The values of each stage need to be mastered to progress to the next, which integrates what's already been developed.

Typical features of the eight stages, each represented by a colour, are as follows (with an emphasis on the more advanced stages). At Stage 1 (Beige), your focus is on basic survival. At Stage 2 (Purple), the practice is surviving, but you have limited understanding of what influences its relative success. At Stage 3 (Red), the business is more resilient, but you may focus on competition and defending territory rather than further defining yourself. At Stage 4 (Blue), you focus on increasing stability and optimizing systems. At Stage 5 (Orange), you have a more developed entrepreneurial focus, pursuing opportunities for growth and achievement. At Stage 6 (Green), you may temper entrepreneurial goals with a more humanistic focus, reconnecting with your core values and engaging with the community.

At stage 7 (Yellow) you seek to reinvent your practice. You value knowledge, competence and flexibility, inviting novelty, and even chaos, to enhance your creativity, uniqueness, pleasure and awareness. You appreciate synchronicity. You have typically moved beyond a medical model to a personal growth model.

At Stage 8 (Turquoise), you integrate previous experience in a holistic and harmonious way. Your business operates smoothly, you joyfully practise your craft, and you attract the clients and opportunities you desire. You experience a state of flow more consistently, including times when optimal performance and synchronicity coincide.[8] This stage is reflected more broadly in the growth of transpersonal psychology.[9]

extent, the link between Roo and my Australian background. The thought immediately came to my mind that 'Tigger' could represent a non-judgmental way of characterizing the high-energy levels I'd experienced through shifts in brain chemistry when I was 'doing a Daedalus', given that others had used that nickname to favourably allude to my high energy levels at the time.

The brain chemistry theme didn't stop there. I returned to Findhorn and discussed what I'd experienced with Anne, whom I knew shared my experience of frequent synchronicity. I told her how my speculations about our potential influence over our brain chemistry had seemingly been affirmed by the remarkable synchronicity I'd just experienced. I told her about the crops and the cows, and the turquoise number six.

My observations about the brain turned out to be prophetic in that evening's class when the course leader introduced some unexpected themes. She said we probably have more potential for change than previously understood. She explained that every cell in our body was renewed at least over a seven-year period. Although I'd referred to six years and she'd said seven, the uncannily repeated theme seemed close enough to be strongly synchronistic. She then added that our brain receptors were sometimes active, and at other times resting, or non-responsive. My intense feeling of numinosity was enhanced as Anne leaned forward to throw me a look of wide-eyed amazement. I was glad that I had expressed my idiosyncratic convictions to her earlier. I took all this as several ticks from the universe that my intellectual intuitions were on the right track.

I experienced further synchronicity while playing the Transformation Game itself. On one occasion I'd just referred to Carl Jung. At that exact second, a bright orange butterfly flew into the room, circled slowly less than a metre away from me, and flew out again. It felt numinous. My fellow participants looked taken aback.

A few days later, a large photograph in the *Guardian* newspaper grabbed my attention. It was of a large butterfly, with similar orange colouring on its wings to the one that had flown into the room. It had the caption, 'New species hatches in lab'. The article related to the accelerated evolution in a new species of butterfly, occurring over just a few generations rather than the typical timeframe of thousands of years. I took this to be a hint that we could potentially speed up the evolution of human thought by allowing for synchronicity and other forms of supra-rational thinking.

Something then struck me as even more remarkable. Next to the picture of the butterfly was a separate story entitled, 'How stem cells can turn back the biological clock'. Apparently some researchers at Edinburgh University had found a way of converting mature brain cells to stem cells, winding back their age to an original form. This was done by fusing embryonic stem cells with brain cells while boosting a gene identified within the stem cells, called Nanog.

The Nanog gene was named as an abbreviation of Tir Nan Og, the 'land of the forever young' in Celtic myth. I couldn't help speculating whether the action of Nanog might be influenced by the experience of novelty, given the core role that novelty seemed to play in other remarkable brain processes such as neuroplasticity and neurogenesis, as highlighted by Ernest Rossi. The juxtaposition of the article with the butterfly photograph, itself a symbol of new life and transformation, made me feel that such fanciful hunches were being endorsed by strong synchronicity.

I then started to guess that any optimistic idea I'd harboured about the potential capacity for us to transform our brain functioning was likely to be conservative compared with the actual living reality. The notion that brain cells could be renewed using the Nanog gene seemed to go further than anything I'd intuitively envisaged.

The outcome of this for me was that I felt even further emboldened to pursue more expansive and optimistic notions of how we can improve our mental health while more actively challenging reductionist and pessimistic brain chemistry models in psychiatry. It felt like a very big tick from the universe.

When I returned from Findhorn, my wife and two young daughters greeted me at the airport. My younger daughter excitedly explained that she'd recently bought some CDs with new songs that she was learning with the help of her singing teacher. She asked me to guess who the songs were about. Coming up with the answer seemed to be a tall order.

Ellie, my younger daughter, gave me a hint: they were based on a Disney character. I then immediately, and confidently, responded that it was the Little Mermaid. That proved correct. Yet another affirmation from the universe! I'd been sitting next to a young woman on the plane from London who'd just been playing the role of the Little Mermaid at DisneySea in Tokyo. She'd explained it was the only Disneyland in the world with a full production of the 'Little Mermaid' show. So I took it she would recently have been singing those songs more frequently than anyone else in the world.

I later wrote to Anne about this incident, given her shared interest in synchronicity. She responded that the Little Mermaid is a creation myth that relates to evolution. The mermaid, as I now understand her, is associated with wishing for a missing soul (perhaps the soul positive psychiatry hopes to provide). This added to my numinous feeling. Even though I didn't well understand the mythical association, it nonetheless further strengthened my conviction that we might accelerate the evolution of our thought processes and awareness if we were to draw on the power of supra-rational thinking.

Approximately seven years after visiting Findhorn, months into the writing of this book, I gave a community talk on 'Using Brain Science for Positive Mental Health'. Before doing so I reflected on my recent experiences. I revisited, for the example, the photo of the sign of the van hire business inscribed, 'Apollo – your chariot awaits'.

I researched Apollo, and learned that he was the god of healing and prophecy to whom the Delphic oracle turned for guidance.[10] That fitted my belief that my intuitions on that run could be applied to mental health and healing even better than the associations I made at the time with the speediness of the chariot.

In preparation for my talk I finally read Ernest Rossi's book, *The Psychobiology of Gene Expression*. What particularly caught my eye was a passing reference to a scientific study on mice that suggested that brain receptors could be open or closed.[11] He described a particular study that showed that younger mice reacted more quickly than older mice because their receptors were open for twice as long. This led me to explore the science further, including attending a number of Rossi's presentations at another Evolution of Psychotherapy conference. (I shall detail what I further learned in the next chapter, as it leads on to a leitmotif of this book, the need for a 'Positive Psychiatry' that incorporates a more optimistic perspective on mental health problems.)

Rossi's explanations of brain chemistry and functioning yielded further symbolic links with the movie *Charlie and the Chocolate Factory*. The movie claims to be about 'the most amazing factory ever!', which mysteriously produces chocolate and other special sweets – something I see as analogous to endogeneous neurotransmitters. There is no obvious means of producing them, since there are no apparently no staff operating the works. Yet it turns out that the factory functions very well through the involvement of the Oompa-Loompas, who engage in all sorts of monitoring and corrective activities to ensure that the right quality of product is made.

I mused after reading *The Psychobiology of Gene Expression* that the Oompa-Loompas could represent what Rossi described as 'immediate early genes'.[12] These genes can be triggered into action within one to two minutes in circumstances such as novelty and numinous experience. In turn, they can switch on other targeted genes, which subsequently produce specific endogenous neurotransmitters, or switch them off, to cease production. One such immediate early gene, zif-268, was switched on within minutes of a person being stimulated by novel or exciting situations.[13] On those grounds I imagine that the numinous impact of strikingly synchronistic experiences could switch on the zif-268 gene as effectively as any other form of novelty.

There were also hints of synchronistic or psychic phenomena in the Oompa-Loompas seeming to be know what was about to happen. The factory's owner, Willy Wonka, appeared to achieve his creative success partly by operating at the border of chaos and order, a characteristic of systems that are most capable of transformational change: his personality seemed highly idiosyncratic and somewhat chaotic, as his name suggests, and yet he oversaw an operation of remarkably sophisticated order.

It seems to me that in our culture we have a great tolerance for wild fantasy scenarios in moviemaking for our entertainment. I think we're much less disposed to consider whether such creative activity might have any connection with the deeper truths of life.

I decided against making references to *Charlie and the Chocolate Factory* in my talk on brain science. I'd briefly done so years earlier, during the period of my 'doing a Daedalus'. Some friends had been concerned about the risk to my reputation. It would have been interesting to see what responses I'd have elicited if I'd covered my most recent speculations prompted by that movie. During the talk there was a rare minor disruption from a performance in the main part of the town hall next door. They were putting on a school production of *Charlie and the Chocolate Factory*.

17

Synchronicity and Brain Science

Making Sense of It All

One of my key aims in this book is to illustrate that intellectual intuition, at times bolstered by synchronicity, can be a powerful way of gaining legitimate knowledge. Intellectual intuition is an undervalued resource. I sometimes call it supra-rational thinking, because the insights gained can go beyond what might be accessible to reason. Carl Jung's conclusion more than half a century ago that modern society has underemphasized the importance of intuitive processes, becoming too rationalistic in outlook, applies just as strongly today. I believe that drawing on synchronicity as a means of focusing one's intellectual intuition is a useful, and underused, wellspring of creativity.

My purpose in this chapter is to describe some of the objective evidence I've encountered to support the validity of my hunches about the brain's undervalued powers. I include some technical material, because I direct it in part to fellow mental health professionals to encourage discussion about the issues involved. First, I'll summarize my core hunches (I've described in previous chapters how I arrived at them).

Firstly, I intuited that we might be able to deliberately influence our brain chemistry by switching on and off endogenous chemicals, or inbuilt neurotransmitters, that directly impact on our brain functioning and mental health.

Secondly, I believed we can deliberately open and close particular brain receptors that are designed to respond to specific chemicals or neurotransmitters, thus mediating their impact.

Thirdly, I believed that the process of deliberately influencing one's brain chemistry in such a way could lead to observable objective benefits, thus differentiating it from a psychosis – I thought of this as inducing a hypomanic wellness as opposed to a hypomanic illness. I believed that if this were to be objectively demonstrated, it could support the evolution of mainstream mental health interventions. It could lead to a more optimistic perspective on our capacity for conscious mental influence over brain processes affecting our mental health.

All these hunches, I felt, were strongly supported by symbolism in the movie *Charlie and the Chocolate Factory*. I believed it would ultimately be shown that we have a wonderful chemical factory in our own brains, over which we can exert much more mindful control than previously realized. There was some connection here, I felt, with shamanic practice (even though I knew little about shamanism).

If our brain responds to any type of chemical substance, such as a particular neurotransmitter, or an externally administered drug, there must have been pre-existing receptors that were designed to respond to those specific chemical substances in the first place. Opiate receptors would not exist if our brains had never been exposed to opiates.

This means that every external drug that has an impact on us must be a second-generation drug. The first-generation drug would have been a pre-existing, endogenously produced one, which the second-generation drug would imitate to activate the same receptors.

Given the right genes, there must be other, perhaps more exotic, chemical substances that our brains can produce. Some of these could lead to hypomanic symptoms. In a sense, such chemicals might imitate endogenous amphetamines, leading to quicker thinking and action, more energy, and a lesser need for sleep.

In my case, I might have inherited from my mother the capacity to produce neurotransmitters that relate to manic tendencies, but nonetheless might have been able to modulate their impact to gain specific benefits, without the typical costs. In other words, I might be able to induce a hypomanic wellness, as opposed to a hypomanic illness.

If any specific brain-affecting chemicals exist endogenously, then why would they not be responsive to conscious influence, especially with practice? If we can develop our conscious capacity to influence our states of mind (through hypnosis, mindfulness techniques and the like), then surely we can deliberately influence our endogenous brain chemistry. That would be a natural process: there might be no need for an external drug to create the effect. If it was endogenous, or internal, the relevant chemical process could be switched on, or switched off, just as a chocolate factory could switch chocolate production on or off.

It was only well into the writing of this book that I came across objective evidence for some of these beliefs. One source of illumination, as I've described, was Ernest Rossi's *The Psychobiology of Gene Expression*. Rossi described the evidence for the remarkable mechanisms behind some quite specific placebo effects. For example, it had been found that when patients with Parkinson's disease were given a placebo, they released more endogenous dopamine in a part of the brain called the striatum: this was demonstrated using sophisticated PET scan technology. The placebo effect worked in a similar way, and led to similar benefits, as externally administered dopamine, which was known to improve the condition.[1]

The investigators in that study understandably thought that placebo effects for any medical condition might similarly be helped by an increase in endogenous dopamine, a neurotransmitter that's also implicated in pleasure and motivation. However, later research showed that placebo mechanisms were far more complex and differentiated than initially supposed. When a person takes a placebo pill, various neurotransmitters can be released, apparently tailored for specific circumstances. For example, a PET scan study showed that placebo effects for pain were mediated by a different neurotransmitter, endogenous opiates.[2] These had their primary impact in a different location, the anterior cingulate cortex and brainstem. Not only was there an increase in opiate production as a result of the placebo effect for pain, but there was an increase in blood flow to those areas of the brain that were rich in opiate receptors. This was a remarkably specific and targeted response.

I later learned from reading *Brain Wars*, by the neuroscientist Mario Beauregard, that method actors show increases in serotonin on brain scans when playing a happy role, and decreases in serotonin when playing a sad role.[3] In other words, we can immediately, and consciously, influence our brain chemistry under some conditions. This is a point that seems to be rarely made, despite its obvious implications for our potential internal influence over our mental health functioning.

Rossi's most recent research spells out further striking evidence for a novelty-*numinosum*-neurogenesis effect (see p.176). He has shown that novel and fascinating experiences, elicited by a creative hypnotherapy technique he uses, have been found to switch on approximately 200 genes following a single 90-minute intervention.[4] The triggered genes include those known to impact on stem cell growth, neurogenesis, dopamine pathways, circadian rhythms, immune response, stress response, cancer pathways, schizophrenia, Alzheimer's disease and Parkinson's disease. In my view, Rossi has demonstrated the existence of an internal biological factory every bit as wonderful as Willy Wonka's fictional one.

Rossi explains that it's novelty in particular, in the form of numinous experience, that switches on the dopamine receptor gene, also known as the DRD4 gene. I now think of this as a synchronicity gene, since few experiences are more numinous than synchronicity. Rossi describes how numinous experience, as well as novel thoughts, have been demonstrated to initiate the release of RNA molecules, which in turn activate DNA to create proteins that ultimately form new stem cells and synaptic pathways. We're continually renewing and rebuilding our brains, especially when we're moved by physical activity, active engagement of our attention, and novel experience.

In tune with my own interests, Rossi and his scientific colleagues now explicitly relate such brain processes to quantum physics, encouraging mental health professionals to learn more about this area. This supports the view that a principle applicable in one field of science can often be found to apply to other fields. One example is the seeming link between synchronicity and 'entanglement', a key concept in quantum physics (see p.32), since they both relate to the principle of immediate, non-local influence.

The next issue relates to the opening and closing of brain receptors. Such a potential mechanism is not often considered. For example, not even Daniel Siegel had heard of this possible mechanism when I asked him about it at his workshop in Melbourne in February 2014. Again, it was Rossi who provided me with the first scientific evidence for this belief. Rossi made reference to a laboratory study that claimed that the improved learning of younger mice relative to older ones was 'due to the length of time the NMDA receptor remains open in the CA1 region of the hippocampus'.[5] NMDA receptors have a central role in learning, and in acquiring and erasing memory: they are therefore fundamental to establishing changes in behaviour.

I got hold of the relevant article by Joe Tsien of Princeton University, entitled 'Building a brainier mouse'.[6] It revealed that NMDA receptors function as 'minuscule pores' that open and close.[7] These same receptors mediate the impact of a number of drugs, including nitrous oxide, which William James used to explore mystical phenomena.[8] I later learned that NMDA receptors are also linked to the development of psychotic symptoms, including hallucinations.

This seemed to strongly support my earlier hunches. Not only were there identified receptors that could open and close, but they included some that were relevant for novel and numinous learning experiences, mystical experiences and psychotic phenomena.[9]

I have since learned of other receptors that use a mechanism involving the opening and closing of pores at the postsynaptic membrane. These include GABAa receptors, which respond to anxiolytic drugs, including benzodiazepines.[10] This suggests that many different types of psychiatric conditions may be influenced by the opening and closing of pores in brain receptors.

Again, why would such mechanisms not be influenced by changes, including deliberate changes, in consciousness? After all, it's well recognized that much of the impact of many psychiatric drugs, including the benefit of antidepressant medication for depression, is barely better than placebo effects alone.[11] Presumably, based on the PET scan findings described earlier, placebo effects involve changes in consciousness that lead to specific biochemical changes in particular areas of the brain. At least some placebo effects have been shown to operate in this way.

If this is the case, we might wonder why such research findings are not more widely discussed. They seem to be extremely encouraging in suggesting that there might be other ways in which we can induce positive changes in our mental state. In my view, the problem is that most psychiatric research is funded by drug companies: they have no incentive to highlight the potential benefits of placebo effects, or any other non-medical ways of influencing our mental health. Their profits primarily result from people believing that they need prescribed medication to achieve such effects.

Not only have mechanisms been identified that involve the opening and closing of particular brain receptors, but some researchers have taken the view that exploring ways to control this process is worthy of commercial investment. For example, in supplementary commentary following Tsien's article in the April 2000 *Scientific American*, it was noted that several people, including Tsien, had teamed up with a venture capitalist to explore this possibility further.[12] They started a company, Eureka Pharmaceuticals, to try to devise a pill that would improve memory by modulating the activity, or degree of opening, of the NMDA receptor. The problem to date seemed to be that the chemical compounds developed tended to lead to *too much* opening of the receptor, flooding it with calcium ions, which could be toxic.

As a result, several researchers described the need to come up with a more modulated way of influencing the opening of these receptors. I can't help wondering whether the use of placebo effects, perhaps enhanced by hypnotic techniques, would be one useful way of exploring this avenue further. It seems relevant that placebo effects for antidepressant medication achieve most of the benefits of such medication, but not the full impact. Could this mean that placebo and hypnotically induced effects might impact on NMDA receptors in a more subtle or modulated way than drugs, an outcome that the Eureka Pharmaceuticals scientists were seeking?

Regardless of the truth or otherwise of such speculation, I believe the potential impact of numinous experience in brain chemistry is greatly underestimated. The work of Tsien and his collaborators hints at the potential usefulness of exploring endogenous ways of opening and closing brain receptors to influence such things as learning, memory and creativity.

As for the value of 'doing a Daedalus' (which I believed was mediated by endogenous brain chemistry, including the opening and closing of receptors), I cannot fully explain my motivations for taking such a seemingly risky approach, as they related in part to my interaction with others in a complex family situation. However, I can say that my mental health has been good since that time, my private practice has thrived, and my family functions well. My career has progressed well since then: for example, I was appointed as a Fellow of the Australian Psychological Society, partly as a result of our nationally recognized practice outcome evaluation research.

In staying motivated and engaged in my profession, I'd say that I've derived as much benefit from synchronistic experience as from any other influence. I find such experience fascinating and appreciate the sense of meaning it lends my work. As I anticipated while 'doing a Daedalus', immersing myself in any synchronistic experiences seems likely to provide rich material and understanding to engage my interest for the rest of my career. Our practice as a whole has also gained many benefits from recognizing and acting on synchronistic opportunities, a feature commonly associated with more highly developed organizations, including psychotherapy practices (see p.182 on the spiral dynamics model).

Over and above these subjectively perceived benefits, time will tell whether my conclusions about my experiences have led to a useful contribution to the psychology and mental health fields. Certainly, I hope they reflect a creative approach that draws on synchronicity to enhance further scientific and therapeutic understanding. I'd argue that my experience of 'doing a Daedalus' was related to mystical experience associated with an emerging process of enlightenment, consistent with entering one of the later stages in Ken Wilber's psycho-spiritual model. If that were not the case, then it might instead represent an example of psychic inflation, or grandiosity. Time will tell whether Daedalus has a contribution to make to psychiatry.

I hope that even scientists will come to accept that exploring synchronicity is not counter to rational, or even scientific, understanding. If it were not for my fascination with synchronistic experience, I'd probably never have been motivated to get to grips with current brain science, or other themes raised in this book. In my view, Ernest Rossi's work is at the forefront of many of these issues. Rossi explicitly describes an overlap between shamanic practices, psychotherapy interventions and processes identified through brain science. Rossi's explanations suggest that traditional shamans have been past masters of drawing on numinous experience to enhance physical and mental health, mediated by placebo effects to influence endogenous brain processes.[13] In my view, Rossi has updated the role of the shaman to embed it within modern scientific and psychotherapy practice. I see him as another modern-day shaman.

In my view, combining Rossi's brain science with the optimistic approach of positive psychology, as described further in the next two chapters, would be a powerful way of enhancing our approach to mental health.

18

A Free Kick from the Universe

From Global to Local

The year before first meeting Martin Seligman, the esteemed founder of positive psychology, I referred to his work in a public lecture, given to mark 25 years of working as a clinical psychologist in Geelong. In one hour I would attempt to sum up my most valued learning from a quarter century of clinical practice. After reading his book *Authentic Happiness* (2002), I felt I'd encountered a genuinely novel approach that would still be referred to in 50 or 100 years' time. The book conveyed optimistic and practical messages for positive mental health, and for life generally. I particularly liked the emphasis in positive psychology on helping to identify people's signature, or core, character strengths.[1] These relate to universally recognized virtues that individuals characteristically display when functioning at their best in various life situations. Seligman convincingly argued that when we deliberately draw on these qualities, we tend to be more effective in whatever tasks or roles we're performing. We also experience more 'flow' – a state of satisfying and stimulating engagement with whatever we are doing.

Upon completing the Signature Strengths Questionnaire in *Authentic Happiness*, I noted that my top strength was creativity, with other core strengths including perceptiveness, judgment and love of knowledge. Spirituality made an unexpectedly high appearance on the list, given that I'm not particularly religious. I recognized that this related to my interest in transpersonal themes, including my experience of synchronicity.

These results emboldened me to back my judgment in speaking, in my Geelong anniversary address, about synchronicity, a phenomenon rarely discussed in modern psychology. Out of the hour, I devoted 20 minutes to positive psychology and 10 minutes to synchronicity. The talk went down well. This strengthened my view that if you wanted to talk about transpersonal issues, it was easier with the general public than with mental health professionals.

Later, as I've described (p.175), I met Dr Seligman in California, at the 2005 Evolution of Psychotherapy conference. About a year after that, a friend phoned to tell me that Dr Seligman was going to address a gathering at his son's school in Geelong that very evening. Shortly afterwards, another friend rang to say they'd arranged for my wife and me to attend. This was exciting. I went along and heard Dr Seligman talk about introducing positive psychology to Geelong Grammar School – the first ever instance of applying his principles throughout an entire organization, with the aim of not only improving current wellbeing but also potentially helping to prevent mental health problems down the track. He argued it was worth exploring such an approach, given limited progress in many areas of mental health, reflected in the fact that the incidence of depression had increased tenfold over the previous 50 years.

After his presentation there was a chance for a brief personal interchange with Seligman. I suggested that his signature character strengths seemed like a practical way of pointing towards a person's potential destiny: there seemed to be a link between identifying core character strengths and helping to find one's destiny according to James Hillman's 'acorn theory' (see p.48). To my surprise and pleasure, Seligman immediately responded that he believed in destiny – I hadn't expected him to acknowledge such a transpersonal-sounding concept.

Seligman and his team were duly appointed to help develop 'Positive Education' at Geelong Grammar School. Dr Seligman was going to relocate to Geelong for six months himself.[2] I wondered at the time whether people recognized just how significant that was. To me, it was just as noteworthy and unexpected as if Paul

McCartney had come to teach music – but potentially more profound and far-reaching in its impact. Given my earlier interest in helping to spread positive psychology principles in Geelong, it certainly felt like a free kick from the universe.

Through these local connections I met Trent Barry, who'd played a key role in Seligman's coming to Geelong Grammar and had generously facilitated my contact with many of the most prominent leaders in the positive psychology field. Meeting people such as Martin Seligman, George Vaillant, Barbara Fredrickson, Chris Peterson and Nansook Park in my own regional back yard, at times in fortuitous informal circumstances at Trent's house, was not something I could reasonably have expected. I couldn't help thinking of the way I'd juxtaposed the topics of positive psychology and synchronicity in my 25th anniversary talk a couple of years earlier. Seligman's arrival in Geelong seemed itself a striking example of synchronicity.

My interest in positive psychology was supported by the active engagement and interest of colleagues in our practice. Clients responded well to it. We usually added the theme of character strengths to the tail-end of more usual cognitive-behavioural therapy for a wide range of problems, including depression and trauma reactions. We incorporated a focus on signature strengths in therapy groups. It seemed to promote a more optimistic outlook for many.

George Vaillant was one of the positive psychology luminaries who visited Geelong Grammar over subsequent years. I was able to attend several sessions of a book discussion group he and Seligman attended to review George's book *Spiritual Evolution* before it was published.[3] I continued to feel that the universe was providing. He later delivered an evening lecture in his typical creative and thought-provoking manner. I was struck by his allusion to people's exaggerated fears of ending up like Icarus: that is, being afraid of aiming too high. I privately thought, it might be right for people to be concerned about 'doing an Icarus', since Icarus did fly too high, fell to earth and was killed. In my view people's exaggerated fears more accurately apply to 'doing a Daedalus'.

At the 2013 Positive Psychology conference in Los Angeles,[4] a number of emerging themes intersected with those I was reflecting on for this book in a way that seemed highly synchronistic. Seligman highlighted the importance of creativity and its core components of imagination, prospection (or making a mental representation of the future), originality, innovation and execution.[5] He argued that such components were teachable. He encouraged a focus in positive psychology on promoting creativity, suggesting that creative people tend to be uncommonly productive in generating lasting social benefits.

Seligman highlighted that at the heart of creativity were positive heuristics, or effective strategies to get things right, as opposed to negative heuristics, or ways to not get it wrong. He added that he was not sure what those positive heuristics were. I was excited hearing this, as I thought such themes pointed to the potential benefit of creatively drawing on synchronicity when looking to the future, or considering future action.

My strategy of combining synchronicity and *kairos* (see p.71) seemed highly relevant to the issues Seligman was raising. The value of being emboldened to act on intuition at a seemingly opportune moment and of being bolstered by the experience of meaningful coincidence – these ideas incorporated many of the components of creativity that Seligman raised.

In general, I believe that much of scientific practice is driven by a fear of getting it wrong. This might lead to a greater focus on rationalistic thinking. Scientists tend to be more timid than entrepreneurs, who by contrast tend to be bolder in aspiring to their goals, often viewing failures as providing helpful experience along the way. I could see that Seligman was encouraging a bolder way of thinking than is usual at scientific conferences. I took Seligman's opening address with its resonating themes to be a tick from the universe for my own approach.

The morning after Seligman's welcoming address I fortuitously encountered him in the foyer, just finishing a conversation, and we went for a short walk together. I was pleasantly surprised when he told me he'd undertaken a Jungian analysis for a year – another indication of his breadth and depth of knowledge. He kindly asked me to send him the manuscript of this book when it was finished. To me, our brief intersection was an example of synchronicity and *kairos* combined.

Positive psychology refers to five pillars of positive mental health: positive affect, engagement, relationships, meaning and achievement.[6] In my view, synchronistic experience demonstrably supports each of these pillars. It's often associated with joyful experience. It helps us to engage with experience, drawing our attention through its numinosity; and with roles and tasks seemingly related to our daimon, or destiny. Synchronicity highlights personal meaning, by definition, since the term is applied to meaningful coincidence. Combining synchronicity with *kairos*, and quickly acting on your centimetre of chance, supports achievement. In my experience, synchronicity also assists positive relationships, the third item on the list. It often seems to be associated with meeting the right teachers when you're ready to meet them; it can encourage conversations about life's deepest themes; and it helps you to connect with others who are accepting of acting intuitively and with a sense of higher purpose, albeit not always in ways that lend themselves readily to rational explanation. Ultimately, synchronicity relates to the spiritual theme of acting with a sense of purpose, beyond selfish interests; and this supports relationships between individuals and, more broadly, within communities.

At this later stage of my career, I have a conviction that we need further evolution of our prevailing approaches in mainstream psychology. We could benefit from a multiplicity of creative new approaches that draw more heavily on intuitive abilities – we could still relate these to a scientific framework. I think we should give further consideration to the work of Carl Jung on synchronicity and dreams in the light of more recent findings in brain science that highlight the potential value of numinous experience.

These days I'm not too bothered if my thoughts perhaps don't seem rational to others. I think it assists creativity to allow for more free-flowing intuition. If they were to take this approach, many within the positive psychology field might be more ready to venture into bolder conceptual territory.

I also believe that leadership that allows for such creativity and flexibility reflects a more enlightened management approach, which could lead to more evolved, healthy and indeed successful organizations, consistent with higher stages of the spiral dynamics model (see p.182). It seems to me that Seligman's call for greater creativity, risk-taking and focus on the future represents enlightened leadership within the broader psychology field.

Using Signature Character Strengths

Drawing on our core character strengths can help us achieve a state of flow. This is one of the most worthwhile, empirically tested and extensively used strategies from the field of positive psychology.

Our core character strengths are our enduring key virtues. Chris Peterson and Martin Seligman identified 24 such virtues recognized across virtually all cultures over the centuries.[7] They include curiosity, persistence, leadership, courage, forgiveness, humour and appreciation of beauty. There's an accessible scientific method for identifying signature character strengths, involving the completion of a Character Strengths Survey. This is obtained by accessing the Authentic Happiness website at www.authentichappiness.org.

When we act on our core, or signature, character strengths to address challenges or goals, we're more likely to be engaged and effective and to find satisfaction in what we're doing.

Our signature character strengths can also help us identify our genius (see p.57). When we're doing things we're passionate about, we're likely to be drawing on our character strengths more fully. The same strengths are probably going to be in use when we're functioning at our best.

In exploring synchronicity, I've drawn heavily on each of my own top strengths, including creativity, judgment, perspective and curiosity, and especially, while writing this book, on my love of knowledge. Perhaps of almost equal relevance, my lowest strength when last tested was self-control! Perhaps only a person with lower self-control would embark on the apparent risks of 'doing a Daedalus'!

PART FOUR

Loud and Clear

19

It's Time for Positive Psychiatry

As I look back on a relatively full career within the mental health field, one thing strikes me above all others. I believe the most common explanations for mental health problems actually cause harm because they are too pessimistic. Apart from this, the prevailing explanations, and especially those from the field of psychiatry, don't fit well with my direct life experience. This includes what I've learned from the personal stories of the thousands of clients I've seen, the clinical research I've conducted with colleagues, and my own experience of actual and perceived mental illness.

The field of psychiatry, and the bulk of its research, are strongly influenced by drug companies with a vested interest in explaining mental health problems in terms of biochemical imbalances in the brain and the need for medication in treatment. In my view, this is a major source of misunderstanding. As clinical psychologist Dr Richard Bentall argues in *Doctoring the Mind*, over the last 50 years there's very little evidence of research to support the simplistic reduction of mental health problems to specific biochemical imbalances.[1]

Typical psychiatric explanations of mental health problems, apart from being too pessimistic, display a number of other problems. These include the following issues of misplaced emphasis: too little on promoting more favourable psychological functioning beyond alleviating symptoms; too much on medication as a treatment; correspondingly too little on psychological and social factors in assessment and treatment; too little on the relevance of past trauma, neglect and/or abuse; and too little on relationships – including clinician–patient relationships, as well as relationships between health practitioners. Moreover, the everyday practice of psychiatry is based on inadequate continuing evaluation of patient progress.

Finally, of particular relevance to this book, psychiatry markedly plays down spiritual and transpersonal phenomena. From my observation, there is very little attention paid to the soul in current psychiatric assessment and treatment. I suspect that psychiatry has largely distanced itself from the soul owing to anxiety about appearing to lack scientific rigour.

I believe that each of these failings could be addressed by developing a more optimistic, broad yet scientifically grounded approach that might be termed 'positive psychiatry'. This could draw on strategies from positive psychology, including its emphasis on strengths, but with a greater emphasis on biological and transpersonal phenomena than is typical in that field.

Positive psychiatry could draw on the paradigm-changing perspectives outlined more than 30 years ago in *The Aquarian Conspiracy* and applied in the Wellness Model.[2] It could draw upon recent brain science that points to a more optimistic view of people's capacity for change.

Dr Martin Seligman's motivation to found the field of positive psychology was largely based on the limited progress he perceived in many areas of mental health intervention. In exploring what could more reliably improve mental health, he surmised that an optimistic outlook could be relevant. His subsequent research found that not only do optimists enjoy better physical and mental health than pessimists, but an optimistic outlook supports better recovery from life-threatening illnesses, as well as better performance in such areas as sport, education, politics and business.[3] An optimistic outlook can even promote longevity. This makes it worthwhile to consider in more detail what optimism actually means.

Seligman defined optimism versus pessimism in terms of people's 'explanatory style'.[4] People typically account for positive or negative outcomes in any particular situation, such as exam performance, in terms of three relevant characteristics. Did the outcome result from factors that were stable as opposed to temporary, pervasive as opposed to specific, and personalized as opposed to external?

Optimists tend to explain positive outcomes as resulting from characteristics that are permanent and stable, pervasive, or applicable across a range of circumstances, and personalized, or subject to their own influence. For example, a good exam result could be attributed to being a capable student who always prepares well regardless of the subject.

By contrast, optimists would explain negative outcomes as resulting from reasons that were temporary, specific to particular circumstances and influenced by external reasons, perhaps including uncommonly bad luck. For example, a poor result could be explained by a disruptive illness. For those who were pessimistic in outlook, the converse of these factors would be applicable. They might attribute a good result to temporary factors, such as having made a number of correct guesses and benefiting from an uncommonly lenient marker, but attribute a poor result to permanent ones, such as perceived lack of academic ability, or having no interest in formal learning.

Those diagnosed with mental disorders such as moderate to severe depression, or bipolar disorder, are often told something to the effect that, 'you have a disease-based illness [poor outcome] that is caused by a biochemical imbalance [that is, a pervasive influence] in your brain. It has a genetic [that is, stable and permanent] cause. The main treatment for this is medication [that is, externally based influence].' By definition, such an explanation is pessimistic.

The person is also often told they might need to take the medication for the rest of their life. It seems to me that by offering such pessimistic explanations, we risk taking some of the potentially most vulnerable people in the community, at their most vulnerable time, and then further undermining their outlook by describing their circumstances in unduly negative terms. I believe the potential harmful, or nocebo, effects of such explanations counteract many of the beneficial effects of the medication, placebo or otherwise, in the longer term. Such explanations might predictably reduce people's sense of self-efficacy, and promote an attitude of learned helplessness.

At times, such simplistic and rigid explanations are even further simplified by implying that there's a single gene causing the person's suffering. For example, a mental health manual delivered to every practising general medical practitioner in Australia in 2004 claimed that 'People with bipolar disorders seem to have a disturbance of chemicals in the brain ... It is likely that *the faulty gene* [my italics] causes the body to produce the wrong balance of chemicals.'[5]

This manual was produced long after such single gene theories were revealed to be extremely simplistic and fallacious. The same manual referred to depression as a 'genetic and biological disorder that is affected by life stress and personality style', the latter exemplified by people who 'are always pessimistic and seem to focus on the bad side of things rather than taking a positive view of the situation'.[6] Paradoxically, while suggesting that such rigidly narrow and pessimistic thinking may contribute to depression, the manual unwittingly endorses such pessimistic thinking itself.

Such statements do not sit well with the finding that many genes have some link to psychotic conditions such as bipolar disorder, and that most people with some such genes do not develop the condition. To add to the confusion, over 1,000 genes have a demonstrated link to depression (often the same ones that are linked to anxiety-based conditions).

Furthermore, approximately half the well-designed scientific studies making direct comparisons have shown no advantage of medication over placebo: a large part of the effectiveness of anti-depressant medications is most probably attributable to placebo effects. Recent brain scan research shows that when depressed patients respond to placebo, their brain changes are almost identical to those changes observed when patients respond favourably to medication.[7]

Many people diagnosed with a range of psychiatric conditions do not share the predicted biochemical imbalances. Simplistic statements attributing mental health problems to genetic causes seem to ignore the dynamic interplay of genes, biochemistry and experience as described by Ernest Rossi in relation to gene expression.

As described in *The Truth About Drug Companies* by Marcia Angell, former editor of the *New England Journal of Medicine*, drug companies spend a great deal more on marketing than research.[8] At times the research itself appears to be barely disguised marketing.

Ever broadening definitions of mental disorders potentially gather more and more people in a diagnostic net. This is seemingly influenced by a bias in drug company-funded research towards promoting medication. For example, major depressive disorder has recently been defined more broadly to include circumstances where someone is grieving normally, following the death of a relative as recently as a few weeks earlier.[9] Pathologizing relatively normal reactions to loss can further compromise mental health.

In our psychology practice we've now conducted research on more than 600 clients whose symptoms fit a *DSM* diagnosis of major depressive disorder. This research shows that, in general, clients who haven't received medication have recovered just as well and just as quickly as those who have.[10] This doesn't mean that we've seen few clients who have benefited from medication – in fact, we've seen many over the years who clearly have, albeit assisted by the strong placebo effect. Many such clients have seemed even more receptive to the positive effects of psychological therapies, with medical and psychological interventions seeming to work well in combination. However, I've no doubt that the emphasis on the widespread need for medication to alleviate depression, especially in more mild or moderate cases, is markedly exaggerated.

There has also been a tendency, as I've mentioned, to underemphasize the relevance of psychosocial influences on mental health problems and their treatment. There seems to have been little mainstream recognition of how psychosocial factors influence biological functioning, including gene expression, rather than the other way around. For example, having novel thoughts, our family environment, our level of social support, or even being a performer acting in a sad or happy role, can change our brain chemistry.[11]

Psychosocial factors are especially underemphasized when past traumatic experiences, and the typical symptom patterns that accompany them, aren't identified. This applies to such conditions as post-traumatic stress disorder and dissociative disorders. When unresolved past trauma and associated psychological complications are identified, there's often good reason to feel more optimistic about recovery, given the commonly good outcomes resulting from applicable psychological treatments.

It can be of great help for people to understand that their mental health problems are consistent with the influence of past traumatic events, to which they might now be able to alter their response. They more readily appreciate that their problems aren't their fault; and they feel more hopeful that there's something they can do to address them.

A number of psychological treatment interventions for trauma reactions work by helping the person alter the way they perceive or remember past traumatic events. This can result in potential improvements not only in their brain chemistry, but also in their physical brain structure itself. Successful treatments can lead to increased volume of the hippocampus, which supports learning and memory functions.[12] At times such interventions may be supplemented by helpful medication.

In my experience, specific treatments for trauma reactions are among the most underused interventions in mainstream mental health settings, given their potential benefits.[13] This seems to be partly because so few psychiatrists have been well trained in the use of such methods.

A large proportion of people with a wide range of mental health conditions, including psychosis, dissociative disorders and borderline personality disorder, have suffered a history of psychological trauma. This often includes past physical or sexual abuse. This history is often missed in assessments. Often in psychiatric hospital settings I've found that reports of traumatic childhood abuse were met with extreme scepticism, in a way that has ultimately worsened the client's condition.

Positive relationships between doctor and patient, or therapist and client, are more important than any particular therapy modality used. The valuable contribution they make has been highlighted by various research projects. Good relationships predictably enhance client motivation and hopefulness, and bolster the placebo effect. Relationships between mental health professionals are also key, but often they are conflictual, with professional rivalries compounded by quite different emphases in assessment and treatment within the different disciplines. In my experience, psychiatrists rarely encourage the novel approaches promoted at higher levels of the spiral dynamics model (see p.182).

Unsurprisingly, there's now research to show that those with mental health problems improve more readily from treatment if their progress is objectively monitored. Routinely measuring progress and reporting the results to clients and others helps to develop a more optimistic mindset about recovery. There are now simple and effective ways of gauging not only clinical progress but also the quality of the therapist–client relationship.

Finally, as a core theme of this book, I believe that mainstream mental health services markedly underemphasize the relevance and importance of spiritual or transpersonal issues in people's lives. As Dr Craig Hassed outlined in *The Essence of Health*, the benefits of actively acknowledging a spiritual dimension in life may include reduced incidence of cancer, heart disease and substance abuse, improved recovery from cardiac surgery, reduced mortality from all causes, and greater longevity.[14] Spirituality also assists reduced incidence of and quicker recovery from depression.

A much broader notion than the practice of religion, spirituality can relate to whatever gives us meaning and purpose in life. However, the term also covers transpersonal and mystical experience. I believe that in order to promote optimal mental health, it's important for mainstream services to more actively consider the kinds of experience that can enhance people's sense of purpose, meaning and interconnectedness. This would include acknowledging the potential relevance of synchronicity.

There are numerous reasons to conclude that synchronistic experiences may provide specific benefits to people's mental health, some of which are related to neuroplasticity. Novel experiences are especially powerful for stimulating neuroplasticity, triggering the release of dopamine, which boosts energy as well as motivation and pleasure in pursuing a goal, and consolidating the new brain connections that support such rewarding activities. As the cases cited in Chapters 3 and 21 of this book show, external circumstances perceived as synchronistic can be especially powerful in promoting therapeutic change.[15]

Many people relate to the notion of synchronicity, which to many implies a real, albeit unseen, transpersonal dimension to life. However, they wouldn't necessarily choose to reveal this to health professionals. They might be concerned about being judged, or misunderstood. There's a general wariness in our culture about acknowledging any experience or perspective that might not sound completely rational.

I believe this concern inhibits many people from disclosing individual experiences and unique perspectives that are central to their personal philosophies. However, such beliefs and experiences might play a useful part in therapy or treatment to promote more effective healing. I've been struck by the fact that many more clients have revealed strikingly synchronistic experiences to me since they learned I've been writing a book on the subject.

The broadening in general medical training to consider such themes as social connectedness, stress management, environmental issues, exercise and nutrition as well as spirituality will no doubt help the next generation of medical practitioners to have a more holistic perspective on physical as well as mental health care.[16]

Further emphasis on the principles of positive psychology would also help – especially assisting patients to adopt and maintain optimistic perspectives about the challenges and opportunities they face, drawing on their particular strengths (see pp.201–2 on character strengths).

I believe the positive psychology field itself could encourage a greater emphasis on spirituality, as well as more active recognition of the potential benefits of numinous experience, including synchronicity, in our biological functioning, including in relation to dopamine release and neuroplasticity. If all these ambitions can be realized, mainstream mental health interventions might become more creative and powerful.

As I've said earlier, and emphasized throughout this book, my daimon relates to promoting the transformation of mental health services in a more optimistic direction. Specifically, I believe it's time for our mental health services to develop 'positive psychiatry'. This should have, as its core principle, optimistic perspectives on our capacity to improve physical and mental health in the face of challenges. There would be a strong focus on biology, including the impact of psychosocial, and indeed transpersonal, experiences on biology. There would still be scope for judicious use of evidence-based medical interventions, including medication, ideally on the basis of more rigorously independent research.

A positive psychiatry approach would adopt a more optimistic, or strengths-based, approach to our understanding of genetic influences. Rather than viewing mental health problems in terms of genetically based medical 'conditions' that are universally seen as negative, we could consider such problems as resulting from underlying biological substrates that may confer advantages, in addition to the more obvious disadvantages.

For example, people with autistic traits might have deficits in social skills, and might become overly fixated on certain interests, but they also tend to have advantages in following routines, persisting with tasks and paying attention to detail. This might predictably assist them in certain work roles (detective? researcher?). As another example, those with dyslexia commonly have advantages in certain types of spatial and creative reasoning: they can also have natural advantages as scientists, engineers and entrepeneurs.[17]

Similarly, I believe those who share a substrate for bipolar disorder may have advantages in creativity, energy levels and quick thinking across their lifespan. They are disproportionately represented amongst poets and stand-up comics. I deliberately drew on such ideas, to seemingly good effect, while 'doing a Daedalus'. Supporting this view, some research shows that creative artists and those with bipolar disorder and schizophrenia share a number of characteristics, including a greater capacity for divergent thinking.[18]

The prevalence of many mental disorders suggests that the biological substrates, or particular genes, that underlie them must provide advantages. Otherwise, they aren't likely to have lasted through such a long period of evolutionary natural selection. Owing to the pessimistic focus in psychiatry, it appears that the advantages of otherwise problematic substrates are rarely appreciated.

Perhaps the key is to be able to draw on the advantages of genetically based substrates, while limiting their disadvantages. For example, we could further explore ways of drawing on the underestimated advantages of dyslexic or bipolar-type genes, while also focusing on ways to limit their negative influence. My personal experience of 'doing a Daedalus', combined with Rossi's experiments of conscious influence over gene expression (see p.190, and Chapter 17, note 4), suggest that we've barely begun to recognize our true potential for conscious influence over our brain chemistry.

Recognizing the advantages might at least compensate for the liabilities of any problematic substrate. In some cases, the advantages might even outweigh the liabilities.

Positive psychiatry would also have a focus on the importance of healthy relationships, including the relationship between the treating clinician and patient. Supportive contact with family members would also be crucial. There would be a strong emphasis on positive relationships between health professionals and other interested parties in their collaborative efforts.

There would be routine evaluation of progress in relevant dimensions, including regular monitoring of the relationship between clinician and patient. There would be a much greater emphasis on spiritual and transpersonal issues, including an invitation to patients to share their personal philosophies and beliefs. This would most probably include a stronger emphasis on intuition on the part of the client and therapist alike.

With regard to mental health problems, there would often be a view that the best answers might well lie in the client. This means that interventions would take a highly individualized and personalized direction, strongly factoring in the client's preferences, perspectives and beliefs.

Promoting positive psychiatry has been an abiding theme in my work for many years. It remains an explicit focus in my regular public talks. Nothing has energized me more on this quest than the repeated experience of synchronicity. It is that, above all else, that directed me towards my daimon.

Principles of Positive Psychiatry

Positive psychiatry, as I see it, would retain a strong focus on biology, but in a more holistic and optimistic way. It would not merely focus on the negative (such as pathological conditions) but would explain problems and interventions in more optimistic terms. This would include a greater recognition of the potential advantages of genes associated with various conditions. It would integrate findings from positive psychology. There would be less overemphasis on medication. Placebo effects would be embraced and enhanced as important components of healing. More recognition would be given to the impact of trauma. Other key features of the approach would be:

- an emphasis on healthy relationships with patients and their families, and with other health professionals and with the wider community
- more regular monitoring, including measurement of wellbeing as well as symptom reduction
- actively engaging with the patient, and looking for answers from within their experience, rather than from outside

- actively encouraging and drawing on the patient's intuition
- considering dreams, as part of the patient's narrative and as a means of promoting more whole personality functioning
- an emphasis on transpersonal issues, including questions of meaning, purpose and values – perhaps using synchronicity to explore such areas
- looking for serendipity and synchronicity to offer fortuitous opportunities and enhance energy, motivation and pleasure.

20

Going to California

One of the key questions about synchronicity is whether it increases when you attend to it. In preparing this book, I had the opportunity to put that notion to the test. In particular, I set aside a month in California between conferences with no other focus than writing. If I were to experience no increase in synchronicity, it would challenge my views about the relevance and meaning of the phenomenon. However, if I were to experience an increase in the frequency and intensity of synchronistic events, and if there were discernible meanings attached to them in relation to my life path, that would support my idea that synchronicity is more than just happenstance.

I arrived in Los Angeles two days before an international positive psychology congress.[1] I learned that Robert Plant, one of my favourite singers, was performing at The Shrine and purchased a ticket. The first time I noticed a numinous feeling was a few bars into his song, 'Going to California'. A person nearby exclaimed that the song, unlike the others Robert Plant had performed, was not in the anticipated set list for the evening – perhaps he'd played it because, as he told the audience, he'd performed in California 40 years earlier to the day. It struck me then, perhaps for the first time, that effectively I'd set a month aside to write about synchronicity in California, a location that represented the heartland of *The Aquarian Conspiracy*, the book that got me interested in synchronicity in the first place. This made me feel more excited, and ready for whatever might happen.

When staying in San Francisco I planned to stack the synchronistic odds in my favour by staying at the Mystic hotel. I didn't read too much into it when I learned that the man on the reservation desk was named Angel. It might be a common name in Spanish, but I found it amusing nonetheless.

The first synchronistic experience I noted was that the room key was adorned with the symbol for the Greek letter psi. This is a prominent symbol chosen for the 6 o'clock position on our practice's mandala sculpture. We chose the psi symbol at the base of the mandala, because it had long been an official symbol representing mainstream psychology in Australia. (All the work we conduct in our practice, regardless of our interest in the transpersonal dimension, is conducted from the base of mainstream psychology.)

Psi is also one of the two symbols we integrated into our practice logo. The other is phi, to represent optimal balance. Seeing the psi symbol on the key as I walked to my room, where my sole purpose would be to write about the numinous topic of synchronicity, gave me a feeling of genuine excitement. I photographed it and emailed the photo to my wife and colleagues. It bolstered the feeling that I was staying in the right place at the right time. It felt like a big tick from the universe.

The feeling intensified when I researched the meaning of the letter psi on Wikipedia. I'd previously thought of it only in connection with mainstream psychology, but there were a few other prominent associations. I was struck to see that it was also related to paranormal phenomena, with specific reference to communication with the dead. This especially intrigued me, as at the recent Positive Psychology congress two well-connected psychologists had confided to me on consecutive nights that they were spirit mediums, and communicated with the deceased. Their brief anecdotes had been compelling.

So: psi linked psychology with synchronicity, since the latter was an example of the paranormal. My interest was compounded when I also discovered at the time that the psi symbol related to wave functions in quantum mechanics.[2] This was based on the work of Schrödinger, a founder of quantum physics, who I later learned was also interested in mysticism.[3]

I felt that this remarkable coincidence had a revelatory quality. I saw it as extremely affirming in relation to the links I was proposing between synchronicity and the three seemingly disparate areas of mainstream psychology, paranormal phenomena and quantum physics. It turned out that each of these areas was uncannily associated with the same symbol, psi.

Sometimes I'm in more of a mood to attract synchronistic experience than at other times. I would now say that this mainly occurs when my soul is most consciously 'playing', to use an expression from Plato.[4] This doesn't happen often. It mainly occurs when I'm away from work and have time in reserve, with plenty of opportunities to look around – for example, when I'm travelling.

I find it helpful to venture out for hours at a stretch with relatively little expectation of where I might go, or what I might find, preferably without a map. I call this 'following my nose'. While travelling, I find this helps my experience to seem fresher – that is, not filtered by advice from tour books or travel brochures. There isn't much to get in the way of spontaneity.

It was in this spirit of adventure that I wandered through China-town and came across the Beat Museum. It was an unexpected find that entertained me for hours. I hadn't been aware of the extent to which the beat poets were interested in transpersonal themes. They set out with hopeful and grand visions of a better world after such disturbing events as the dropping of the atom bomb. They celebrated experience and were wary of others' expectations. They were interested in how life is, rather than how it was meant to be. These themes resonated with me around the experience of synchronicity.

I was moved by the beat poets' creativity and humour, not to mention their groundbreaking unconventionality. They inspired a search for meaning while almost seeming to do the opposite. As I explored the museum, my sense of numinosity grew. I felt an extra connection with them when I learned that their principal venue was the Six Gallery.

The last thing I read before leaving the museum felt like the overriding reason to have visited. Kerouac wrote, 'Don't mind critics

... don't mind the stuffy academic theses of scholars ... they don't know what they're talking about ... they're way off the track. They're cold ... you're red-hot ... you can write all day ... you know what you know.'5 I took that to be strong encouragement on the threshold of my month of writing. I felt fortified.

I spent the whole of the next day writing. My subject was some of the most difficult material that I'd ever tried to negotiate. I had a sense of conviction that I was on the right track. This feeling was reinforced that evening when I completed a section of writing and went downstairs to the Mystic hotel bar in a spirit of celebration. I liked the music and film noir atmosphere.

After ten minutes I struck up a conversation with an Iranian woman on the next bar stool and her English husband beside her. They had come from Dubai, on holiday. We discussed the sights we'd each seen so far. I emphasized to the husband how much I'd loved visiting the Beat Museum. He promptly informed me that he hadn't heard of the museum, but that he'd completed a two-year thesis on the beat poets for his college degree in London. I call that strong synchronicity.

A few days later, I had a run of synchronistic experiences when taking a few hours off for a bus-top tour. The tour guide's commentary started with a warning about cheap haircuts in Chinatown. I'd just messaged friends about the unfortunate result of having had an especially cheap Chinatown haircut the previous day. Soon afterwards, he pointed out a church with a seemingly inappropriate street address of 666. Again, I noticed the recurring sixes. Soon afterwards he made an extended reference to three black birds on a building façade, an uncanny reminder of a client who informed me that his most frequent synchronicity occurred in the form of repeatedly encountering three birds.

I then saw a series of posters advertising a photographic exhibition of the work of Allen Ginsberg, the beat poet. That resonated strongly. It was at the Jewish Contemporary Art Museum. I had no map and wasn't sure where it was.

When I later alighted from the bus at Union Square, where I'd started, I felt like walking further in a different direction, following my nose. I eventually passed a promenade where I noticed people seated at a small outdoor café, with a tall, attractive building beyond. Before it, lower down, was an interesting architectural projection, like the prow of a ship poking out into a space. I decided to walk to this building.

As I got closer, I noticed a poster on its wall. It advertised an exhibition of photographs taken by Allen Ginsberg. Yes, it was the Jewish Contemporary Art Museum. It was a long way from where I'd thought it might be. Then I noticed a second poster. It advertised an exhibition of 100 years of spiritual art. It was called 'Beyond Belief'. I liked the title. Maybe that was what I was there to see. I'd have to wait until the next day, though, when it reopened after a public holiday.

Next day I went straight back to the 'Beyond Belief' exhibition. I loved the prominent quotes on the wall as I ascended the stairs. One was from Mark Rothko: 'The most important tool the artist fashions through constant practice is faith in his ability to produce miracles when they are needed.' In a way I felt that was what I was attempting to cultivate through the practice of 'following my nose'.

I noted Philip Guston's quote, 'Everything means something. Anything in life, in art – any mark you make has meaning, and the only question is what kind of meaning.' I strongly agreed with that. It reminded me of the meaning I'd derived from the repeated psi symbol.

I agreed with the sentiments of Karen Armstrong, a British author and former nun: 'Like art, religion has been an attempt to find meaning and value in life, despite the suffering that flesh is heir to.'

The 'Beyond Belief' exhibition was organized around such themes as 'Divine Architecture', 'Loss and Redemption' and 'Without End' (that is, the limitlessness of the divine). One section was intriguingly titled 'Hidden and Revealed'. Its introductory explanation included a reference to *satori*, the Zen notion of sudden enlightenment 'without reference to words and intellectual concepts'.

The section that particularly captivated my interest was 'The Secret Language'. The introduction went as follows: 'Many consider modern art, like religion, to have its own secret language, with levels of visual, literary or symbolic meaning that the viewer may or may not be equipped to decode. The artists in this section use letters and symbols in their work, asking us to "read" their art in order to ascertain its meaning.'

My attention was soon drawn to a Jackson Pollock painting, *Guardians of the Secret*. The caption explained that Pollock's emerging style was influenced by Carl Jung's exploration of the unconscious. Pollock was apparently also fascinated with, and inspired by, the Native American culture to which he was exposed in his childhood. In this painting, he'd supposedly adapted and abstracted 'symbols, totems and masks associated with shamanistic ritual'. I read that 'the hieroglyphic markings in the center of the work – commonly interpreted as "the secret" – cannot be read or fully understood, suggesting an otherworldly mystery never to be solved.'

I looked at the painting. I was captivated by it. Then – bang! Right there at the bottom of the central rectangle was the unmistakable symbol of psi. It was in equivalent position to the psi symbol centrally located at the bottom of our practice mandala sculpture. It no longer just represented mainstream psychology. It was no longer just additionally linked to paranormal phenomena and quantum physics. Throw in shamanism as well. It was surreal and all so real, all at once.

I then felt that the symbol psi was a key that was just as capable of opening a secret related to mental health and transformation as the door of my hotel room. I hadn't yet read of how Ernest Rossi had related some of the most creative forms of psychotherapy with Shrödinger's wave functions in quantum physics[6] as well as shamanism[7] when explaining recent advances in brain science, all while highlighting the central role of numinosity. That was another revelatory moment yet to come.

In the meantime synchronicity served as the instrument to help me appreciate these links. That was my preferred form of intellectual intuition, if you will. I felt I was following my personal destiny. I felt energized. I kept on going.

I then visited the Ginsberg exhibition. I was struck by the guide's reference early on to one of Ginsberg's favourite phrases: 'Notice what you notice.' I felt that was a perfect description of what I aim to do when I follow my nose. Notice what you notice. Sometimes the synchronicity just hits you without needing much symbolic interpretation – like the room key at the Mystic hotel. Other times it nags at you a bit, and then the meaning sinks in. As soon as I heard that phrase it felt like something had landed, or become permanently embedded in my understanding.

On the evening I arrived in Marin County, in a peaceful place to write, I decided to drive to the Point Reyes lighthouse. By the time I arrived, it was after dark. As I walked towards the lighthouse, with no one else around it started to feel spooky. It was something of relief to return to the car. Just after I started driving off, I thought I saw a flash of silver to my left. I glanced across to see two pairs of shining eyes. It looked like two grey wolves. I'd never seen a wolf in the wild before.

I got back to the house and looked up wolves and Marin on the internet. I soon realized that what I'd seen were coyotes, which were more common. I then Googled the symbolism of coyotes. The first thing I read suggested that coyotes represented 'an ending which makes way for new beginnings'[8] and were thus symbols of transformation. The entry said that 'when the coyote comes into our awareness, or presents itself as a totem, we're tapping into a high-voltage energy – crazy!' Wow! I felt ready for whatever would come.

I didn't have to wait long. As I've described earlier (p.133), it came in the form of the heart-shaped illumination appearing on the page, just as I started to write about my experiences of being hospitalized with depression years earlier, and remembered my lack of self-compassion. It helped the writing flow.

The evening after writing that chapter I went to visit a friend of my wife's who lived a half-hour's drive away. We'd planned a walk in the valley behind her house before dinner. I mused on the drive there that writing a chapter on being hospitalized for depression was perhaps not the best preparation for socializing, regardless of an underlying theme of transformation. I needn't have worried, as my host and I quickly found a shared wavelength. Our walk was peppered with numerous specific references to and experiences of synchronicity over a couple of hours.

Carmel was a literary agent whose first publishing job, I soon learned, was with the publisher of *The Aquarian Conspiracy*. At one point I asked if she practised meditation. She explained that just on the other side of the hill there was a meditation centre run by Jack Cornfield. He was the most prominent meditation teacher I knew of, and I'd attended one of his presentations at the most recent Evolution of Psychotherapy conference. As we walked on the track, Carmel saw a rarely encountered shed snakeskin, a common symbol of transformation. She started telling me of a synchronistic experience involving a hawk. At that very second we heard a hawk call nearby. Our walk was then accompanied by the howl of a lone coyote, another symbol of transformation. This all contributed to a numinous feeling which no doubt shaped our subsequent dinner conversation replete with spiritual themes.

Several days later I moved to Point Reyes Seashore Lodge. After the first day of writing I went on a short walk nearby. Returning from the track to the lodge, I became inexplicably lost on the short and direct return route. I came to an unsurfaced road. I was soon struck by the sight of a sign for a spiritual retreat on adjacent farmland. It was associated with the Vedanta branch of Hinduism, about which I then knew little. Trudging back towards the main road I encountered an elderly man walking a dog. As we were passing each other, I slipped into our brief exchange that I was there to write a book. He paused, turned around and enquired what it was about. 'Synchronicity,' I responded. His ears seemed to prick up.

He suggested that we me move to some shade. I asked him whether he knew anything about the retreat. He then gave me a remarkable extended lesson on such diverse topics as Vedanta philosophy and mysticism; the Indian mystic, Vivekenanda, and his impact on the West; John Rockefeller's associated induction into philanthropy; past lives; Aldous Huxley's writing; the Dalai Lama;

Hatha Yoga; and a renewed rise in spiritual practices in the United States. In between he gave me a few tips on writing and book publishing. I learned that Ray (this was his name) had written a book called *The Spiritual Athlete* after receiving a government grant. He ended our encounter by exclaiming, 'Now, this is synchronicity!'

By this stage the numinous feeling was so strong that I felt like a character in a Carlos Castaneda novel. Apart from describing some of the history of the Vedanta retreat next door, Ray suggested that I visit its library. I did so, but not before meeting him for one further time and sharing an Indian meal.

What stood out for me most from this extended conversation was Ray's emphasis on not getting too caught up in synchronicity itself, including the apparent significance of the repeated number six. He urged me to be more focused on fundamental spiritual principles. He warned me that if I became overly excited about such a phenomenon as the repeated six, I could just keep on encountering it for years to come, but then wonder, down the track, 'What was all that about?' It could be futile.

'Wow!' I thought. Here was synchronicity advising me to not get overly hung up on synchronicity! I enjoyed the paradox. As they say, when the pupil is ready, the teacher will come.

I visited the Vedanta library on my last afternoon in Marin. I only had an hour, so I did what I commonly do when there's relatively brief time and much rich material. I followed the intuitive whim of picking up first this book, then that one, opening each one at whatever page, and being receptive to whatever meaning might spring forth. I just followed my nose.[9]

The first book that caught my eye included a chapter by Aldous Huxley. He suggested that if we sought to learn or research something with too little guidance from a 'working hypothesis', then we'd have no rational theory for making sense of observed facts: little progress would be made. However, if we placed too much emphasis on our working hypothesis, then we'd mainly tend to find out what we already knew. We'd tend to discover only what we'd been taught to believe.

The Library Angel

In the early 1980s I met a client who told me about his curious ability to walk into a bookshop and find material that was especially applicable to his circumstances and interests at the time, simply by looking at books at random – or apparently at random. This has prompted me to try the same approach, albeit irregularly, ever since. I often find it helpful.

Arthur Koestler, the great writer, attributed this skill to the work of 'The Library Angel', adding that finding the right words at a crucial moment can have a profound impact. He related a personal example of 1937. Imprisoned by Franco's regime, he was about to be executed. Looking for some comfort in a dire situation, he read a Thomas Mann novel containing a reference to a Schopenhauer essay on death, which suggested that death was just a transition to another existence, a reunion with a cosmic oneness. This reading comforted Koestler so greatly that when he was miraculously rescued by the Red Cross he wrote to Thomas Mann to thank him for his inspiration. Minutes before Mann received Koestler's letter from the postman, he had the urge to pick up Schopenhauer's essay and read it for the first time in 40 years.[10]

To call on the Library Angel is to allow serendipity to guide you when you've limited time to seek information, and no obvious way to target the most meaningful material. I know of at least one university lecturer who has encouraged their students to explore this approach. I found it most helpful with only an hour available to read from so many books in the Vedanta library.

I find the Library Angel helps me most consistently when I'm feeling playful, or spontaneous, or in a state of flow. Give it a try some time, in a bookstore or library. See what 10 minutes of browsing yields. To the extent that what you've read is meaningful to you, it's likely to be of some benefit. If little comes from the experience on any particular occasion, it doesn't matter. It's taken little of your time, and has helped you check in with yourself at a deep intuitive level.

In my view, this helped to account for the lack of recognition of synchronicity in modern psychology. In the interests of being sufficiently scientific, research has often stuck closely to what was already known, while making only minor adjustments. This can stifle creativity and fresh perspectives. Synchronicity was too big a stretch, given the constraining effect of past working hypotheses.

Huxley also made reference to the law, or dharma, that must be obeyed – a 'Tao, or way which must be followed' for people to achieve their final or true purpose. That reminded me of James Hillman on the subject of daimon and destiny.

A second book opened randomly at a section on the 'nothingness' of things, and described how language distorts reality by implying causality. The passage highlighted the oneness of all things despite illusions of 'individuation', and how the world is but a dream, or mirage. Such notions might seem ludicrous if they didn't fit so well with quantum physics.

Another book referred to Vivekenanda, the Eastern mystic, and his significant impact on John D. Rockefeller, who subsequently turned to philanthropy. Uncannily, I'd already learned from Ray that his book was funded by a government grant that he'd learned about from a philanthropic neighbour who turned out to be a member of the Rockefeller family.

My eye was next drawn to a book flap with a series of quotes from Vivekenanda. One stated, 'All souls are playing, some consciously, some unconsciously. Religion is learning to play consciously.' As I read these snippets of Vivekenanda, I felt that I was playing more consciously.

An obvious overlap with my usual interests was a section of books on R.D. Laing, the British psychiatrist who challenged the medical establishment for ignoring the 'creative and spiritual potential of the human mind'. He lamented the failure to recognize a link between the mystical experience of so-called schizophrenic individuals with 'those experiences which are the living font of all religions'.

Laing referred to a man who was 'judged mad' by Western society standards, but whose beliefs were utterly consistent with the experiences of 'enlightened souls of Hindu or Buddhist faiths'. He saw such experiences as a form of 'enlightened normality'. This clearly relates to the theme of differentiating between psychosis and *satori*.

Again, I was struck by the extent to which a relevant teaching might come to us, or be reinforced, when we're open to it.

I had many other synchronistic experiences in my two weeks in Marin County. For example, a few hundred yards down the road from the creekside home I rented in Inverness was a bookshop called 'Spirit Matters'. When I told the woman serving that I was writing a book on synchronicity, she immediately volunteered that in the past two weeks she'd spontaneously developed a new mantra, 'I am open to synchronicity and serendipity and listening to the cues the universe sends me.'

One day I had a kayak-rolling lesson. A few days later my sister told me she'd read about the kayak rolling of Canadian Inuits. This coincidence prompted me to wonder further about the symbolism. There must be something more to it. Of course! The four-stage model of transformative change! Stage 1 – tracking along and then tipping; stage 2 – upside down, in the dark night of the soul; stage 3 – an epiphany when finally righting the craft, seeing daylight and regaining control; and stage 4 – a joyful consolidation when paddling off again, bolstered by further knowledge and experience of how to deal with such a challenge.

Synchronistic experiences in California strengthened my awareness of interconnectedness and meaningful intersections. The repeated experience of the psi symbol, above all else, bolstered my view that synchronicity might be a mystical phenomenon, but that it wasn't invalidated by a scientific outlook and potentially could be justifiably associated with mainstream psychology. Many of my synchronistic experiences seemed to relate to the implicit theme of transformation. My experiences supported my interest in continuing to write, and my belief in my destiny being related to themes of mental health and transformation.

After I left America for the CBT conference in Lima, there were early signs that the heightened synchronicity might continue. My wife joined me at the hotel, where we'd yet again been allocated the sixth room on the sixth floor, room 606, in a hotel of 300 guest rooms.

Co-presenting at a conference session with the psychologist who'd helped me get through my severe depression all those years ago was a welcome coincidence that further underscored the theme of transformation. If I hadn't gone through that experience of depression, I doubt that I would have subsequently undertaken the research I was presenting, or written a book on synchronicity. It's all part of the twists and turns of life. Finding meaning in the twists and turns only enhances the experience.

In my experience, synchronistic ticks from the universe are powerfully energizing. They lend conviction and a sense of life purpose, and bolster commitment to your life path. I believe that recognizing synchronistic experience is a positive heuristic – that is, an effective strategy to help you lead a fuller life of deeper meaning. It's clear that many others feel the same way.

21

Told in Confidence

Client Stories

I haven't systematically collected anecdotes or client reports of synchronicity, though I've heard such stories from clients so often, and from the earliest days of my own interest in the subject, that they've been a key influence in shifting my own rationalistic mindset.

However, as a psychologist, I first and foremost practise cognitive-behavioural therapy (CBT) – I like the rigour that goes with pursuing an integrated therapy approach, and especially one that's evidence-based. Now, there's a basic principle in CBT about 'treatment fidelity'. This means that therapists are meant to adhere to relatively circumscribed principles and practices, including the scientific principle of using minimal inference to account for what's observed. Typically, mystical notions of any sort would be excluded from consideration. In CBT, such ideas might be referred to as 'magical thinking'.

As a result, I've rarely pursued mystical notions, nor systematically referred to synchronicity with my clients, lest it compromise 'treatment fidelity'. It was a different matter if clients brought up such material themselves. In the early days I'd respond to this by telling my clients that focusing on such experiences may go beyond my brief as a therapist: it was seemingly beyond the psychological realm. However, I told them that I drew on such experience in my own life. I suggested that my own experience of synchronicity seemed to be a positive sign that my life was on the right track. I couldn't help thinking that might be the case for them too. We would nonetheless evaluate their progress in therapy in the usual way, with reference to repeated, objective questionnaires to gauge symptom change. Sometimes I couldn't resist commenting that, from a purely personal point of view, I thought their synchronistic experiences might be an even more meaningful indicator of their progress than the questionnaires.

At the CBT world congress in Japan in 2004, I encountered the psychologists Arthur and Christine Nezu. They provided evidence that discussing spiritual issues with a client, after checking with them whether they wished to do so, typically enhanced the benefits of therapy.[1] Given their established pedigree in the field, I felt that this gave licence for me to discuss synchronicity and transpersonal issues with clients more freely and openly. Nonetheless, it rarely became a focus.

However, this pattern has changed. Over recent months, during the writing of this book, clients have divulged to me more examples of striking synchronicity. I am more ready to discuss such issues now, even within my formal clinical role.

I believe that even within the framework of CBT, and the aligned field of positive psychology, it's best to allow scope for clients to discuss transpersonal experiences. Transpersonal themes are arguably a key aspect of people's further development. This is suggested not only by the work of Carl Jung, Ken Wilber, Deepak Chopra, Amit Goswami, and others explicitly associated with transpersonal themes, but also by such mainstream pioneers as Abraham Maslow (see Chapter 2).

In my experience, acting on synchronicity commonly enhances effectiveness and wellbeing. It promotes creativity. Responding to synchronicity can also bolster personal meaning and sense of purpose, thus enhancing mental health. It has stood the test of time in engaging people's interest across a range of cultures. These are some of my rationales for now more explicitly considering the synchronistic experiences of my clients, and their interpretation of them. I would now consider this to be a valid adjunct to CBT.

The following client examples involve situations where an active processing of synchronistic experience appears to have been helpful. In each case, the clients agreed to discuss such experiences in therapy, and gave permission for relevant material to be used here.

Some months ago, while preparing this book, there was one client I thought I'd contact for a follow-up and to ask him about any experiences he might have had with synchronicity. It was Alan, who'd been diagnosed with schizophrenia by five psychiatrists. He'd shown an exceptionally good recovery after leaving the mental health system – he'd discontinued his medication and left the public mental health system with the eventual acceptance of his psychiatrist. I changed his diagnosis to a dissociative disorder to reflect that I didn't believe he was psychotic, but his difficulties were probably influenced by complicated traumatic circumstances in childhood.

I thought of contacting Alan because I thought his story best illustrated some of the themes I wished to raise in advocating the development of 'positive psychiatry'. I didn't need to contact him. After 20 years of having no contact, Alan phoned to refer himself to me again. That was synchronistic in itself. When we next met, it was evident that he'd fared relatively well throughout the intervening period. He hadn't shown any signs of psychosis since I'd last seen him.

During the first of our renewed sessions, Alan described having faced increased stresses over the past couple of years, including mid-life and work stresses. I mentioned I was writing a book on synchronicity. It was only at that point that he told me that on the day he left mainstream psychiatric treatment, his aunt chose to replace all the opals in her jewellery with amethysts to bring better fortune for him. She'd reportedly attributed part of Alan's recovery to this.

Alan said that he'd recently decided to procure amethysts and put them around his house. He said he wasn't particularly superstitious, but regardless of whether this contributed only a placebo effect, it could still make some real difference, he felt, given the proven usefulness of placebos. As he spoke, he didn't appear to me to be irrational or lacking in intellectual rigour. I learned for the first time that as a young student he had been offered a full scholarship to a prestigious secondary school.

Alan also went on to relate some amusing stories about his uncommon water divining abilities, describing how he'd converted one or two sceptics with his demonstrations. It became apparent that there were important aspects of Alan's subjective experience that he'd never discussed with me, perhaps because they hadn't appeared to be sufficiently rational. They included experiences of a transpersonal quality, or ones based on strong intuition.

I believe that Alan's uncommonly good recovery in his early adult life was based on him adopting a more optimistic perspective for his future than the one offered to him by mainstream psychiatry. He backed his intuitive judgment as to how he might best progress. I suspect that seeking to dismiss some of his idiosyncratic ideas – about amethysts, for example – would not be rational, merely rationalistic.

I wonder what proportion of clients I've previously seen have censored discussing personally important intuitive beliefs with me because they wouldn't be acceptable to a rationalistic viewpoint.

I recently became aware of another, perhaps more compelling, example. Eric is a man in his early 30s with a history of severe alcohol and drug problems. I saw him for approximately 15 sessions over several months before he booked into an overseas rehabilitation programme. He recently returned and has shown extremely good progress. He hasn't relapsed in 12 months, despite having left a supportive residential environment and facing various personal challenges.

At a recent session, I told Eric I was writing a book on synchronicity. Straightaway he told me that he lived by synchronicity ('meaningful coincidences'). He divulged this startling example.

Eric had been feeling suicidal earlier in our contact. I was aware of this, but perhaps not to the full extent. At one point he was kneeling before a window, crying, with the barrel of a 9mm pistol in his mouth. He slightly chipped a tooth on the barrel. He was about to pull the trigger. He suddenly noticed a black bird, like a raven, looking towards him from about 20 metres away. He'd previously shot many of them. It suddenly took flight directly at him at full speed. It smashed into the window pane immediately in front of him and fell down dead, 'like a kamikaze pilot'.

Eric put down the pistol. He had a 'brief moment of clarity'. His immediate thought was that the black bird had sacrificed itself for him. Soon after that, he went online and booked himself into a rehabilitation programme in Thailand. He discontinued all drugs and alcohol. He added that he hasn't shot one of those birds since … 'and I'm alive!' He was clearly so struck by the uncanny nature and timing of the bird's life-saving intervention that he felt he was meant to live.

Eric told me that he had seven friends who'd committed suicide over the previous two years. He explained that he hadn't mentioned the black bird incident to me because it might have seemed like 'borderline psychotic behaviour'. He nonetheless felt that the incident had strengthened his motivation to the point where he was only one of two people he knew of from the rehabilitation facility who had left and remained alcohol and drug free for more than a year.

He now highlights the importance to him of meaningful coincidences. He told me, 'I've been getting these messages all my life. When I'm in touch with me and my inner feelings, I'm aware of good things happening around me … that's my higher power. That's synchronicity.'

He continued: 'Those moments are stamped in my head when they happen … life will throw you opportunities every single day. It's whether you're present or aware enough to notice. Living in the present is a gift … I love being aware. By being aware I recognize when these moments happen. When you experience [them] once, I want to make sure I can experience them more. So I want to stay more aware.'

He described a direct impact of this on his drug-taking. 'The longer you stay clean, the more your life will revolve around synchronicity. What happens is supposed to happen. If shit happens, it's supposed to happen. If it isn't happening, it isn't meant to. That's my higher power. My higher power throws moments to me through synchronicity. He hears my requests and sends it through.'

There were nonetheless some hints that Eric could be susceptible to 'psychic inflation'. For example, he said: 'it's like I'm a supernatural person.' He told a friend that he believed he might evolve into the Buddha. It seemed to me at this point that it might be helpful for me to place this power of his in the context of other people's experiences.

Eric had said he now saw similar black birds as representing his higher power. I told him that black birds were a common shamanic symbol. This seemed to further reinforce the healing theme running through his own experience. We talked a little more about others' experiences of synchronicity. It seemed that Eric and I from this time on could share a further depth of experience that I believed would support his ongoing recovery.

I don't see any of this as inconsistent with CBT. I believe that the most plausible inference to account for Eric's experience is that many coincidences compellingly seem to go beyond chance. I consider his beliefs to be evidence-based when considered in the light of countless reports of others' similarly uncanny experiences. I fail to see how the totality of such reports, from Jung's anecdotes onwards, can be dismissed as a series of sheer flukes. Such an inference might be minimal, but I don't find it believable.

I've known several other clients who've experienced sudden, unexpected disruptions to a serious suicide attempt. On many occasions they've responded to the timing of the disruption as being more than coincidence, concluding that they were meant to live. This has understandably seemed to assist their recovery, which at times has included speedy recovery from severe depression. I believe that they've had numinous experiences, rather than merely being superstitious after the fact.

Another encounter with black birds figured in a shared synchronistic experience with another client, which further deepened our therapy relationship. Francis suffers from chronic schizophrenia, a long-standing condition. He clearly appears to benefit from anti-psychotic medication. We've met on about 15 occasions.

Francis is a poet; he might have been a priest. He finds his religious beliefs highly sustaining. He'd told me that he commonly encountered a particular example of synchronicity, which we'd briefly spoken about. He frequently saw birds in threes – not twos, nor fours, but threes. We didn't discuss at first what this might have meant to him. Francis mentioned that I might be interested in the work of a Master Charles, a Vedic monk, who has often referred to synchronicity.[2]

A few months later, whilst on the bus tour in San Francisco, I was uncannily reminded of Francis. When passing the Civic Center the guide pointed out a seemingly idiosyncratic feature. High on the façade of one of the buildings there were now three black pigeons nesting: he said there used to be two, but now there were three. This resonated with me.

Later, in Peru, I went on a tour to a valley where the main attraction was seeing condors in flight. The tour operators indicated that visitors would typically encounter about 10 birds. On this occasion there were three. The third took a while to appear, leading many tourists to call out in the end that there weren't two, but three. This resonated even more strongly.

When I next met with Francis, I told him of the incidents with the three birds. We'd now shared a related experience, I said. I then asked him whether he attributed any meaning to what he'd witnessed. He replied that, to him, the three birds represented the Trinity. I suspected that he'd noticed the two Trinity symbols on our practice sculpture in the front yard. He suggested that the three birds appearing together were like a living reminder of his spiritual beliefs. He added: 'Suffering is the compost in the garden of the soul.'

I was struck by Francis's elegant statement and how it might help him adjust to the rigours of chronic schizophrenia. I jokingly told him I planned to plagiarize him. I later asked Francis what our discussion of our shared synchronistic experience had meant to him. He said it further added to his sense of connection and trust with me. I felt that it added more balance to our interactions: I was now more able to witness the depth of his wisdom. It didn't seem to detract at all from our capacity to identify some of his distressing thoughts as delusions. Indeed, it seemed to have helped differentiate authentic experience, what was worth attending to, from delusions that needed to be set aside.

I read the above passage to Francis before including it here. He thought one thing had been left out, so he suggested it as an addition. 'Your response', he reminded me, 'was threefold – body, mind and soul.' That's true. Like I said, he's wise!

I shared a number of synchronistic experiences with another client in an even more profound way, especially after our therapy contact was terminated. When Terry first came to me, he explained that he loved the mandala sculpture with its symbols in our practice front yard: he took this as an indication that he'd come to the right place. He'd written a book on organizational change that had a very similar mandala on the cover.

I was only able to help Terry to a limited degree with his persistent depression over our nine months of therapy contact. However, he and I saw each other again about a year and a half later, after he'd learned I was writing a book on synchronicity. We met at a local café where we could discuss our shared interest in more detail. It was only then that we recognized there was an uncanny overlap in the content of our synchronistic experiences and the way we responded to them. To convey this, I need to provide some background information.

Almost a year after Terry discontinued therapy, I returned to California, six months after my visit described in the previous chapter, to attend the latest Evolution of Psychotherapy conference. While there, I kept wondering about the repeated motif of the psi symbol, which had featured in my recent synchronistic experiences. Somehow, I felt, it must relate to the body.

I asked myself, what does the symbol look like? My immediate thought was that it's somewhat like a priest, or minister before a church congregation, with arms upraised. That seemed to fit. That posture seems to connect us, while centred on the ground, to something above – a link between physical and spiritual worlds.

Soon afterwards, I attended a presentation by Robert Dilts, called 'Exploring the Pattern That Connects'.[3] He'd previously highlighted aspects of posture that support an open mindful state, such as being upright and centred. In this presentation, he invited his audience at one point to stand and adopt postures that would embody or symbolize the stages of creative change. When he introduced the illumination stage, I spontaneously struck a pose. Dilts himself, as well as the woman in front of me, adopted the same psi-like posture of outstretched arms as I did. That felt so synchronistic that I took a photograph as a record.

My feeling that the psi symbol was related to a transcendent stance was reinforced when soon afterwards I saw Ernest Rossi end a therapy demonstration with outstretched arms, after his client had adopted a similar posture while being led silently through a therapy process that he later revealed had elicited profound change in him. Again, it struck me that the psi-like posture was a poignant symbol for connecting the physical and spiritual worlds – a connection that tends to be missing in Western culture.

A year later, I met with Terry at the café. It turned out that he'd kept a pictorial record and extensive diary of a remarkable run of synchronistic experiences he'd had in 1995 and 2008. On each occasion, he'd encountered repeated images of people with their arms outstretched, in a psi-like pose. One such image was the main illustration on the front cover of the Picador version of Jung's *Man and His Symbols*, which we both owned.

Terry had noted in his diary that he felt a 'dopamine rush' from his synchronistic experiences. They led him to feel that he was on his true path: he was pursuing his implicit life purpose, consistent with themes highlighted by Jung and Maslow. He graded the intensity of his synchronistic experiences from mild to strong in terms of 'Hmmm', 'Wow' or 'Omigod!' He particularly encountered synchronicity when he was 'in a heightened state of wholeness'. If he deliberately set out to experience it, he failed.

Terry said that during his synchronistic runs, he often felt on a high, to the point at which it seemed manic. He commented in his diary that he'd read somewhere that these could be called 'bipolar manic episodes'. Twenty years earlier, he'd presented his ideas about synchronicity and symbolic imagery in a few lectures to management students at a university where he taught organizational psychology, but he'd been warned by a fellow academic that his presentation threatened his credibility.

Terry's reported experiences seem to me to illustrate the difference between psychosis and *satori*. They related, I believe, to a process of enlightenment, rather than poor mental health. In my opinion part of his difficulty with persistent depression resulted from others not fully appreciating his perceptiveness and wisdom: this led him at times to be out of kilter with his social environment. I think he was at least 25 years ahead of his time!

I wonder whether I would have been able to help Terry more as a therapist if I'd asked him directly about his attitude to transpersonal or spiritual experiences, and been bolder in declaring to him my own interest in synchronicity. It seemed to be very affirming to him to learn afterwards of the extent to which his synchronistic experiences, and many of his views about their potential relevance, were shared. It seems noteworthy that these days even some of the most mainstream therapists, such as Donald Meichenbaum of CBT fame, are advocating a greater consideration of a client's spiritual views, even to the point of probing for them.[4]

I recently encountered something in a newspaper that reminded me of the only other former client I was tempted to contact while writing this book. There were indications that she might have an interest in transpersonal themes. I thought she might have some interesting stories on synchronicity, even though I don't recall discussing the subject with her in the past. However, I didn't contact her, as I hadn't seen her for over five years: it might have been too intrusive. But then her partner contacted me to make an appointment. I told him I'd been thinking of contacting Michele in relation to the book I was writing on synchronicity. He pointed out that as we were speaking, she was at home reading a book on Jung.

Just like quantum physics, psychology tells us that we partly shape our reality by what we observe and how we observe it. In my experience, a client's recognition of synchronicity is often not only convincing and meaningful, but also uplifting. It commonly supports an optimistic worldview, even in challenging situations.

I think it would be a pity to dismiss such worldviews as irrational, or based on magical thinking. As the examples here suggest, many clients view such experiences as having profound relevance, fitting with their life experience. The numinosity of such experience seems to lead many clients to be more open to, and capable of, transformative change.

I shall add just one more client story. I think the cosmic prankster had something to do with this one. One morning I saw an elderly gentleman for the first time. He was preoccupied by his sense of foolishness and his apparently fading capabilities reflected in a minor car accident just days earlier. He asked me whether I'd ever had a car accident, the only client in over 30 years to have done so. Yes, I replied. I'd in fact had one that very morning. There was only one other car in the street at the time – and it was stationary! His mood seemed to pick up after that.

A well-known leader in the trauma field, John Briere, has a favourite expression to bridge the gap between therapist and client: 'We are all bozos on a bus.'[5] That morning it was a case of 'We can all be bozos behind a wheel.' Life can be a leveller.

22

Unwrapping a Gift from the Universe

At the 2013 Positive Psychology congress, Mihaly Csikszentmihalyi began the closing address with the optimistic quote from John W. Gardner, 'We are continually faced with a series of great opportunities, brilliantly disguised as insoluble problems.'[1] Csikszentmihalyi asserted that the future evolution of the human race would be influenced by our choices and free will more than ever before, given the nature of the problems we face. These included overpopulation, the degrading of the physical environment, youth unemployment, the drug problem and an ageing population. He challenged all those present to consider how we might address such problems in future. He concluded by saying that positive psychology is about changing the world, urging the audience, 'Help make it happen!'

Help make it happen. To me, this strongly echoed the final sentence of *The Aquarian Conspiracy*: 'The Aquarian Conspiracy is you.' In my view, Csikszentmihalyi's strong call to action cries out for creative originality. I'd argue that in order to best address these challenges, we need to go beyond rationality and draw on other capabilities, including intellectual intuition, or what I call 'supra-rational thinking'.

Many scientific discoveries have been assisted by intuitive insights. It's only when we more fully combine our left brain and right brain abilities, so to speak, that we'll achieve our best in tackling the world's problems. Drawing on intuition, and the sense of oneness that commonly follows from it, would encourage more collaborative approaches to such issues as dealing with climate change, accommodating refugees and providing accessible health care.

As a specific goal of this book, I should like to encourage further ways of evolving our prevailing approaches in mainstream mental health care, as I've said. I believe we can make more progress by drawing more on the intuition of the client as well as the therapist, and by having a greater focus on spiritual and transpersonal growth. Noticing synchronicity, and reflecting on its personal meaning, can help us achieve this.

At the 2013 Evolution of Psychotherapy conference I learned that positive psychology was making inroads in many countries at a political level. Seligman had met with Prime Minister David Cameron of Britain and President Xi Jinping of China. Things have progressed a long way since the organization-wide experiment at Geelong Grammar School. I also learned from Rossi that numinous experience can switch on hundreds of genes, and that when we sleep, the walls of brain cells become permeable, opening up to be flushed of toxins.[2] This further opened up for me the vision of an astonishing flexibility in our mental hardware.

The possibilities are truly beyond what I'd previously envisaged. I'm even more motivated now in my attempts in my own field to stand on the shoulders of such giants as Jung, Rossi and Seligman. I'm even more convinced of the need for a field of positive psychiatry, weaving in a more optimistic focus, a greater emphasis on intuition and the transpersonal, and incorporating the latest heartening findings from brain science.

At a personal level, developing our intuitive abilities and spiritual selves is likely to enhance our creativity and wellbeing. In my personal experience, combining synchronicity and *kairos* has provided a powerful instrument to address the most challenging problems I've faced. During such periods, including during the writing of this book, this approach has helped me to remain energized, to feel positive emotions, to be engaged, to find meaning and achievement, often in the context of enhanced relationships.

Sometimes transformative change seems to follow mainly from the input of an inspiring leader, such as a Gandhi or a Mandela. Their achievements have been monumental. But perhaps we need the genius to be more widespread than the occasional charismatic and inspiring leader. Maybe the responsibility needs to be more shared. That was what preoccupied Jung. He believed in individuation – not just for himself, but for all. That's what Jung thought would be required to address the problems of his day.[3]

As Csikszentmihalyi added, nowadays we realize that, when it comes to addressing the world's problems, there's no pilot in the cockpit. If we don't take responsibility we'll crash.[4] So: there might not be a pilot. The steering seems to be down to us. But there might just be a navigator. At least at times. Sometimes when you most need it. Sometimes when you're most ready and open to be guided. That's what synchronicity is to me. Experiencing synchronicity, and appreciating its personal meaning, is like unwrapping a gift from the universe – one that points to the way forward.

Synchronicity relates to our inner life and experience as much as to any objective, outer experience. If it's defined in terms of uncanny and meaningful coincidence, this means things that seem like a coincidence *to you*, seem uncanny *to you*, seem meaningful *to you*. Not to anyone else. Synchronicity doesn't have to be recognized by others as meaningful, although that can be helpfully affirming. It's highly personal. Yet without personal change, personal positivity, the global changes we need will never happen. Achievement starts in the spirit.

In encountering synchronistically the repeated pattern, or fractal, of psi, as I've described (pp.218–19, 222 and 238), I felt I was receiving a gift from the universe that was tailored just for me. My sense of receiving such a special gift felt further confirmed soon afterwards. When I returned home from the Evolution of Psychotherapy conference, I saw there was a package for me. It was from the Australian Psychological Society. I opened it. It was a gift. It was a round silver pin. At the base was the word 'Fellow'. I'd recently been elected a Fellow of the Australian Psychological Society. It felt powerfully reassuring to belong in the village.

I looked at the APS symbol in the centre of the pin and briefly lamented that it had superseded the former symbol, psi. The new symbol represented a tree of knowledge, like an evergreen fir, at the intersection of a light and dark circle. I liked it. I looked at it more closely. I was struck. It felt numinous. It *was* psi, but stylized. It was more of a Y shape. In fact there were several psi forms, nested vertically, tapering at the top to form the tree of knowledge. The APS Fellow pin, a symbol of formal achievement in my chosen field, was a fractal of psi! That seemed to fit.

As I sign off, I remember all those years ago when I set out to challenge John Travis with his caftan, seagull pictures and so-called 'wellness model'. A thought comes to mind. It's the same notion that I began with. I hold it with the same conviction.

> a transpersonal world
> with numinous forces
> throughout and beyond
> is beyond belief.

Notes

Introduction, pp.1-6

1 Cambray, J., *Synchronicity: Nature and Psyche in an Interconnected Universe*, p.89.

2 Ibid.

3 Jaworski, J., *Synchronicity: The Inner Path of Leadership*, p.175.

Chapter 1: What Is Synchronicity?, pp.9-24

1 For a history of Jung's development of the concept of synchronicity, see Cambray, J., *Synchronicity: Nature and Psyche in an Interconnected Universe*, ch.1, 'Synchronicity: The History of a Radical Idea'.

2 Jung, C.G., *Synchronicity: An Acausal Connecting Principle*, p. 25.

3 Jung, C.G., *Man and His Symbols*, p.41.

4 Cousineau, P., *Coincidence or Destiny: Stories of Synchronicity That Illuminate Our Lives*, reports 80 striking examples of synchronistic phenomena, including this one; many of them are well documented.

5 See Main, R., *Revelations of Chance: Synchronicity as Spiritual Experience*, pp.14–15.

6 Ibid., p.15.

7 Jung, C.G., *Synchronicity: An Acausal Connecting Principle*, p. 15.

8 Main, R., *Revelations of Chance*, ch.5, 'Multiple Synchronicities of a Chess Grandmaster'.

9 See ibid., pp.105–8.

10 See O'Connor, P., *Understanding Jung, Understanding Yourself*, pp.16–18.

11 See ibid., pp.22–30.

12 Jung, C.G., *Man and His Symbols*, p.58.

13 See Main, R., *Revelations of Chance*, ch.7, 'Synchronicity and Spirit in the *I Ching*'.

14 For a description of Jung's interactions with Pauli, Einstein and other scientists, see Cambray, J., *Synchronicity: Nature and Psyche in an Interconnected Universe*, pp.9–20.

15 See Jung, C.G., *Memories, Dreams, Reflections*, pp.320–4.

Chapter 2: Spooky Action at a Distance – Synchronicity, Science and Spirituality, pp.25-37

1 Cambray, J., *Synchronicity: Nature and Psyche in an Interconnected Universe*, pp.9–10.

2 Kumar, M., *Quantum: Einstein, Bohr, and the Great Debate about the Nature of Reality*, p.158.

3 See Wilber, K. (ed.), *Quantum Questions: Mystical Writings of the World's Greatest Physicists*, including writings by Heisenberg, Shrödinger, de Broglie, Pauli and Eddington.

4 Ibid. See, eg, Schrödinger's references to Vedantic philosophy in ch.8, 'Oneness of Mind'.

5 See Capra, F., *The Tao of Physics*, ch.2, 'Knowing and Seeing'. I owe much of my understanding of quantum physics to Fritjof Capra's books, *The Tao of Physics: An Exploration of the Parallels between Modern Physics and Eastern Mysticism* and *The Turning Point: Science, Society, and the Rising Culture*, especially ch.3, 'The New Physics'.

6 Another example of superposition is that a particle can be in two or more states of motion, or 'spin' at one and the same time. Ford, K.W., *101 Quantum Questions*, p.203.

7 Ibid., p.260.

8 Baker, J., *50 Quantum Physics Ideas You Really Need to Know*, pp.60–3.

9 For example, when a subatomic particle is observed through a microscope, the photons of light that enable one to see the electron could bounce off it and unpredictably alter its movement. Ibid., p.66.

10 As Einstein described, it's the theory we adopt that decides what we can observe. Baggott, J., *The Quantum Story*, p.94.

11 See Capra, F., *The Tao of Physics*, for an extensive description of such parallels.

12 Schrödinger, E., *My View of the World*, trans. C. Hastings, Cambridge University Press, Cambridge, 1964, ch.4.

13 Schrödinger's approving references to Vedantic philosophy regarding a unity of consciousness are also detailed in Wilber, K., *Quantum Questions*, pp.87, 96–7.

14 From Capra, F., *Uncommon Wisdom: Conversations with Remarkable People*, Bantam, New York, 1988, 'Howling with the Wolves'.

15 Capra, F., *The Tao of Physics*, p.160.

16 Einstein reportedly mocked Bohr for evoking 'voodoo forces' and 'spooky interactions'; Kumar, M., *Quantum*, p.312. Also see Marin, J.M., '"Mysticism" in quantum mechanics: the forgotten controversy', in *European Journal of Physics*, 30 (2009), pp.807–22, available at www.academia.edu/260503.

17 From an article on 'Religion and science' by Albert Einstein in *The New York Times Magazine*, 9 November 1930, pp.1–4.

18 Baggot, J., *The Quantum Story*, p.109.

19 From Capra, F., *Uncommon Wisdom: Conversations with Remarkable People*, Bantam, New York, 1988, 'Howling with the Wolves'.

20 Ibid.

21 The English translation of a Mexican proverb referred to by Dr Rogelio Diaz-Guerrero at the International Congress of Psychology in Sydney, 1988.

22 For a more detailed description of these issues, see Capra, F., *The Turning Point*, ch.2, 'The Newtonian World-Machine'.

23 Descartes, R., *Philosophical Writings*, ed. E. Anscombe, and P. Geach, Nelson's University Paperbacks, London, 1972. See Third Meditation, 'Concerning God: that He Exists'.

24 Capra, F., *The Turning Point*, pp.41–2.

25 See Southwell, G., *Philosophy of Science Ideas*, p.51.

26 Cambray, J., *Synchronicity*, p.38. However, William Newman, Professor in the History and Philosophy of Science at Indiana University, claims that many scientists of Newton's day believed in transmutation of metals: he argues that Newton's life-long interest in alchemy, about which he wrote over a million words, did not reflect the interest in mysticism with which it is currently associated. Newton reportedly

kept his writings on science and religion separate. Presented at a lecture at Melbourne University, 'Why Did Isaac Newton Believe in Alchemy?', 1 September 2014.

27 See Wilber, K. (ed.), *Quantum Questions: Mystical Writings of the World's Great Physicists*, ch.12, 'Science and Religion'.

28 This expression appears to relate to the 1927 remark by J.B. Haldane, evolutionary biologist, that 'The universe is not only queerer than we suppose, but queerer than we can suppose.' Similar expressions have been attributed to the physicists Werner Heisenberg and Arthur Eddington.

29 Bohr once reportedly told Heisenberg that an idea he put forward 'isn't crazy enough to be true'. See Ferguson, M., *The Aquarian Conspiracy*, p.151. Einstein is reported to have expressed similar sentiments, eg: 'If at first the idea is not absurd, then there is no hope for it.'

30 See Ford, K.W., *101 Quantum Questions*, pp.247–53.

31 See Peterson, C., *A Primer in Positive Psychology*, pp.292ff, for a brief history of psychology and religion, and research on religiosity and wellbeing.

32 See Frager, R., and Fadiman, J., *Personality and Personal Growth,* 6th edn, Pearson Prentice Hall, New York, 2005.

33 Rowan, J., *The Transpersonal*, p.28.

34 Ibid., p.30.

35 See ibid., ch.3, 'Wilber and Therapies' for an extensive description of Wilber's model of psycho-spiritual development.

36 See article in *Salon* internet magazine, 'The dark legacy of Carlos Castaneda' by Robert Marshall at www.salon.com/2007/04/12/castaneda.

37 Bolen, J.S., *The Tao of Psychology*, p.4.

38 Hassed, C., *The Essence of Health*, see ch.3, 'Spirituality'.

39 Peterson, C., *A Primer in Positive Psychology*, p.295.

40 Presentation on 'Trauma, Spirituality and Recovery' at Evolution of Psychotherapy conference, Anaheim, California, 14 December 2013.

41 Peterson, C., *A Primer in Positive Psychology*, p.293.

Chapter 3: Ghostly Encounters – Seeing the Future, Healing the Past, pp.38–47

1 See Beauregard, M., *Brain Wars: The Scientific Battle Over the Existence of the Mind and the Proof That Will Change the Way We Live Our Lives*, HarperOne, New York, 2012.

2 See Radin, D., *Supernormal*.

3 See Jung, C.G., *Memories, Dreams, Reflections*, especially ch.11, 'On Life After Death'.

4 Ibid., p.334.

5 Ibid., p.335.

6 Ibid., p.117.

7 Ibid., p.356.

8 HuffPost/YouGov poll of 1,000 adults, 17–18 December 2012.

9 Jung, *Memories, Dreams, Reflections*, p.333.

10 Ibid., p.347.

11 Ibid., p.352.

12 See Bem's detailed YouTube presentation, 'Feeling the Future', at https://www.youtube.com/watch?v=YAAXS1TK6bM.

Chapter 4: Synchronicity and Your Life Path, pp.48–57

1 Hillman, J., *The Soul's Code: In Search of Character and Calling*, pp.6ff.

2 Ibid., p. 9.

3 Bolen, J.S., *The Tao of Psychology*, pp.87ff.

4 Goswami, A., *Quantum Creativity*, p.131.

5 Rowan, J., *The Transpersonal: Spirituality in Psychotherapy and Counselling*, p.28.

6 See Jung, C., *Man and His Symbols*, pp.161ff.

7 Campbell, J., with Moyers, B., *The Power of Myth*, p.120, as cited in Jaworski, J., *Synchronicity: The Inner Path of Leadership*, p.135.

8 Chopra, D., *Synchrodestiny*, p.116.

9 Ibid., p.137.

10 Ibid., p.140.

11 Jaworski, J., *Synchronicity: The Inner Path of Leadership*, p.52.

12 Ibid., p.57.

13 Article in the *Sunday Times*, 27 July 1980, as quoted in ibid., p.77. This article refers to David Bohm's book, *Wholeness and the Implicate Order*, Routledge & Kegan Paul, London, 1980.

14 Jaworski, J., *Synchronicity: The Inner Path of Leadership*, pp.80–1.

15 Ibid., p.83.

16 Ibid., p.84.

17 Ibid., p.175.

18 Campbell, J., with Moyers, B., from *The Power of Myth*, quoted in ibid., p.135.

19 Jaworski, J., *Synchronicity: The Inner Path of Leadership*, p.185.

20 Ibid., ch.17, 'Encountering the Traps'.

21 The following material is largely based on a workshop by Robert Dilts, 'The Hero's Journey as a Roadmap for Managing Crisis and Healing', at the Evolution of Psychotherapy conference, Anaheim, California, 12 December 2013.

22 Ibid.

23 See Rossi, E.L., *The Psychobiology of Gene Expression*, ch.6, 'Positive Psychology Replaying the Four-Stage Creative Cycle'.

24 From Michael Leunig's delightful presentation, 'Short Notes from the Long History of Happiness', at the 'Happiness and Its Causes' forum, Melbourne, 16 June 2013, at www.youtube.com/watch?v=nhR34 E2NHYs.

25 Jung, C.G., *Man and His Symbols*, p.227.

Chapter 5: Shifting Worldviews, pp.61–71

1 See Ferguson, M., *The Aquarian Conspiracy*, p.247.

2 Ibid., p.56.

3 Ibid., pp.71–2.

4 Ibid., pp.163–9.

5 Ibid., see ch.4, 'Crossover: People Changing'.

6 Ibid., p.87.

Chapter 6: Something Is Happening – A Career Shaped by Coincidence, pp.72–82

There are no notes for this chapter.

Chapter 7: The Synchronistic Matchmaker – Flirting with Numerology, pp.83–91

1 As described by Joanne Walmsley, http://numerology-thenumbersand theirmeanings.blogspot.com.au/2011/05/number-6.html.

2 Ibid.

3 www.astronlogia.com/2011/03/13/numerology-meaning-of-number-66.

4 www.mysticboard.com/numerology/30800-number_606_in_a_dream.html.

5 Main, R., *Revelations of Chance: Synchronicity as Spiritual Experience*, p.207.

6 'Mal Walden relishes synchronicity and wonders if he was too sensitive to work in the media', interview with Michael Lallo reported in *The Age*, 30 November 2013. See www.smh.com.au/entertainment/lunch-with--mal-walden-20131128-2yawn.html.

7 The following Tarot material is based on a presentation by Evelynne Joffe, director of the Institute of Esoteric Studies in Melbourne, at a Transpersonal Psychology Interest Group meeting of the Australian Psychological Society in Melbourne on 22 February 2013.

Chapter 8: Revealing Dreams – Watch Out for the Shark!, pp.92–102

1 O'Connor, P., *Understanding Jung, Understanding Yourself*, especially ch.9, 'Dreams and Symbols'; and *Dreams*.

2 Jung, C.G., *Man and His Symbols*, p.33.

3 Ibid, p.34. See also Jung, C.G., *Modern Man in Search of a Soul*, p.15.

4 Jung, C.G., *Dreams*, pp.29ff.

5 Jung, C.G., *Memories, Dreams, Reflections*, p.410.

6 See O'Connor, P., *Dreams*, p.107ff, for a further description of Shadow figures and their meaning.

7 Ibid., p.139–40.

8 See Jung, C.G., *Memories, Dreams, Reflections*, pp.199–200.

9 Jung, C.G., *Man and His Symbols*, pp.58–63.

Chapter 9: A Wider World – Blessings and Mishaps, pp.103–111

1 See www.ucl.ac.uk/news/news-articles/1210/121004-serendipity-more-than-a-happy-accident.

Chapter 10: Hell on Earth – Into the Abyss, pp.112–121

There are no notes for this chapter.

Chapter 11: Return to the Light – The Self Regained, pp.125–133

There are no notes for this chapter.

Chapter 12: Wisdom on Tap – Learning from a Mentor, pp.134–143

There are no notes for this chapter.

Chapter 13: A Confession – Hypomanic Wellness, pp.144–152

1 See Surprise, K., *Synchronicity: The Art of Coincidence, Choice and Unlocking Your Mind.* p.59. John Rowan makes the same point in *The Transpersonal: Spirituality in Psychotherapy and Counselling,* p.265.

2 Surprise, K., *Synchronicity*, p.59.

3 See ibid., ch.6, 'Satori in a Can'.

Chapter 14: Doing a Daedalus, pp.153–166

1 Directed by William Arntz, Betsy Chasse and Mark Vicente; produced by Samuel Goldwyn Films; released in 2004. According to Wikipedia, the film has been criticized as pseudoscience. It nonetheless aims to bring a number of mysterious findings associated with quantum physics (such as superposition) to mainstream attention, and to explore their potential links with philosophy, also bringing out the potential health implications. A general theme of the film is to question the extent to which we objectively perceive reality, and to explore how our particular view of reality may shape our experience.

2 Emoto has elaborated on his ideas, and included supporting photographs, in his book, *Hidden Messages in Water*, Atria, New York, 2005. His claims remain controversial.

3 Directed by Tim Burton; produced by Warner Bros.; released in 2005.

4 *See the Sun* album by Pete Murray, released by Sony BMG in September 2005.

5 These songs were from the Pearl Jam album, *Rearviewmirror* (Greatest Hits 1991–2003), released by Epic Records in November 2004.

6 *Diagnostic and Statistical Manual of Mental Disorders*, 4th Edition, American Psychiatric Association, Washington, D.C., 1994.

7 Halifax, J., *Shaman: The Wounded Healer*, Thames and Hudson, London, 1982.

8 Jung, C.G., *Memories, Dreams, Reflections*, pp.178–9.

Chapter 15: Seeing the Sun, pp.167–174

1 *See the Sun* album by Pete Murray, released by Sony BMG in September 2005.

2 See Rowan, J., *The Transpersonal: Spirituality in Psychotherapy and Counselling*, ch.3, 'Wilber and Therapies'.

3 See ibid., pp. 100–1.

4 See ibid., p.102.

5 Ibid., p.102.

6 See ibid., pp.265–6.

7 Ibid., p.266.

Chapter 16: Signposts to Enlightenment – From Anaheim to Findhorn, pp.175–187

1 The term 'psychotechnology', as described in my Chapter 5, was coined by Marilyn Ferguson in *The Aquarian Conspiracy*, to refer to therapy interventions designed to induce transformative change.

2 Szasz, T., *The Myth of Mental Illness*, Paladin, London, 1984; first published 1961.

3 Published by Innerlinks, Inc., 2003 (original edn 1987).

4 See Beauregard, M., *Brain Wars*, ch.6, 'Beyond Space and Time: Psi', for a neuroscientist's description of the 'remote viewing' achievements of Joe McMoneagle, for which he was awarded the US Legion of Merit.

5 See Grodzki, L., *Twelve Months to Your Ideal Private Practice: A Workbook*, Norton, New York, 2003, p.262.

6 See ibid., pp.191–2.

7 See ibid., pp.195ff.

8 Ibid., p.262.

9 Ibid., p.194.

10 The classics scholar Martin Litchfield West associates the Oracle of Delphi, or 'Pythia', with shamanistic practices (see http://en.wikipedia.org/wiki/Pythia, note 21).

11 Tsien, J., 'Building a brainier mouse', Scientific American, 282 (2000), pp.62–8, referred to in Rossi, E.L., *The Psychobiology of Gene Expression,* p.209.

12 Rossi, E.L., ibid., p.13.

13 Ibid., pp.154–5.

Chapter 17: Synchronicity and Brain Science – Making Sense of It All, pp.188–195

1 De la Fuente-Fernandez, R., Ruth, T., Sossi, V., Schultzer, M., Calne, T., and Stoessl, A., 'Expectation and dopamine release: mechanism of the placebo effect in Parkinson's disease', *Science*, 293 (2001), pp.1164–6, cited in Rossi, E.L., *The Psychobiology of Gene Expression*, p.247.

2 Petrovic, P., Kalso, E., Petersson, K., and Ingvar, M., 'Placebo and opioid analgesia – imaging a shared neuronal network', *Science*, 295 (2002), pp.1737–40, cited in Rossi, E.L., *The Psychobiology of Gene Expression*, p.249.

3 Beauregard, M., *Brain Wars*, pp.72–3.

4 Workshop presentation by Drs Ernest Rossi, Kathryn Rossi, Mauro Cozzolino, Giovanna Celia and David Atkinson, 'The Next Step in the Evolution of Psychotherapy: Facilitating the Psychosocial Genomics of Creating Consciousness', at Evolution of Psychotherapy conference, Anaheim, California, 12 December 2013.

5 Rossi, E.L., *The Psychobiology of Gene Expression,* p.209.

6 Tsien, J., 'Building a brainier mouse', *Scientific American*, 282 (2000), pp.62–8.

7 N-Methyl-D-aspartate receptors are receptors found in the nervous system that are implicated in such processes as learning, memory and neuroplasticity. They are capable of 'synaptic plasticity' in that they can

vary in their structure. They are found at both a post-synaptic and pre-synaptic level. They can modulate the release of neurotransmitters as well as synaptic connections.

8 Rowan, J., *The Transpersonal: Spirituality in Psychotherapy and Counselling*, p.28.

9 Eg, see http://en.wikipedia.org/wiki/NMDA_receptor_antagonist, including diagram of simplified model of NMDA receptor activation. See also references to 'ligand-gated channels', eg http://en.wikipedia.org/wiki/Ligand-gated_ion_channel, on how receptor function is mediated by channels which open and close.

10 See http://en.wikipedia.org/wiki/GABAA_receptor, for reference to anxiety-reducing effects mediated by 'increasing the frequency of opening of the associated chloride ion channel'. See also http://web.williams.edu/imput/synapse/pages/IIIA6.htm, for an illustration of the action mechanism of the ion channel opening.

11 See Bentall, R., *Doctoring the Mind*, pp.209ff, for a reference to the relevant research.

12 See article by Carol Ezzell, staff writer, 'The search for a memory-boosting drug: smarter mice are only the first step', *Scientific American*, 282 (2000), p.68.

13 See Rossi, E.L., *The Psychobiology of Gene Expression*, p.243.

Chapter 18, A Free Kick from the Universe – From Global to Local, pp.196–202

1 See blog 'Identifying Signature Character Strengths' at the Free Education: Blog section of our practice website, www.chrismackey.com.au. This section includes many other blogs on positive psychology and other topics related to mental health.

2 See Seligman, M.E., *Flourish*, ch.5, 'Positive Education: Teaching Well-Being to Young People'.

3 Vaillant, G., *Spiritual Evolution: How We are Wired for Faith, Hope, and Love*, Broadway, New York. 2008. This book describes some of the biological basis for positive emotions. Vaillant, a psychiatrist, is recognized as one of the foremost early leaders in the positive psychology field.

4 3rd World Congress on Positive Psychology, Los Angeles, 27–30 June 2013.

5 From the opening lecture at the above conference by Martin Seligman and Roy Baumeister on 'Prospection and Positive Psychology', 27 June 2013.

6 For further elaboration of these pillars of wellbeing, summarized by the acronym 'PERMA', see Seligman, M.E., *Flourish*, ch.1, 'What Is Well-Being?'

7 Peterson, C., and Seligman, M., *Character Strengths and Virtues*.

Chapter 19: It's Time for Positive Psychiatry, pp.205–216

1 For example, see Bentall, R., *Doctoring the Mind*, including ch.8, 'Science, Profit and Politics in the Conduct of Clinical Trials'.

2 See Ferguson, M., *The Aquarian Conspiracy*, ch. 8, 'Healing Ourselves'; and Travis, J.W., and Ryan, R.S., *Wellness Workbook*.

3 See Seligman, M.E., *Learned Optimism*.

4 See ibid., ch.3, 'Explaining Misfortune'.

5 World Health Organization, *Management of Mental Disorders*, Australian 4th edn, WHO, Sydney, 2004, p.208.

6 Ibid., p.193.

7 Doidge, N., *The Brain's Way of Healing*, p.26.

8 See Angell, M., *The Truth About Drug Companies*, p.xv and ch.3, 'How Much Does the Pharmaceutical Industry Really Spend on R. & D.?'.

9 The latest version, *DSM-5, Diagnostic and Statistical Manual of Mental Disorders*, 5th Edition, Arlington VA, American Psychiatric Association, 2013, has been strongly criticized for broadening definitions to include seemingly normal reactions as mental illness. For example, see 'Lateline', TV interview at www.abc.net.au/lateline/content/2013/s3763502.htm, where Emma Alberici talks with Dr Allen Frances, who compiled previous versions of *DSM*.

10 This data is included in our research slide presentation, 'Treatment Outcome Data for Clients Seen Through Better Access Scheme', available at the 'Free Education: Research' section of our practice website, www.chrismackey.com.au.

11 See Beauregard, M., *Brain Wars*, pp.72–3.

12 For example, see Moustafa, A., 'Increased hippocampal volume and gene expression following cognitive behavioural therapy in PTSD', *Frontiers in Human Neuroscience*, November 2103, at www.ncbi.nlm.nih.gov/pmc/articles/PMC3819529.

13 This particularly includes the use of Eye Movement Desensitization and Reprocessing (EMDR), a therapy technique developed by Dr Francine Shapiro, which involves bilateral stimulation of the brain. Mental health professionals might refer to outcome data included in our research slide presentation, 'Outcome Data for Clients with Trauma Reactions', available at the 'Free Education: Research' section of our practice website, www.chrismackey.com.au.

14 See Hassed, C., *The Essence of Health: The Seven Pillars of Wellbeing*, ch.3, 'Spirituality'.

15 Hippocrates urged physicians not only to provide their own skills but also to enable their patients, attendants and *the external circumstances* (my italics) to do their part as well (see Doidge, N., *The Brain's Way of Healing*, p.vii.) Such external circumstances might include synchronicity and serendipity.

16 I've witnessed this broadening of training first hand through interaction with medical students at Deakin University, Geelong, in roles as a lecturer or tutor.

17 See Eide, B., and Eide, F., *The Dyslexic Advantage: Unlocking the Hidden Potential of the Dyslexic Brain*, Hudson Street Press/Penguin, New York, 2011.

18 See Nettle, D., 'Schizotypy and mental health among poets, visual artists, and mathematicians', *Journal of Research in Personality*, 40 (2006), pp.876–90.

Chapter 20: Going to California, pp.217–229

1 3rd World Congress on Positive Psychology, Los Angeles, 27–30 June 2013.

2 As also illustrated later by Bruce Gregory at a workshop presentation by Drs Ernest Rossi, Kathryn Rossi, Bruce Gregory and Brigitta Gregory, 'The RNA/DNA Epigenetic Dialogues of the Creative

Unconscious: Are Quantum Dynamics Involved?', at the Evolution of Psychotherapy conference, Anaheim, California, 11 December 2013.

3 From Wilber, K., (ed.), *Quantum Questions: Mystical Writings of the World's Great Physicists.*

4 As Plato wrote in the Laws, 'Man is made God's plaything, and that is the best part of him ... Therefore every man and woman should live life accordingly, and play the noblest games ... What then is the right way of living? Life must be lived as play.' Cited in Klein, D., *Travels with Epicurus,* Text Publishing Company, Melbourne, 2012, pp.61–2.

5 Excerpt from framed quote on display in Beat Museum, San Francisco.

6 Rossi, E.L., *The Psychobiology of Gene Expression,* p.29.

7 Ibid., p.243.

8 www.whats-your-sign.com/animal-symbolism-coyote.html.

9 The following references to material from the Vedanta library are without citation as I did not take details of specific books when spontaneously selecting books, seemingly at random, from various shelves.

10 Cousineau, P., *Coincidence or Destiny?: Stories of Synchronicity That Illuminate Our Lives.*

Chapter 21: Told in Confidence – Client Stories, pp.230–240

1 Drs Arthur and Christine Nezu, workshop on 'Spirituality-Guided Behaviour Therapy (SGBT: Where East Meets West)', presented at the World Congress on Behavioural and Cognitive Therapies, Kobe, Japan, 20–24 July 2004.

2 See http://synchronicity.org/master-charles-cannon.

3 'Exploring the Pattern That Connects', Robert Dilts workshop, presentation at Evolution of Psychotherapy conference, Anaheim, California, 15 December 2013.

4 Meichenbaum, D., presentation on 'Trauma, Spirituality and Recovery' at Evolution of Psychotherapy Conference, Anaheim, California, 14 December 2013.

5 Dr John Briere, workshop on 'New Directions in Trauma Mindfulness', Melbourne, 19 May 2011.

Chapter 22: Unwrapping a Gift from the Universe, pp.241–244

1 Closing presentation at 3rd World Congress on Positive Psychology by Mihaly Csikszentmihalyi and Jeanne Nakamura, 'Role of the Future in Positive Psychology', 30 June 2013.

2 Workshop by Drs Ernest Rossi, Kathryn Rossi, Mauro Cozzolino, Giovanna Celia and David Atkinson, 'The Next Step in the Evolution of Psychotherapy: Facilitating the Psychosocial Genomics of Creating Consciousness', at Evolution of Psychotherapy conference, Anaheim, California, 12 December 2013.

3 See Lachman, G., *Jung the Mystic*, p.205.

4 Closing presentation at 3rd World Congress on Positive Psychology by Mihaly Csikszentmihalyi and Jeanne Nakamura, 'Role of the Future in Positive Psychology', 30 June 2013.

Bibliography

Angell, M., *The Truth About Drug Companies*, Scribe, Melbourne, 2005.

Baggot, J., *The Quantum Story: A History in 40 Moments*, Oxford University Press, Oxford, 2011.

Baker, J., *50 Quantum Physics Ideas You Really Need to Know*, Quercus, London, 2013.

Beauregard, M., *Brain Wars: The Scientific Battle Over the Existence of the Mind and the Proof That Will Change the Way We Live Our Lives*, HarperOne, New York, 2012.

Bentall, R., *Doctoring the Mind*, Allen Lane, London, 2009.

Bolen, J.S., *The Tao of Psychology: Synchronicity and the Self*, Harper One, New York, 2004; first published 1979.

Cambray, J. *Synchronicity: Nature and Psyche in an Interconnected Universe*, Texas A&M University Press, College Station, 2009.

Capra, F., *The Tao of Physics: An Exploration of the Parallels between Modern Physics and Eastern Mysticism*, 5th edn, Shambhala, Boston, 2010; first published 1975.

—— *The Turning Point: Science, Society, and the Rising Culture*, Flamingo, London, 1983.

Chopra, D., *Synchrodestiny*, Random House, St Ives, 2005; first published 2003.

Cousineau, P., *Coincidence or Destiny: Stories of Synchronicity That Illuminate Our Lives*, Conari Press, Canada, 1997.

Doidge, N., *The Brain's Way of Healing*, Scribe, Melbourne, 2015.

Ferguson, M., *The Aquarian Conspiracy: Personal and Social Transformation in Our Time*, Tarcher/Putnam, New York, 1980.

Ford, K.W., *101 Quantum Questions*, Harvard University Press, Cambridge, MA, 2012.

Goswami, A., *Quantum Creativity*, Hay House, New York, 2014.

—— *The Quantum Doctor*, Hampton Roads, New York, 2004.

Hassed, C., *The Essence of Health: The Seven Pillars of Wellbeing*, Random House, Sydney, 2008.

Hillman, J., *The Soul's Code: In Search of Character and Calling*, Random House, Sydney, 1996.

Jaworski, J., *Synchronicity: The Inner Path of Leadership*, Berrett-Koehler, San Francisco, 1996.

Jung, C.G., *Dreams*, Routledge, New York, 2002.

—— *Man and His Symbols*, Picador, Aldus, London, 1978; first published 1964.

—— *Memories, Dreams, Reflections*, Flamingo, London, 1983; first published 1963.

—— *Modern Man in Search of a Soul*, Harcourt, London, 1955; first published 1933.

—— *Synchronicity: An Acausal Connecting Principle*, Princeton University Press, Princeton, NJ, 1973; first published 1955.

Kumar, M., *Quantum: Einstein, Bohr, and the Great Debate about the Nature of Reality*, Norton, New York, 2011.

Lachman, G., *Jung the Mystic*, Tarcher/Penguin, New York, 2013; first published 2010.

Main, R., *Revelations of Chance: Synchronicity as Spiritual Experience*, State University of New York Press, Albany, NY, 2007.

O'Connor, P., *Dreams*, Methuen Haynes, Sydney, 1986.

—— *Understanding Jung, Understanding Yourself*, Methuen Haynes, Sydney, 1985.

Peterson, C., *A Primer in Positive Psychology*, Oxford University Press, New York, 2006.

Peterson, C., and Seligman, M., *Character Strengths and Virtues*, Oxford University Press, New York, 2004.

Radin, D., *Supernormal*, Deepak Chopra Books, New York, 2013.

Rossi, E.L., *The Psychobiology of Gene Expression: Neuroscience and Neurogenesis in Hypnosis and the Healing Arts*, Norton, New York, 2002.

Rowan, J., *The Transpersonal: Spirituality in Psychotherapy and Counselling*, 2nd edn, Routledge, Hove, 2005.

Seligman, M.E., *Authentic Happiness: Using the New Positive Psychology to Realize Your Potential for Lasting Fulfilment*. Random House, Sydney. 2002.

—— *Flourish: A Visionary New Understanding of Happiness and Well-Being*, Free Press, New York, 2011.

—— *Learned Optimism*, Random House, Sydney, 1992.

Southwell, G., *Philosophy of Science Ideas*, Quercus, London, 2013.

Surprise, K., *Synchronicity: The Art of Coincidence, Choice and Unlocking Your Mind*, New Page, Pompton Plains, NJ, 2012.

Travis, J.W., and Ryan, R.S., *The Wellness Workbook*, 3rd edn, Celestial Arts, Berkeley, 2004; first published 1981.

Wilber, K. (ed.), *Quantum Questions: Mystical Writings of the World's Great Physicists*, Shambhala, Boston, 2001.